A REFUGE FOR MY HEART

I heartily recommend this book to all who want to know God in a deeper way than they have ever known him before. Full of Biblical illustration, this is a great resource for leaders and followers alike. **Jill Briscoe**
International Speaker/Author

In a profound way, the author is using the example of different Bible characters to bring Godly wisdom to the pain and struggles of our daily living. This book is a wonderful aid to spiritual growth and knowing God! **Nick Nedelchev**
President of the European Evangelical Alliance

I have had the great pleasure of ministering with Eleonore van Haaften in different parts of the world and am very impressed with her gifts as a speaker, author and Bible teacher. Her book has enriched my own walk with God. **Robyn Claydon**
Lausanne Senior Associate for Women in World Evangelisation

Noor van Haaften is a very gifted woman who has a great ability to communicate with people of all ages in a wide variety of cultures. I have had the privilege of working with her in a number of international situations and have always been impressed by her keen mind, her sweet spirit and her deep love for the Lord and His cause. **Stuart Briscoe**
Former Senior Pastor, now Minister at Large of Elmbrook Church, USA

This moving book will be of great help to all Christians.
Elizabeth Catherwood

My friend Noor cares deeply about the Word of God, as well as sharing that Word with people around the world. I know you will enjoy her insights in this poignant and personal book.

Joni Eareckson Tada
International speaker/author

I highly recommend this book to anyone who desires to learn more about God's loving care for us, even in the darkest days.

Lindsay Brown
General Secretary IFES

Noor van Haaften has an amazing ability to bring to life Biblical characters and draw out timeless yet contemporary principles to challenge and comfort us today. **Pam Johnston**
Focusfest Ministries/Evangelical Ministries, N. Ireland

This book is an encouragement to go deep with God, and to find him as our deepest security. The whole work draws us into a closer walk with God, and shows how the Scriptures speak to our condition, whoever we may be. This is a profound work which offers deep encouragement and understanding to anyone who reads it with an open mind. **Dr Michael Green**

A powerful book, plumbing the depths of God's sovereign love. I found myself reading, rereading, and soberly pondering. This book, coming to me in my old age, has indeed been a refuge for my heart, reminding me to hide in God. It has been balm for my soul. **Elisabeth Elliot**

A Refuge For My Heart

Trusting God Even When Things Go Wrong

Eleonore van Haaften

Christian Focus Publications

Christian Focus Publications publishes biblically-accurate books for adults and children. The books in the adult range are published in three imprints:

Christian Heritage contains classic writings from the past.
Christian Focus contains popular works including biographies, commentaries, doctrine, and Christian living.
Mentor focuses on books written at a level suitable for Bible College and seminary students, pastors, and others; the imprint includes commentaries, doctrinal studies, examination of current issues, and church history.

For a free catalogue of all our titles, please write to:

Christian Focus Publications,
Geanies House, Fearn,
Ross-shire, IV20 1TW, Great Britain

For details of our titles visit us on our web site
http://www.christianfocus.com

First published in 1997 by Hodder and Stoughton, London

Translated from the original Dutch by Mariette Woods and Eleonore van Haaften

ISBN 1-85792-684-6

Published in 2001
by
Christian Focus Publications
Geanies House, Fearn
Ross-shire, IV20 1TW, Great Britain
www.christianfocus.com

Printed in Great Britain by Cox & Wyman Ltd, Reading
Cover Design by Owen Daily

To my mother Johanna Struik Dalm.
She lives increasingly in the past,
but knows that her present and future
are safely kept in God's hands.

The eternal God is your refuge, and underneath are the everlasting arms.
Deuteronomy 33:27

I long to dwell in your tent forever and take refuge in the shelter of your wings.
Psalm 61:4

Contents

Part 2

Foreword

I knew a man who suffered a major heart attack in which his blood pump almost packed up. For his recovery after surgery a wide range of medications was combined, and his diet was substantially changed. All contributed to his subsequent wellbeing, and he remains thankful for the resources of modern medicine. Scripture speaks of the heart often, usually, however, with reference not to the blood pump but to that which it mirrors, namely the dynamic core of our personal selfhood, where action and reaction, awareness, thought, understanding, discernment, desire, emotion, integration, self-absorption, wilfulness and folly all originate. This is where God's knowledge of us is focused: 'the LORD looks at the heart' (1 Sam. 16:7); 'I the LORD search the heart' (Jer. 17:10).

Fallen human beings have bad hearts, and face spiritual death, but heart surgery, liberating and life giving, performed by the Holy Spirit of God, is an apt way to characterize the regenerating union with the risen Christ that makes us into Christian believers. And following this, our new heart becomes the source and centre of our Christian identity, the true growth-point of our ongoing change into the image of our Saviour. So every bit of our life as believers should express, safeguard and reinforce against undermining the goals, values, desires and convictions of which our heart is now the home. Such is the way of holiness, as the writer of this book knows and shows.

A refuge is a safe place where one is shielded from destructive forces, and can rest while getting one's breath back, and where one may gain fresh strength for further conflict. Eleonore van Haaften explores most sensitively the range of circumstances and

11

experiences that make Christian hearts cry out for a place of refuge. She tells us what it means to hide in God as our refuge, and she brings out the varied resources of hope and help from the triune God that between them guarantee recovery from the hurts our hearts have felt. All the remedies have their place in a unified recovery strategy, though each one will mean more to some sufferers than to others. This is a thoughtful book, calling for thoughtful readers.

To make her point van Haaften profiles, among others, Naomi, the widow with her bitter heart; Joseph, the purchased and gaoled slave with his battered heart; Leah, the wife with (I think) her obtrusive squint and her humiliated heart; and King David, with half his life blighted by his susceptible and thoughtless heart. Her own heart for people enables her to diagnose the heartaches in these life stories in a sure-footed and profound way. Then she tells us how God the Son and God the Father are there for us to hide in, and how what we may call (using a medical phrase in a van Haaften sense) heart events should teach us that in God's family being matters more than doing, and the rock-bottom reality of the refuge relationship (trust and dependence) is the most important thing of all. The communication here is deep to deep, just as it is heart to heart; Eleonore shows us how we may know God better, and leaves us longing to do just that. What a good book this is– medicine and diet in one. Reading it did me good, and will I think do you good too. All our hearts need constant overhaul, and I cannot imagine the Christian who will not be enriched by what is written here. I commend this book with real and grateful enthusiasm.

J.I. Packer

Preface

I can't quite remember when and how my fascination with the lives of the two Old Testament ladies Ruth and Naomi began, but I'm not over it yet! Most people will remember their story as one where life's tragedies are overshadowed by romance and a happy ending: the young widow Ruth remarries and her second marriage is blessed with a son. Her mother-in-law Naomi, once bitter and disillusioned, rejoices and shares in the happy circumstances of the loving new couple and their baby boy who is one of Jesus' forefathers.

It is, however, not so much the end of the story that fascinates me, exciting though it is, but rather the preceding events. We meet Ruth and Naomi, both widowed, on their way to Bethlehem. What makes Ruth's way of coping with distress so different from Naomi's? Why is Naomi bitterly blaming the Lord for her misery whereas Ruth seeks refuge with him, thereby indicating that she still trusts him? And what does 'hiding under the wings of the Almighty' (that which Ruth did, see Ruth 2:12) actually mean?

We all know moments when our world appears to fall apart and everything seems to go wrong. How do we react when we are hurt and disillusioned? Some of us will try to restore things, cost what it may. Unable to accept what has happened, we turn bitter and start questioning God. Others, however, find that their faith and relationship with the Lord deepen in the very 'pit experiences' which bring us down. Some seem to get stuck, whereas others can continue living, having grown even richer in the process of learning to cope with their pain.

In this book we look at five biblical characters, who knew our kind of ups and downs, joys and sorrows. Whilst they may have been bewildered about the events in their lives, we have the privilege of seeing things from a wider perspective as the Bible offers us a fascinating overview. It helps us to begin to understand something of God's dealings with his people as we get an overwhelming glimpse of his holiness and faithfulness.

The people we study were at times and for different reasons empty-handed. We can identify with each situation they faced, which makes a study of their response to it and the way in which they coped, a very interesting exercise. We are challenged to compare notes: how did they and how do we respond to adversity? We shall find that the way in which we come to terms with our disappointments is closely related to the question whether we go through these moments of despair with or without the Lord.

Life is such that we shall at times be empty-handed, but each time we find that the Lord fills our hands again, irrespective of what caused our misery. He does so in his time and in his way, which may not always be our idea of solving problems! Yet, when considering the lives of Naomi, Ruth, Joseph, Leah and David, we recognize God's hand, even in perplexing moments. He holds, guides and blesses his people and reveals himself throughout biblical history as almighty and totally trustworthy. He also reveals himself as a hiding place for those who seek him and walks with us in and through the valleys of life. David says: 'My heart is steadfast, O God.... For great is your love, higher than the heavens; your faithfulness reaches to the skies' (Ps.108:1and 4). His experience, as well as that of many others, can encourage us.

Acknowledging God as the Almighty One is one thing, learning to take refuge with him, or to hide in him, is another. The former can be merely a matter of the will, and stay at mind level. The latter is a matter of the heart, and is a relational question. The Almighty also becomes Abba, Father. Acknowledging becomes knowing. Knowing God implies security in this world, where we won't be spared adversity. We can choose to carry on rather than stand still; we can choose peace instead of anxiety. Ruth chose the better part and in her hiding with God, she gave evidence of her faith in his goodness and sovereignty, a faith that was stronger than her sorrow. In surrendering to the Lord, her heart found peace and a home.

What does it mean to hide with God? This is what we look at in the last five chapters of this book. Hiding with God is one of the most difficult, yet one of the most precious things we can experience. It is difficult because time and time again we are tempted to think that we can manage on our own. We find it easier to trust ourselves, other people or even circumstances, rather than to trust God. It is difficult because we are often far removed from the reality of walking with God. Our hurried existence keeps us so occupied with worldly things that we have become alienated from heaven. Besides, a childlike trust and hiding in our heavenly Father seem to go against everything we know or think we know.

Maybe that is why we need to experience moments in life when we are, as it were, stripped of our securities – be they people, things or circumstances that are familiar and dear to us. Moments of empty-handedness and helplessness. Moments when we crave for security, comfort and restoration. Often it is the very valleys of life that drive us into the arms of God. There we find that 'pit experiences' can become depth experiences: when hiding with God, we find security, healing and new strength. Under the wings of the Almighty we will taste something of God's love, which David says, is 'better than life' (Ps.63:3).

The major part of this book was written in Austria, the country where, at the age of eighteen, I met the Lord. There my first steps in spiritual growth took place, at international conferences, sitting at the feet of great Bible teachers, who taught me and others principles from God's Word, being themselves visual aids of what walking with God means. Later on I spent seven years in Austria, as a staff worker for the International Fellowship of Evangelical Students (IFES), during the challenging days of pioneering the Austrian Student Mission. Many years have gone by since those early days: years of Christian growth (with both failures and successes), years of active involvement in Christian ministry, with young people and students, in women's ministries, in speaking, writing and working with the media. Early in 1995, over twenty-five years after my conversion, I returned for a short sabbatical period to the place where it all began. Surrounded by the majestic Alps that so clearly speak of God's greatness and sovereignty, I began working on this book in which I would like to join the biblical heroes in bearing witness to God's faithfulness and goodness in the lives of his children. It is my sincere desire that, together with David, we shall be able to say: 'Taste and see that the Lord is good; blessed is the man who takes refuge in him' (Ps. 34:8).

I owe many thanks to my friends who were willing to read through the manuscript, offering helpful comments. Among them Dr Paul van der Laan (church historian) and Mrs Wil Doornenbal, MA (psychologist), who provided valuable comments and suggestions from their own field of expertise. Dr Carl Armerding (Old Testament scholar) helped me during my research period, offering useful study material. My sister, Mariette Woods, spent many hours translating the major part of this book into English and Anne Roberts painstakingly checked the language, spelling and grammar, thus reviving her own mother tongue after years of living in foreign countries! My sincere thanks to them all as well as to the many wise men and women who in the past years have challenged me in my thinking and taught me about the things of God through their lectures, books and lives.

Part 1

1
Empty Hands

As long as we live on this globe we will know disappointment and sorrow, for painful experiences are inevitable in a broken world inhabited by imperfect people. Time and time again things will go differently from what we had hoped. Expectations, however well-founded, will not automatically go according to plan and we keep having to find a way to carry on. This will be easier for some people than for others; there are those who seem to possess a tremendous elasticity enabling them to adjust, whereas others find it almost impossible. Some people struggle with questions of faith, others find that it is their very faith that enables them to rest in whatever it is that happens to them. Some feel that God is far away at these times while others, on the contrary, feel that God is nearer.

The very fact that each individual is different, makes it difficult to appreciate someone else's struggle or pain and to really stand alongside them and understand what they are going through. We imagine that we understand where the other person is or how they feel, just because their experience seems similar to what we or people we know have gone through. However, even though there may be points of recognition and even when we feel we can identify with the other person to a certain degree, we must realise that each individual and each experience is unique.

Sometimes it is impossible to pinpoint the exact cause of certain painful events in our lives. Someone may fall prey to illness or to a handicap. A stillbirth, or the ailments that can come with old age, or death itself, are calamities that leave people standing empty-handed. Just as is the case when we are faced with natural disasters (interestingly called 'acts of God' by insurance companies!), here man is overcome and unable to interfere or change the course of events and nowhere else is he quite so aware of his own helplessness as in situations he can neither fully understand nor master.

In the following three chapters (including this one), we look at Naomi and her two daughters-in-law Ruth and Orpah, who were confronted with the death of their loved ones as well as with childlessness. Then, in Chapters 4 - 9 we go to Joseph, Leah and David who experienced suffering which was either caused by other people and/or themselves or brought upon them as a result of their obedience to God. In all cases we consider things perplexing and painful and attempt to discover how the people involved dealt with their particular circumstances as well as how God dealt with them.

Naomi, Ruth and Orpah

The story of Naomi, Ruth and Orpah is recorded in the book of Ruth, in the Old Testament, where, in just four chapters, the main events in their lives are described: an account of tragedy and love in the lives of ordinary people. The story begins with a severe famine in Judah which causes Elimelech to emigrate with his wife and two sons to the land of Moab. After they settle there, Elimelech dies and subsequently the two sons marry Moabite (i.e. heathen) women. Both these marriages remain childless and both wives are widowed after having been married for approximately ten years. The author of the book of Ruth manages to compress all these major events into just five verses (Ruth 1:1-5) and we realise that what is now left is a three-woman household consisting of Naomi and her two foreign daughters-in-law, Ruth and Orpah.

Twice it is said of Naomi that she 'was left', firstly after the death of her husband ('and she was left with her two sons', Ruth 1:3) and then after the death of her sons ('both Mahlon and Kilion also died, and Naomi was left without her two sons and her husband', Ruth 1:5). The three words 'she was left' simmer with emotion, communicating disillusion, heartbreak and profound shock. How desolate she must have felt – a lone foreigner in a strange country, stripped of all that was familiar and secure to her.

Even though it isn't mentioned specifically, it goes without saying that Naomi's daughters-in-law were also deeply affected by the events. Having married foreign men may well have made them strangers in their own country, and when they became widowed after ten years of (childless) marriage, they were also on their own again, stripped of their identity and of a future that had seemed secure. Where, in such a situation, does one find an anchor in life, what is there to build on, who is there to give support?

The three women were left empty-handed, a feeling that Naomi put into words when, upon her return to Bethlehem, she said: 'I went away full, but the Lord has brought me back empty'(Ruth 1:21).

The whys in life

Confrontation with a major personal disaster automatically raises questions as to the reason behind it. We have this urgent inner need to understand, feeling that once we can 'place' things, we can more easily get to grips with them. It is indeed true to say that the more insight we gain into the background of events, the better we shall be able to identify ways in which we can work towards solving or alleviating our painful circumstances and emotional pain. But the problem is that in vast matters like, for instance, death or childlessness – the calamities Naomi and her daughters-in-law faced – the cause of events isn't always crystal clear. In fact, more often than not, it isn't clear at all. Sometimes, in our striving to find a satisfying answer, we continue probing so long and go so far that our search becomes unhealthy, leading to problems that are both unnecessary and oppressing. This is particularly the case when, having tried all other options, we have started on an inward path, looking for personal guilt that has called God's wrath over us.

Assessment of our circumstances, including reflection and self examination is a good thing, provided we do it in a healthy way, recognizing outside causes as well as our personal role where that is appropriate without digging and searching endlessly for imaginary things. We must realise that probably more often than not we will not find all the answers (and solutions) we desire, and some whys may remain with us forever (although they can change in intensity or urgency). That is particularly true for events too great or too definite for us to influence, moments when we stand, as it were, in naked helplessness.

The book of Ruth doesn't tell us whether Naomi ever asked herself (or God!) what she had done to deserve the loss of her husband and sons (and with them also potential future generations). Some people claim that, as people of God, Naomi and Elimelech should never have moved to a heathen country where other gods were worshipped. They feel that this step marked the beginning of their downfall and misery, which was no more (and no less) than God's punishment. We don't know if people ever said things of such a nature to Naomi or if she herself thought about her circumstances in that light. Did she question the wisdom of their decision to move from Bethlehem to the land of Moab? Did she, on looking back, feel guilty about the fact that both her sons had married heathen women? Did she consider the death of her husband and sons and the childlessness of both her daughters-in-law as God's punishment for wrong decisions and deeds of the past? These things are not mentioned, yet such reasoning is not uncommon. When we face inexplicable pain, it can be quite tempting and even natural to start thinking and arguing in terms of personal guilt and blame; when all other options are ruled out, it seems the most plausible inference. However, once we set off on the track of 'sin-leads-to-punishment-leads-to-grief' therefore 'grief-means-punishment-implies-there-was-sin', soon enough we start turning ourselves inside out, looking for mistakes we made or sins we committed, all in order to discover the cause of our trials. It is good to take stock of our painful circumstances in order to get things into perspective and self-examination is part of that exercise, but it can get out of hand and lead to an unfair struggle with 'if onlys'. Unfortunately, even if we don't do it ourselves, there are always others who will point out the possible (or likely) link between our sins and whatever tragedy is happening in our lives, but even though this can at times be necessary and the right course of action, it is not always true and can be unnecessarily destructive.

When Job had lost his home, children and possessions, his friends first sat with him for seven days and nights without saying a thing (Job 2:13)– they didn't attempt to find words of comfort or explanations in order to help him to cope better with his tragedy. Hats off to their wisdom! When, however, the disaster continued and no answer or solution was provided, they came with well meaning advice and words that, Job said, tormented and crushed him (Job 19:2). They suggested that he had sinned, and advised him to submit to God and repent (Job 22:5,21). Such words are often the product of helplessness. We want to be able to explain things and feel we need to provide answers in order to help our suffering friends, but we need to realise that keeping silent and putting an arm around the other person is a far greater blessing than speaking in rash and thoughtless judgement.

Faith and trust

When it is not possible to identify clearly the cause of our misery, our urgent whys can take hold of us, affecting not just ourselves (in depression or bitterness), but also our view of God and consequently our faith. Sometimes, in our helplessness, we point to God as the author of our grief.

This is what Naomi did after the death of her husband and two sons. In Ruth 1:13 she says 'the Lord's hand has gone out against me!' and in verse 20: 'the Almighty has made my life very bitter' and in verse 21: 'the Lord has brought me back empty' and 'the Lord has afflicted me; the Almighty has brought misfortune upon me'. In her questioning Naomi seemed to have reached the point where her trust in God's goodness was wavering. She came to see im as the One who doesn't only allow evil in our lives, but who actually distributes it, deliberately putting it upon us. What Naomi didn't see is, that because of God's sovereignty, there can be good hiding behind negative things. It is difficult to discern that in moments of pain.

Did Naomi still trust the God of Israel? Interestingly, she kept calling him the Lord, the Almighty, even whilst she blamed him for all her misery. She confessed that she still believed in the existence and sovereignty of God, but she seemed to have lost her faith in his goodness, at least for herself. In Ruth 1:8 and 9 Naomi says to her daughters-in-law: 'May the Lord show kindness to you' and 'May the Lord grant that each of you will find rest in the home of another husband'. As for her own life, however, she believed he had made it bitter and he had turned against her. It seems possible that we still have faith for someone else, even when we have lost all hope for ourselves. When we do that we have allowed our circumstances to shape our view of God. To us he has become someone inconsistent in character, he is good to some of his children and cruel to others. Therefore, when bad things are happening to us, God apparently doesn't love us any more and it would be unrealistic to expect anything good from him. The truth is that, when this is our attitude, we create a distance between ourselves and God.

With Naomi, we see two things happening. In Ruth 1:13 she contrasts her own grief with that of her daughters-in-law and comes to the conclusion that her grief is greater: 'No, my daughters. It is more bitter for me than for you, because the Lord's hand has gone out against me!' Not only had she lost her husband and sons, but on top of this she was convinced that the Lord was against her. Incapable of looking beyond that double sorrow, Naomi became inward looking and fell into self-pity. She also became bitter and angry, particularly towards God. When our pain is simply overwhelming and our whys continue too long without being dealt with, they can turn into reproach and subsequently into destructive negativism as we see happening here. Upon arrival in Bethlehem, Naomi said: 'Call me Mara, because the Almighty has made my life very bitter' (Ruth 1:20). Mara means bitterness, while her own name, Naomi, meant loveliness. But that loveliness was no longer apparent, she had become a miserable, pitiable woman. Bitterness leaves its marks and this was the case with Naomi; people did not recognize her any more, such was the change in her (Ruth 1:19).

Hiding with God

How was Ruth affected by these trials? She reacted quite differently. When she chose to accompany her mother-in-law to Bethlehem, she stated very clearly: 'your God (will be) my God' (Ruth 1:16). Then, in Ruth 2:12 we are told that she found refuge under the wings of the Almighty. Here we meet with that wonderful concept of hiding in God which is the main theme of this book. The very fact that Ruth discovered that God could be her hiding-place and that she could find refuge under his wings shows that, contrary to her mother-in-law, she hadn't lost faith in God's goodness, but still trusted him. In fact, her turning to God in her need was nothing less than a declaration of faith; she was able to surrender and let herself and her sorrow rest with God. It speaks of the beginning of a personal and intimate relationship. Hiding with God is more than just saying : 'I believe that God exists'. A person can keep talking about God as the Almighty One without ever entrusting his life to him or entering into the precious friendship that God desires to have with his children. That alone makes for empty hands.

Each time I read that Ruth found refuge under the wings of the Lord, I am moved by the implication of these words. They communicate a wonderful mystery, which isn't always grasped.

Sometimes certain negative events make us lose our trust in people, sometimes we lose faith even in ourselves. Sometimes, and especially when we feel utterly helpless, our trust in God can be shaken or lost. When all our resources are used up and we, like Naomi, are left standing empty-handed, the feeling of emptiness can overtake us. It can take control of our hearts and thoughts. The questions in our heart can grow into a black cloud hovering above us, affecting our view and perception of God and consequently affecting our faith. Rather than coming closer, we seem to draw away from the Lord. Hiding in him, however, communicates the very opposite, a nearness, the sheer wonder of which cannot be put into words. It is the response to God's unconditional welcome; he invites us to take shelter with him and longs to enfold and cover us – pain, questions and all!

The imagery of taking refuge under God's wings is one of snuggling up to our heavenly Father, looking for warmth and comfort and the safety of 'home'. It involves both trust and trustworthiness. Taking refuge with the Lord is perhaps not always a conscious choice. In our state of desperation, it is the only way, our only hope, there is nothing else left to do. Our search for God often starts in times of trouble and then turns into a growing process, in which our relationship with him deepens and we learn increasingly to rest in him.

We all know how painful and exhausting the struggle with whys can be. Unless dealt with, questions can begin to possess and torture us to the point where we are desperately going around in circles, unable to find a solution, unable to relax or sleep. We find that not just our mind, but our heart and whole being are in turmoil. As Christians we know we can cast our cares upon the Lord, but we seem sometimes to not quite know how to go about it. How do we seek the Lord when we are deeply distressed?

The way in which we communicate our painful questions to God tells much about the nature of our relationship with him. It is like what happens in human friendship: with a friend who is not so close I may share some facts about what is going on in my life, but whilst doing so I carefully hold back my emotions. With a close friend, however, I dare to let go and share not just my problems but all that goes with them inside me, my feelings and tears. Rather than just presenting them with the facts, I present them with myself and come close enough to allow them to feel my pain. Similarly if I have a rather formal relationship with God, I might just state what is going on in my life, delivering my needs and questions at his doorstep, I may go as far as shaking my fist in fury, showing my indignation and inability to understand what is going on, but I do not show the deeper confusion and pain within and don't draw near enough for that to be touched. When we know a distant God, it is difficult to draw near. Like the elder son in the parable of the prodigal, we may find ourselves standing at the back door, deeply upset but unable or unwilling to go inside and talk. If, however, we know the Lord as a Father-Friend, we can go in for a private talk where we present to him not only our whys, but our very selves. We can draw near enough (and stay long enough) to be touched by him. This is a part of the practice of hiding with God and when we learn to come to him in this way, we shall experience what the author of Psalm 94 says in verse 19: 'When anxiety was great within me, your consolation brought joy to my soul'. The psalmist doesn't say that his questions were answered or his problems solved, but he testifies of God reaching out to him with comfort so deep (reaching his very soul or heart) that his burden seemed lighter; he went from great anxiety to joy.

Interestingly, the Hebrew word used for heart suggests much more than just the centre of our emotions. It is a concept that includes our whole being – feelings, thinking and all! Therefore the consolation that Psalm 94 speaks about is total, bringing peace both in thoughts and feelings. I see in verse 19 how someone moves from thousands of restless thoughts and reasonings to an oasis of rest and refreshment where he is totally restored so that he can carry on. The restoration lies not so much in solutions (which is just as well as it is likely that many of our questions will remain unanswered!) as it is brought forth by being with God. It is as the psalmist says: '...your love, O Lord, supported me' (v 18).

We find the same idea in Paul's letter to the Philippians. In Philippians 4:7, he speaks about 'the peace of God that will guard our hearts and minds in Christ Jesus.' It is actually amazing that when we go to the Lord with the thoughts and questions that occupy us, he is not out so much to satisfy our minds as he is to comfort our hearts. In doing that the Lord touches the core of our problem, for our anxiety goes much deeper than just mind level, hence the expression to 'pour out one's heart' (one's whole being). It is that deep that God wants to reach into man, pouring out his peace which transcends understanding. He does that in the hiding place, in a private and intimate encounter on a one to one basis. There, in the inner room we will find that our questions can be overshadowed by the comfort and solace that the Lord gives in our heart or soul. David puts it like this in Psalm 131:2 'I have stilled and quieted my soul; like a weaned child with its mother, like a weaned child is my soul within me'.

The importance of acceptance

When confronted with painful events, one feeling dominates. We long for things to be reversed; everything should be like it was, or even better than before tragedy struck. But the fact is that some things are irrevocable, they cannot be undone and others can only be partly restored. When a loved one has died, or a baby is born with a severe handicap, there is nothing we can do to change that. The only option is that we find our way in the given situation. The steps we need to take in order to make that possible are firstly, to recognize or acknowledge and secondly, to accept the facts. Unless we reach the latter stage, we cannot really progress, but will, like Naomi, keep on struggling and remain bitter and bound.

Recognising the fact that we are unable to change certain things does not automatically mean that we also accept them. It is quite possible that what we know to be true in our minds is turned away at the gate of our heart and emotions. If the latter is the case, we can go on for ages fighting to change or put right the situation, clinging to dreams that need to be left behind. As long as we keep doing that, the pain continues to be acute and intense and we will find that there is nothing quite as draining as to keep struggling when deep down we know that our efforts won't do any good. Once we have reached the point that we can accept a given situation, we won't only find inner peace but gain other things as well. Freed from a bitter struggle against the unwanted, we can now discover what possibilities (rather than impossibilities) lie before us. This will enable us not only to handle things better, but we will find that where we were drained of energy before, we now find new and unexpected strength and courage.

I once met a man whose wife was suffering from Alzheimer's disease. There had been indications of it for quite a while and finally the medical diagnosis confirmed what had been feared. In the period immediately following the diagnosis, this man did all he could to turn the tide. He kept pointing out his wife's forgetfulness to her, correcting every mistake she made. Meanwhile, he was feverishly trying to find out all he could about recent developments in medical research, hoping to find something that would benefit her. For all involved it was a sad and tense situation. The husband was desperately seeking any means that would change things, knowing all along that it was impossible. He was struggling with his own helplessness as well as with his grief over the loss of his partner with whom it was increasingly difficult to communicate. He was also becoming socially isolated; people were beginning to avoid him as visits inevitably turned into a confrontation, causing even more stress.

This man needed to turn around full circle in his thinking, accepting the reality of his wife's disease, heart-rending though it was. The moment that happened, he was able to move forward. He acknowledged that Alzheimer's had been diagnosed, that the diagnosis was correct and the disease progressive. His acceptance of the facts meant that he was now able to face their implications also, daunting though they were: his beloved wife would become more and more confused and dependent, she was deteriorating mentally as well as physically. Consequently their relationship would change: from being her husband and lover, he would increasingly have to be her nurse and he would need help in caring for her. Accepting these things liberated him, which in turn enabled him to keep going day by day rather than go under in the given circumstances. Things hadn't changed, but he himself had changed. Whereas before he was totally focused on his wife's deterioration and had become a prisoner of his own frustration and fear, he was now able to be more relaxed as well as interested in other things; after seeking help at home he began spending time with friends and socialising again, which greatly improved the entire situation.

Because of its nature, acceptance will seldom be an instant decision. It is rather the fruit of a gradual process of change in our thoughts and feelings. It is not the same as resignation which carries in itself a sense of hopelessness and being (or feeling) forced to give up. A mark of true acceptance is that it is voluntary, which is why its effect is liberating. When acceptance is forced, it has an element of reluctance mixed in with it. This results in a continuing and painfully strenuous effort to reverse things and a situation where we do hardly more than survive. It is good to realise this and to take our time to face our pain and work things through as best we can in order to become free people.

Confrontation with pain automatically results in grief that has to be dealt with. It is like a mourning process, which is needed not only when we bury someone, but also when we face other losses such as our health, position or reputation, financial security, a relationship or future plans. Each time we need to go through different stages before we reach the point of acceptance. We may struggle with unbelief, denial and anger, all of them normal reactions which are part of coming to terms with our grief and whys. Unless we manage to overcome these negative emotions, we will get entangled in the chains of our own hopeless struggle. When, however, we do (with the loving help of those around us) arrive at the point of acceptance, we are increasingly able to let go of what is past, including the dreams we held for the future, and this sets us free to go forward. Even if we feel that we do so with empty hands, we may still lift them up, thus remaining open to (unexpected) blessing. That makes acceptance open-ended and eliminates fatalism.

Back to Naomi, Orpah and Ruth, what happened to them after their bereavement? Orpah decided to return to her own people in the land of Moab. We aren't told exactly how she reacted or what her situation was like later on, in the Book of Ruth she sadly disappears from the scene. But Naomi and Ruth stayed together, they decided to leave the past behind and start afresh in Bethlehem. Their move signified the end of a certain period in their lives. For Naomi, the death of her husband and sons remained a fact: she had to live on alone and decided to do so in her home country. Things were no different for her daughter-in-law Ruth, except that she did not return to familiar surroundings and people. She chose a new direction and in doing so took a big step of faith.

Naomi and Ruth each had their own unique experience and pain and each reacted to it in her own way. Both acknowledged that they were now on their own and that they had to somehow carry on with life. But their attitudes were very different. Naomi had set out on an inward path. She became stuck in self-pity and bitterness, whereas Ruth, in her hiding with God, had found freedom. One was restless, the other possessed a quiet assurance in the midst of her own turmoil. The older woman accepted her circumstances with reluctance; she was bending under her load of disappointment and pain. The younger woman seemed to have left her worries and grief with the Lord in whom she had found refuge. She was able to stand up straight and go forward with hope. We see in the Book of Ruth how Ruth could take the initiative and get on with things. Her zest and courage were stimulating; she was able to carry her mother-in-law along. It seems that her finding refuge in God gave her the strength that she needed to move on in a positive way. She accepted what happened and her acceptance liberated her – in and with God she had a new hope for the future.

The experience of pain seems to be able to take us in one of two possible directions: one person in their helplessness will become depressed and rebellious, whereas the other finds peace.

It is sad to see how some become distanced from God, and somewhat of a mystery to see the opposite happening to others who seem to be driven to God. He is the One who remains the same in all circumstances. Throughout the story of Ruth and Naomi we see him both present and in control, he is never helpless nor at a loss even when his children are suffering. Moreover, he is not just there from the beginning to the end, but he is actively present as the One who is in charge of things, controlling, overseeing and guiding. When the story of Naomi and Ruth unfolds, we discover that God's ways with his children are wonderful, meaning both precious as well as wondrous (in that we will not always be able to fathom or understand what is happening to us). Realising that should make us cautious and teach us not to be quick to provide answers and solutions (or to reproach God!) when we are faced with events that we cannot place, they may simply be beyond us.

In fact we have little or no idea what is happening behind the scenes. As Christians we do know, however, that sometimes visibly, more often invisibly, Someone is keeping an eye on us, holding and guiding our lives safely in his hands. The moment that we start to take refuge in him is in fact the moment that our empty hands are refilled. The wonder of being with God fills and restores us and strengthens our feeble knees, so that we can start afresh on the path which he has laid before us. Ruth found peace and new energy, not just for herself but for others as well. She didn't desert Naomi, in fact she was a tower of strength and a great comfort to her. The truth is, once you find a hiding place in God, you are in a position to be a blessing to others, even when you are going through a difficult time yourself.

Serenity Prayer

God, grant me the Serenity
to accept the things I cannot change;
Courage to change the things I can,
and the Wisdom to know the difference.

Living one day at a time;
Enjoying one moment at a time;
Accepting hardship as the pathway to peace.

Taking, as he did, this sinful world as it is,
Not as I would have it;

Trusting, that he will make all things right if
I surrender to his will;

That I may be reasonably happy in this life,
And supremely happy with him forever in the next.

Reinhold Niebuhr

2
Moving On

When someone is left empty-handed, for whatever reason, there are a number of things that need to be done. Inevitably the time will come when choices need to be made regarding how to continue. Because each person and each experience is unique it is impossible to lay down rules or principles that can be generally applied. Naomi, Ruth and Orpah were all in the same boat, their lives had been intertwined for a number of years, they were related and bonded together by the men they loved and married. The two younger women had a few other things in common as well, they may have been roughly the same age and came from the same culture, having both grown up in the land of Moab. Their husbands were brothers and they both had childless marriages. Naomi, however, was older. Herself a Jewess, she had grown up in Judah, but later on she moved and settled abroad with her family. When her sons died she had already been widowed for years. We saw earlier how the death of her sons was the last in a series of disappointments and how her grief took root and grew into bitterness. Her daughters-in-law had their own pain, but they reacted differently. The story of these three women illustrates how it works in life; each of us faces our own unique situation and have our own choices to make regarding the future. Therefore it is impossible to predict how someone will react when faced with the pain and perplexities of life.

Choices and decisions

In Ruth 1:6 we are told that after the death of Naomi's two sons, there was news that the famine in Judah (the reason why Elimelech and Naomi had moved to Moab) had come to an end. Following this news, Naomi and her two daughters-in-law prepared to return to Bethlehem in Judah. Naomi probably longed to go back to the place where her roots were, there was nothing left to keep her in Moab, no husband, no sons, no grandchildren.

It is often said, and rightly so, that we need to be careful not to make hasty decisions after a dramatic event has taken place in our lives. It can happen that one acts impulsively and later regrets the decisions made and steps taken, simply because more time was needed to work things through as well as to carefully consider new possibilities and their consequences. Remarrying too soon after the death of one's spouse, a sudden move or other radical changes are examples of premature decisions that people can regret deeply later on. They find they weren't ready for such a major step and consequently struggle to adjust to their new situation whilst they still have to come to terms with the events that preceded it. Often they feel trapped and would give anything to undo the present situation. Meanwhile they aren't the only ones suffering; the people around them are also affected by their distress. Many a spouse of someone who remarried too soon after being widowed or divorced is bewildered by the problems that arise in this new relationship, only to find that the cause of friction and pain is a belated but deep mourning process within their partner.

The reverse can also happen. A disastrous event can leave one paralysed by shock, unable to face up to reality. Rather than making hasty decisions, in fact none at all are made. Sometimes people withdraw into their own world. I once knew a man who, following his mother's death, wouldn't open his curtains for weeks, because he couldn't face life going on, and particularly spring coming. Why should he make the effort to get up when the most important person in his life was gone? One can also deny reality by refusing to make even the most basic adjustments. It is just too painful and confrontational. I stood by close friends who recently lost a son and know how putting his last lot of dirty washing into the washing-machine was a heart-wrenching experience, as was going through his books and writings, but it needed to be done. Sometimes the clothes and possessions of a deceased person can be left untouched too long, his or her room almost becoming a shrine or a place which suggests that nothing has happened and that he or she could return any moment. These things are unhealthy and if they continue too long, they hinder the process of coming to terms with what has happened, which in turn hinders moving on and damages the person(s) involved.

One thing is certain: life goes on. A widow can be so overwhelmed by grief that she feels her life is over. The same goes for the man who learns that he is terminally ill; or the parents who have a severely handicapped baby; for the boy who finds himself paralysed after an accident; or the woman who is confronted with her husband's unfaithfulness. They feel as if life has come to a complete standstill, there is no other reality than their own and nothing else matters. Don't talk about 'life abundant' (John 10:10), this is 'grief abundant' and the most one can do is to try and survive.

A young widow once told me how grateful she was that she had young children who required attention and care. 'After my husband died, I would have loved to just stay in bed and never get up again', she said, 'but the children had to get dressed, they needed food and clean clothes and assistance with their homework. They kept me going and helped me to get back on my feet again!' Her situation illustrates how there is always a moment when we need to return to the daily routine of life, picking up things where we left them and taking up the responsibility for our own lives again, maybe with some help initially but then on our own. This is the first (obvious) step in any given situation of grief.

We don't know how long Naomi waited before she moved house, but the moment came when she packed her things and went. Her decision was one that seemed obvious in her situation, it probably wasn't sudden but had taken shape over a period of time. And so she returned to Bethlehem, a decision which later turned out to be not only wise but also far-reaching in its consequences. But at the time she had no idea of the implications, she just followed her heart and head. Sometimes seemingly ordinary and obvious decisions are the wisest ones!

We must realise that Naomi, in returning to the land of her forefathers, didn't just go back to her physical roots, but also to her spiritual roots, as Judah was the land of the God of Israel. There she wanted to try to rebuild life with both her daughters-in-law, Ruth and Orpah. Ruth 1:7 makes it clear that the three of them started out on the journey together. But then Naomi urged the two younger women to return to their own roots and relatives. She realised that she had no resources and next to nothing to offer them. Being a widow herself, she would have to fall back on her relatives and couldn't guarantee that they would be willing to take on two foreign women as well! And even if there would be a place for them to live, what more could she offer Ruth and Orpah? No marriage, no future, only uncertainty. Which kinsman-redeemer would be prepared to marry a non-Jewish woman in order to maintain Elimelech's name (note Ruth 4:5)? These questions must have occupied Naomi's mind and made her decide to send her daughters-in-law back to their own relatives ('Go back, each of you, to your mother's home... May the LORD grant that each of you will find rest in the home of another husband', Ruth 1:8-9). I believe that it was extremely painful for Naomi to tell her daughters-in-law to leave her, but in her eyes there was no other way; her advice was based on her own helplessness to be of any use to them, in no way was it selfish. This family was bonded by love (Ruth 1:8, 14 and 16).

Naomi's return to Bethlehem seemed obvious and was a wise decision, not just momentarily but also ultimately. Remarkably, the suggestion made to Orpah and Ruth to return to their own relatives seems at first sight to have been just as obvious and wise. Yet from a heavenly perspective it was wrong, because it was a step back. Ruth and Orpah were in fact asked to choose between returning to their own relatives and gods or joining Naomi in her return to the land and the God of Israel. It was a choice therefore between serving false gods (Ruth 1:15) and serving the only true God of Israel (Ruth 1:16). Consequently it meant either regressing or progressing, captivity or freedom. The momentous consequences of either choice make it clear beyond any doubt how pivotal prayer for God's guidance and wisdom is, even for steps that in our limitedness we consider logical and good. We must bring our total situation before the Lord and weigh carefully and prayerfully also the loving (but not always wise!) advice given to us by fellow believers.

Sometimes we need to make decisions when we are unable to foresee the consequences. One choice will lead us on, another choice may set us back. What place does God have in our decision making as well as in our newly-chosen situation? Orpah chose the way that seemed safest to her, she took her situation into her own hands and returned to the (relative) security of her family and an environment without God. Following that decision she disappeared into obscurity. Ruth, however, resolutely stated that she desired to follow the God of Israel. This was a very radical decision, implying that she definitely let go of her identity as a Moabite woman, choosing to become a woman of God. She was also quite outspoken about not wanting to abandon her mother-in-law ('Don't urge me to leave you or to turn back from you', Ruth 1:16). Humanly speaking Ruth took a risk in going to Judah, but she nevertheless dared to go. It is likely that living with her in-laws had shown her something of the God of Israel, enough to dare to take refuge under his wings (Ruth 2:12), entrusting her future to him and his people. I ascribe Ruth's courage not merely to herself, but to what she found in God; he himself was her fountainhead of strength and enabled her to keep going and to brave a new situation. Her attitude testifies to a peace that only God can give, the peace which transcends all understanding and will guard our hearts and our minds in Christ Jesus (Phil. 4:7). How we need that peace that prevents our thoughts from running away with us and that serenity that stands even in the most vexing circumstances, enabling us to carry on calmly and steadfastly as we face the unknown.

For Ruth the unknown was the impending stay in Bethlehem as well as the long journey to get there, extra difficult maybe because she travelled with a sad and bitter companion, Naomi.

Yet she stayed with her, and once they had arrived in Bethlehem the two of them set themselves to the task of finding a place to live and the means to provide a living for themselves (Ruth 2).

Grief and bitterness

Some people sincerely believe that the mark of a true Christian is that they are continually grateful and glad. They base their conviction upon Paul's words in 1 Thessalonians 5:16, where he says: 'Be joyful always'. Add to this the 'we are more than conquerors' (Romans 8:37) and there is the setting for a sincere belief in our being commissioned to maintain a cheerful and victorious attitude in all circumstances and, cost what it may, there is no room for tears. Therefore, if someone does grieve and does so for longer (or more intensively) than was expected (or allowed!), they obviously lack in faith. For people who hold this view, grief is the same as defeat, whereas gladness is victory. There is, however, a lot more to Paul's words.

When talking to people who personally know pain, these things often come up. Those grieving are told that it would be a more powerful Christian witness if they were grateful and glad instead of sad. The parents who lost a child at birth should be happy that they already have a child or are young enough to have other children; the wife whose husband had an affair should be grateful that he broke up his relationship with the other woman and wishes to restore his marriage; the man who is handicapped as a result of molestation should be glad that he is still alive. A woman, in the last stage of cancer, received a letter in which she was rebuked for the fact that she grieved about her impending death and having to leave her loved ones. She was told that she should rejoice in the fact that soon she would be with the Lord. What the letter actually communicated was that the writer was disappointed about the dying woman's faith and her lack of testimony. Such remarks are deeply hurtful. They emphasize one side of things but do not leave any room for the process of pain and mourning that we need to go through in order to come to terms with our situation.

How good it is to know that the Lord Jesus has an altogether different view of grief! During his years on earth, he too knew sorrow and he allowed it as a natural reaction to pain. Think of his tears after his friend Lazarus died, of his grief over the short-sightedness and unfaithfulness of people, over the betrayal by his close friends and the pain of his own loneliness in his suffering. He was a man of sorrows and familiar with suffering, says Isaiah 53:3. Jesus was also someone who noticed other people's tears. When, after his resurrection, he saw Mary Magdalene crying at his empty tomb, he asked her: 'Woman, why are you crying?' (John 20:15). He didn't reproach her because of her tears, but he gently probed her, allowing her to unburden herself and tell him what bothered her.

We see the same thing happening with Naomi, who somehow couldn't get over her grief. God allowed her time and space for her feelings, even for those of bitterness. Throughout the book of Ruth I see God's presence and patience lovingly and faithfully extended to this woman who had reached the point where she had become negative and inward looking. God never reproached her for her 'wrong attitude', but let her be and, more than that, he met her in her situation and blessed her.

When people tell you that it is time you to pull yourself together and stop mourning, you may know that the Lord has room for your sorrow and enough buckets to hold all your tears. But it is also true to say that when we come to him with our grief and meet his grace (and space!), our grief changes, or rather, it is given a companion! For the sheer experience of the presence of God gives birth to gratefulness. It sometimes washes away our grief whilst at other times it somehow becomes a partner of it. I believe that joy and sorrow aren't opposites, they can exist side by side. It is neither one or the other, they go together. When I am deeply distressed and seek refuge with my heavenly Father, I can, in my distress, experience an overwhelming sense of gratefulness which comes very close to joy. This is not based on what happened or is happening, but solely on God's goodness and greatness that I meet when I hide with him. In other words, I am grateful for who he is, and can rejoice in him even in oppressing circumstances. I find that in his presence my pain changes. Peace comes into it, the sting is removed and the pain is overshadowed by his endless love and comfort.

There is a continuing painful situation in my own life that I am unable to change. My mother suffers from senile dementia. I knew her as a strong woman with an infectious enthusiasm for the Lord as well as for life. She used to be adventurous and loved to take on all sorts of people and projects, she was always interested in what I did or what concerned me. My mother was converted when she was over sixty years old. Her age didn't stop her from getting involved in different kinds of Christian activities and she did so with great zest and commitment. During the years that I lived abroad I knew I could give her address to people who were travelling and needed a roof over their heads. They always found a warm welcome, sympathy, food and a bed. At present this same mother is totally helpless, restricted both in mind and body. Confined to a wheelchair, she spends her days in a special ward for old people who suffer from senility. Sometimes it is possible to have a reasonable conversation with her, but mostly not. Sometimes she recognizes me, sometimes not.

I find my visits to her very painful. At times I can cope with the situation fairly well, at other times I experience so much pain that I weep buckets in my car whilst driving home after a visit. Initially my helplessness and frustration brought me to the end of my tether, there was no way in which I could cope with the oppressive questions and protests in my mind. The whys of the destructive degeneration of a valuable person, the whys of my mother's own visible grief and confusion. But those things have changed. It would be untrue to say that my questions have totally evaporated or that I have no problems in dealing with the situation, for at times I feel as helpless and frustrated as in the beginning, yet in the midst of all this, peace has been given. My visits to my mother are different from what they used to be like. Today, most of the time when I am with her, I can accept that she is the way she is. Whereas before, I often felt impatient and frustrated and saw only negative and painful things, I now find I can be grateful for the good moments and can adjust to another level of communication and accept a reversed mother-daughter relationship. Things are not the way I (or my mother!) would like them to be and that pain will remain, maybe for the rest of our lives. But the peace that God has given has somehow created room to see and enjoy the good and precious moments spent with a precious person. I myself could not have brought that about, that inner peace is the fruit of hiding in God. When I enter painful situations like this one, hidden in God's safe protection and surrounded by his peace, I experience that he is the One who carries me. And that makes me grateful and gives joy even in the midst of pain.

Coping with our negative feelings

As we saw earlier on, Naomi was given space to grieve and even to utter her negative feelings towards God. Mercifully God allows us to come to him , whatever state we are in! How I wish that, as a Body of Christ, we would learn to reflect more of that same attitude of unconditional love and acceptance and would unlearn our impatience towards one another as well as our rash condemnation of those whose attitude or behaviour is not up to our standard or expectations. We can be quite forward in telling people how they should behave and what should change, whilst maybe all that is needed is some (spacious!) sympathy.

Whilst saying this, I don't deny that there needs to be a limit to negative feelings: for if they go on endlessly, we will spiral down and reach a pit of deep despair which will affect our faith, ourselves and those around us. This is what Naomi was beginning to experience when, incapable of coming to terms with her triple bereavement, her quest for answers brought her to the point where she blamed God. Somewhere and somehow her grief had had the opportunity to take root and grow into something fierce and destructive; she indicated herself that she had turned into a bitter woman.

It is sometimes said that bitterness is solidified grief and I think we have an example of that here. When never called to a halt, grief, which in itself is a healthy emotion as a proper and necessary reaction to pain, can develop into an unhealthy one.

This happens when it isn't dealt with properly and consequently takes root and grows and starts bearing bitter fruit. Somewhere in the process of mourning and coming to terms with grief and pain, destructive emotions (like anger or bitterness) can subtly get mixed in and they can grow to the point where they begin to master our mood, like tares shooting up among the wheat, choking it. It is very difficult to discern when and how this happens, but it is clear that one factor that stimulates growth of negative emotions is the space that they are allowed. We need holy wisdom and discernment to help one another in these complex areas.

There is something else: bitterness towards God isn't only destructive for ourselves, the main evil in it is that it implies a judgement towards the Holy One. As human beings we can never call God to the bar to face a human inquisition. The idea that we should require of him that he explain and defend himself is ludicrous, it is unjustified and unjustifiable. It cannot be allowed, but...God allows it. He allows us to share our deepest feelings and confusion with him as long as he sees fit. It is never our right to do so, it is his grace that allows our protests to be shouted towards heaven and grace that they arrive and are heard there! Note how in the psalms we often come across bitterness and anger, sometimes spoken, sometimes indeed shouted. God is blamed for the fact that he remains silent or seems unjust. The psalmist shakes his fist towards heaven and ... God allows it. But time and time again there is also the point of a miraculous change of attitude. The protester is silenced and stands in awe before God, expressing his devotion and praise. We see that happen in Psalm 73 where Asaph shows great indignation about the prosperity of the wicked. He wonders what the point is of trying so hard to be faithful to God when those who couldn't care less seem to live carefree and successful lives. In verses 21-22 Asaph says that his heart was grieved and his spirit embittered, he says of himself that he was like a brute beast before God. Until! Until he came to the Lord and his eyes were opened to reality. This happened when he entered the sanctuary of God (verse 17), this is when he sought God's presence or came to hide in God. At that moment of truth his attitude turned around one hundred degrees and he said: 'I have made the Sovereign LORD my refuge' (verse 28). This is the best thing we can do as that is where we find life and can shed our bitterness which kills and destroys. We are allowed whys as a cry of our heart but never as a demanding accusation towards God. Whys can exist but should never dominate our thinking and drag on so long that they take root. Rather, they should be brought to and poured out in the sanctuary, this is in God's presence.

3
God Fills Our Hands

Human helplessness is nowhere more clear than in situations where we are faced with things we cannot control. When we have lost a loved one, are struck by an incurable and progressive illness or have lost home and hearth through a catastrophe, our eyes are opened to our own limitations as well as to the vulnerability of our very existence. We know that we are incapable of altering the situation in the sense of undoing it. The option left to us is that we must find our way in the given circumstances. Personally, we often feel that we have reached a cul-de-sac, but we are actually standing at a crossroads from which it *is* possible to proceed. We saw earlier that in order to be able to do this, we need to accept the facts, however painful. The next step that is asked of us is that we adjust accordingly, which requires courage and adaptability.

Naomi and her daughters-in-law had their fair share of disappointments and difficulties. In the previous chapter, we saw how the three women reached a point where they were faced with the necessity of making a choice regarding the direction they should take. Two of them remained loyal to the God of Israel and, in doing so, moved forward. Their choice was a good one, yet one could ask whether it was a guarantee of restoration. If and when we follow the Lord, will our hands be automatically filled again and, if so, what does it imply? We shall consider that question in this chapter.

We are still following Naomi and Ruth, first en route to Bethlehem and later as they settle there. At this point it would be a good idea for you to take a pause and read the whole book of Ruth (if you haven't done so already). You will then have an overview and consequently a better understanding of the principles found in their history.

Can one say that the hands of Naomi and Ruth were filled again? My conclusion is that indeed they were, even though it may not have happened in quite the way they (or we) imagined. If we expected a new marriage for both Naomi and Ruth, we may have been disappointed because only Ruth was given a new husband. Naomi, however, remained single. Yet she also experienced restoration in the sense that she 'came home', not just to Bethlehem, where once again, she was amongst her own people, but deeper still, in her renewed trust and joy in the Lord. Over and beyond that, she was also profoundly blessed by the birth of Ruth's son Obed whom she looked after. Ruth 4:16 and 17a tell us how '...Naomi took the child, laid him in her lap and cared for him. The women living there said, "*Naomi* has a son". (It is just as well that Ruth and Naomi had a very close relationship (Ruth 4:15), or Naomi's deep involvement with the baby might have caused tension with her daughter-in-law!)

Surprises

I once heard Dr. Larry Crabb tell how as a four-year-old, he accidentally locked himself up in the bathroom. When efforts to open the door from the outside had proved futile, his parents assured him through the keyhole that he need not worry as help would come. Overwhelmed by the possibility that he might have to spend the rest of his life in the bathroom, Larry kept his eyes glued to the doorknob which he expected would be the key to his deliverance. Then, at the peak of agitation, because no help seemed to come forward, he heard a sound behind him and to his immense relief, he discovered his father standing on a ladder in front of the window. Help had come, but from a different and unexpected direction.

Larry's story is a parody of what happens between us and our heavenly Father. We stand empty-handed and cry for help, but we have our own ideas about how we should be helped or what ingredients are needed to put an end to our distress. We long for a new partner or for physical healing; we wish our loneliness would end; our financial problems be solved; or an unpleasant colleague or neighbour transferred. These wishes aren't automatically fulfilled. Yet God is the same faithful One whether situations change or not. He looks at each individual, desiring to bless and to fill empty hands. Sometimes his answer comes from an unexpected angle and takes us by surprise, sometimes what he does isn't very obvious. We can be so obsessed by the things that do not happen that we fail to notice God's blessings.

Now let us look at Naomi, who, although blinded by her bitterness, was nevertheless richly blessed by the Lord. From looking at her situation, I want to suggest four areas of blessing that can easily remain unnoticed and therefore immobilised (meaning its potential remains unrecognised and therefore unused), when we are, as it were, helplessly spinning a cocoon in our misery.

a) Consolation in friendship
One of the great blessings in Naomi's life was the presence and faithfulness of her daughter-in-law Ruth. Naomi may not have been aware of the fact that the Lord himself was reaching out to her through Ruth. Dulled by disillusionment, she may not have recognised that what happened was in fact much more than simply human support offered to her.

We are not told what happened during that long journey to Bethlehem. We know that even after Orpah had left, Ruth remained steadfast in her determination to stick to her mother-in-law (Ruth 1:14-17). Naomi finally accepted Ruth's choice. As far as we know she did not waste any more words about it, the matter was settled. Maybe she felt at that point that it wouldn't make much difference, she felt alone and deserted anyway. But she wasn't, for Ruth travelled alongside her. The name Ruth means companion and I believe that the Lord gave Ruth to Naomi as such. She wasn't travelling alone, there was someone standing close by her through whom the Lord communicated his love and faithfulness. Sometimes, when we are blinded by bitterness or pain, God by his grace, gives us people on our life's journey as visual aids in whom we can recognise something of himself.

How does one stand by someone who is grieving? What does it mean to meet someone in his Name, to be as Christ to him? A mother, who lost her son following an unfortunate accident at school, wrote a very moving poem that expresses what comfort and friendship entail in times of distress.

Friends
> They stayed
> when laughter disappeared
> and our faces became lined with grief,
> when only one story was left,
> which needed to be repeated
> over and over again
> about the boy,
> happy and talented,
> do you remember,
> do you remember
> and then...
>
> When others,
> whom we had believed were faithful,

disappeared,
they stayed,
their hands resting firmly on our shoulders

In those days
we grew ages older

And they?
They kept us from going under
in gales of grief,
in hurricanes of sorrow
and through them
we knew,
God hadn't deserted us.

          (written by Riec Kolman, translated from Dutch)

Who were the people capable of giving comfort to these grief-stricken parents? They were not the ones who kept trying to find answers or who tried persistently to cheer them up at a time when space was needed for grief. They were not the people who, driven by their own helplessness, exclaimed in all sincerity that the time had come to stop mourning. They were not those who indicated that they had expected a more positive reaction from a believer than this overwhelming sorrow. They were not those who said: 'Look at all that you still have, there are so many good things left in your life!' They were the people who *were with them*. They *listened*, they did not say anything but *dared to be silent*. They were the people who dared to *touch and hold* the other person, thus communicating love and warmth. They were people who know an inner freedom that enables them to give another person freedom and space. They are often people who have themselves known grief and who have come to understand that, when in pain, we need a place of refuge. Ruth knew that. Like Naomi, she also carried a load of sorrow, yet somehow she had sufficient strength left to be a source of support and comfort to her mother-in-law, without becoming absorbed by her depression and negativism. Here we see the younger generation strengthening the older one and a woman from a heathen background, showing mercy to a daughter of Abraham. These things were only possible because Ruth herself had learned to take refuge in God. Where Naomi blamed him for her distress, Ruth came to the right place with her questions and grief; she found refuge under the wings of the Almighty, there where God's loving kindness is tangible in all that it comprises – love, comfort, restoration and rest. Once she had found a new identity and security in God, she was able to reach out to others, offering them profound comfort and communicating hope.

Is that not exactly what Riec Kolman attempts to communicate in her poem? When her family was grieving over the loss of a young son, they found some friends vanishing. These friends were unable to face up to the confrontation of deep grief as it made them painfully aware of their own helplessness. They were unable to cope with always having to listen to the same story being told. They couldn't stand hearing this overwhelming sorrow being expressed over and over again. So they disappeared. All that is said about those who stayed is that they stayed close enough to touch their friends where they were, putting their arms around them. That was what mattered, that was most important. No talking, no answers, but simply being there, showing empathy and communicating nearness. The parents experienced that as a precious token of God's presence and comfort. This is how he so often chooses to work and act in people's lives, meeting us in and through others and using their arms or hands to convey his comfort. Thus it sometimes happens that we take refuge with another person and there discover something of God as he uses that other person to reveal to us some aspects of his character. We too, can at times be a shelter to someone else. We are able to be that when we ourselves have discovered him to be our hiding place, where we can come with our own grief or in our intercessory prayers with other people's pain. People who have learnt that, have usually also learnt to be silent.

Naomi had a companion in Ruth. That is in fact one of the ways in which the Lord filled her empty hands again. Friendship is a great and precious gift. We need to develop an eye for that and thereby come to appreciate more of what is given to us in our friends.

b) The blessing of intercessory prayer

One very special area in which friends can deeply bless one another is that of prayer. When someone's world is clouded over and grief is overwhelming, friends can reach out by lifting them through the clouds to God's throne of grace in intercessory prayer. We can do that for others, others can do that for us and in doing so we mobilise 'the things of God' that surpass even the best things we can give one another.

When we have reached the end of our tether and are unable to escape the reality of our own helplessness and pain, the Lord God is still the omnipresent One and our great Helper. When confused and yet required to make choices and decisions, when we need to reflect on things past and present in order to know how to carry on, we can seek God in prayer for ourselves as well as for others and rely on his presence with us. He wants to lead his children into truth and freedom. It is possible that our view of God is marred because we are overwhelmed by pain or have become blocked by our own questions. Maybe we are dumbfounded and in such turmoil that we are unable to pray. When this happens to us or others, friends can help one another, not so much by their good advice, but firstly and foremost by their faithful presence and always by their continuing intercession.

I know of some people who pray for me regularly. At least two of them do so each day. Their faithfulness in prayer is to me one of the strongest and most profound proofs of friendship. When people uphold one another in that way, their bond is deepened which makes sharing possible, even the sharing of things that are very painful. It is a very precious experience to realise that someone knows my deeds and anxiety – in as far as I have felt free to share these, for true friendship doesn't force things – and is praying about them. There is no greater thing that friends can give one another than a true commitment to prayer. It is a big thing to give as well as a huge commitment to make and we need to be very careful not to make rash promises in this area. It is easier to say: 'I'll pray for you' or to end a letter with words like 'You are in my prayers', than to actually do it! The promise is sincere, the fulfilment of it sometimes slack. When we say or write such things we need to be true to what we say.

It is an awesome thing to realise that the Lord Jesus himself is continually interceding for us. He is the perfect example of faithful prayer and intercession, both during his life on earth and now, as our High Priest in heaven. It is fascinating to see how, during his life on earth, prayer was both necessary and natural, it was top priority. Luke's Gospel, in particular, records several moments when Jesus made time for and sought a lonely place, away from other people, to be with his Father. I have often wondered what they talked about, but these moments between Father and Son were so intimate, that I realise it is none of my business. However, I am certain that Jesus included his friends in his prayers. His words to Peter, who he knew would disown him after his arrest, testify to that. Jesus says, in Luke 22:31-32, 'Satan has asked to sift you as wheat. But I have prayed for you, Simon, that your faith may not fail'. Imagine praying for someone who you know is about to betray you! Praying for their survival and spiritual growth, when you yourself are facing the deepest suffering! This is caring about others, this is carrying others on one's heart! John 17 records how, on the brink of his arrest, Jesus prayed, not only for himself, but also for his disciples as well as for all believers. He prayed that they might be one and that God would protect them and sanctify them. The Lord isn't only watching us from a distance, he isn't just registering that we go through painful or bewildering experiences, but he is actively present and involved with us at all times.

The Lord Jesus didn't only intercede for us during his life on earth, but also now, following his ascension into heaven, he is our supreme intercessor. In the letter to the Hebrews, we read how Jesus is seated at the right hand of God as our eternal high priest. Hebrews 7:25 says that he always lives to intercede for those who come to God through him. How does he know what to pray for or how to intercede? The focus is on our salvation, just as was the case when Jesus prayed for Peter. Jesus knows of all things that hinder our faith and walk with him. Would he, who himself lived on earth as a man, not be aware of or understand what things occupy or oppress us? Hebrews 4:15 states: 'For we do not have a high priest who is unable to sympathise with our weaknesses, but we have one who has been tempted in every way, just as we are...' The sentence doesn't finish there, a few more words are added and they are the pivotal point of Jesus' high priesthood: '(He).. was without sin'. The very fact that Jesus did not give in to temptation makes him into our perfect High Priest, whose throne of grace we can approach 'with confidence, so that we may receive mercy and find grace to help us in our time of need'(Hebrews 4:16). Here we meet a God, who isn't struck down helplessly by life's events, he is able to abide with us and intervene in our time of need.

As our high priest, Jesus prays for us and he invites us to pray as well, thus calling on us to have our share in mobilizing heaven to pour out mercy and grace in our time of need. But it goes even further than that. The Lord is graciously aware of our weakness when it comes to prayer: in the Garden of Gethsemane, he found his disciples sleeping, 'exhausted from sorrow', as Luke puts it in Luke 22:45. Parallel passages (Matt.26:36-46 and Mark 14:32-42) say that Jesus had to wake them three times and each time Jesus urged them (and particularly Peter!) to be alert and pray that they would not fall to temptation. Sleepy, prayerless disciples are in essence weak disciples. So are disciples who have an undeveloped, 'vague' prayer life; they don't really know how to pray and what to pray for. Well, disciples haven't changed since those early days! But these facts, disturbing though they are, do not leave Jesus disillusioned and ready to give up on us. Rather, he wants to help us by his Spirit and this is what he promises us when it comes to prayer: 'In the same way, the Spirit helps us in our weakness. We do not know what we ought to pray for, but the Spirit himself intercedes for us with groans that words cannot express' (Rom.8:26).

We are being upheld in prayer and we are urged to pray ourselves with hands lifted up (in praise and thanksgiving), but also with empty hands, when we are at a loss and don't know how to handle our situation or how to proceed. What is more, even in our own weakness, we may, as God's 'royal priesthood' (words from 1 Pet.2:9), intercede for others.

c) God's guidance

Naomi's return to Bethlehem seemed the logical and natural thing to do after the death of her sons. There was nothing to keep her in the land of Moab and the primary reason for their departure from Bethlehem many years ago, was no longer valid as the famine had come to an end in Judah. It was an obvious move, Naomi did not need a long time to think about it.

Unfortunately decisions don't always come that easily, particularly when we are in the midst of turmoil or mourning.

When our world just seems to have fallen apart and we are busy trying to pick up the pieces, it is almost impossible to have a clear assessment of our situation and to be able to draw conclusions as to what course of action is required. We may find ourselves enveloped in a paralysing cloud of uncertainty and even though we pray and pray for an awareness of God's presence and for his guidance, we often feel unable to move and incapable of making out which way to go. How can we discern and understand God's voice? If it were up to us, we would be very happy in some situations (and maybe not at all in others!) if the Lord's voice would be clearly audible and he would tell us exactly what to do.

It is true to say that in most cases it doesn't work like that. A number of our Old Testament friends had the privilege of hearing God speak directly to them. When Abram was called by God to go on a journey, Genesis 12:1 simply states: 'The Lord had said to Abram..' and of Moses it is said: 'The Lord would speak to Moses face to face, as a man speaks with his friend...' (Ex. 33:11). When Elijah was tired and depressed the angel of the Lord spoke to him. Later on, when he was staying in a cave on Mount Horeb, he heard the voice of the Lord again (1 Kings 19). Samuel at a very young age was called by God himself (1 Sam. 3). There are numerous instances mentioned in the Bible, both in the Old and New Testament, where people heard God's voice. In the book of Acts for instance, Philip is spoken to by an angel of the Lord, who tells him to go to a certain road. Having arrived there, the Spirit tells him specifically what he is to do next (Acts 8:26 and 29). In Acts 10, we read that both Cornelius and Peter heard God speaking directly. These are just a few of many examples.

Whilst I do believe that these things still happen, I think it is realistic to say that more often than not we would love to hear God's voice speaking to us directly, only to find that we don't hear him speaking in that way. This is not a book dealing specifically with God's guidance and therefore I do not want to go into the subject too deeply here. I do, however, want to say a few words about it, as it is so crucial that we discern God's way in and out of situations where we stand empty-handed and helpless. Let me say firstly that it is often in these very situations, where we long to hear just something or even anything from God, that it seems as though heaven is made of impenetrable brass. At such times we realise how crucial it is to have God's Word hidden in our hearts and stored up in our minds; it is like a life-saving raft that we can hold on to when all the other securities have disappeared in the waves. During the times when our feelings are temporarily numbed and our eyes are blinded by tears, we can continue on our 'automatic pilot', knowing what is good and also what is not. We must hold on firmly to what we know about and of God. We can also count on the presence of his Holy Spirit, who wants to direct us, also through what seem to be our 'own' decisions. Sometimes we cannot do anything else than what seems obvious, but we need to break through the impasse and take some sort of action. Sometimes in hindsight, we can see how God used even unimportant or obvious events to unfold his unique plan for our lives. He doesn't always work in a spectacular way, but more often invisibly and quietly.

We see this happening with Naomi and Ruth. The events that followed their arrival in Bethlehem seem at first sight to have been no more than a few minor and lucky coincidences. With hindsight, however, these seemingly small details were crucial and necessary parts of a greater plan. In Ruth 2 we read how Ruth went to work in order to provide a living for herself and her mother-in-law and how 'as it turned out' she ended up on a plot of land belonging to Boaz (verse 3). He happened to be a relative of Naomi's deceased husband, 'one of our kinsman-redeemers' (verse 20). This meant that he was the one who could have a major role concerning the future of these two widows [1]. When Ruth was working in Boaz' fields, he noticed her and subsequently invited her to join his servant girls (verse 8). He gave Ruth very special favours, she was allowed to eat with the harvesters (verse 14), who had received orders to leave Ruth to glean where she wanted. They were told to pull out stalks from their bundles of barley and leave them for her to pick up (verses 15-16). No wonder she exclaimed:'Why have I found such favour in your eyes that you notice me - a foreigner?' (verse 10). I believe the answer is that God had directed Boaz' eyes to her and had set his heart into motion!

When the time came that Boaz had a personal interest in Ruth and wished to marry her, there was first another kinsman-redeemer, who had the right of priority (Ruth 3:12). When Boaz went and sat down by the town gate, we read: 'The kinsman-redeemer he had mentioned came along' (Ruth 4:1). Is that still just mere coincidence, or had God's plan been set into action? Initially the kinsman-redeemer was interested in buying Elimelech's piece of land that Naomi wanted to sell, but he was not prepared to accept Ruth as part and parcel of the deal (Ruth 4:5-6). This meant that Boaz and Ruth were free to marry. Interesting is the comment of the witnesses at the gate about Boaz' and Ruth's forthcoming marriage. They said: 'May the Lord make the woman who is coming into your home like Rachel and Leah, who together built up the house of Israel!' (Ruth 4:11). Considering the law and culture, these words are quite moving as well as stunning, for Jewish men were not allowed to marry non-Israelites. Ruth, the foreigner, was recognised and acknowledged as one of God's people. Clearly, God's hand had moved events as well as people's hearts.

d) A widening horizon, a new perspective
Sometimes pain makes us lose hope, we stop believing that there could still be any good prospects for ourselves. Hopelessness, like helplessness, is a form of empty-handedness. When, in our grief,

and depressing circumstances, a spark of hope and joy becomes visible, we can see in that, a sign of God's faithfulness as well as of his desire to give us hope beyond hope and joy instead of mourning. We can, through our tears, catch a glimpse of his presence and love and thus catch a new vision for potential change. This is what happened to Naomi.

When Ruth returned from working in the field, her hands had been filled with an 'ephah' of barley (Ruth 2:17). The Lord richly blessed the work of her hands; there was ample food for herself and for her mother-in-law: an abundant harvest! These things may seem trivial at first sight, but God himself was working out his plans for Ruth and Naomi. How important it is that we develop 'spiritual eyes' that are tuned in to God in order to recognise his ways. His guidance is not always immediately visible or clear but the fact that we don't discern it doesn't mean that he is passive. It is quite fascinating to see that Naomi, who in her bitterness actually didn't have much faith left in God's goodness, suddenly began to see that God had a hand in the events. When she saw her daughter-in-law return from work with an abundance of barley, Naomi was happily surprised and asked Ruth where she had been gleaning that day, adding 'Blessed be the man who took notice of you!' (Ruth 2:17-19). When Ruth informed her that she had been working on Boaz' land, Naomi began to realise that he could well be an instrument in the hand of the Almighty. Aware of God's goodness to her daughter-in-law (and to herself also), she now remembered the goodness that the Lord showed her and her family in the past (verse 20). This realisation seemed to bring about a turning point – Naomi's apathy vanished and her bitterness and despondency turned into hope; she was once again able to look forward beyond the here and now and became actively involved with the exciting developments evolving around Boaz and Ruth. I find it extremely encouraging that even Naomi, initially depressed and bitter, could become an instrument in the outworking of God's plans regarding these two, plans that reached far beyond the immediate circumstances as a part of God's great plan of redemption.

e) Abundant blessing

Given Boaz, Ruth was blessed with a new husband and, unlike her first marriage, this second marriage was blessed with the birth of a son, Obed (Ruth 4:13). Ruth, the Moabitess, who courageously chose to follow the God of Israel and then did what seemed obvious, thus became a link in a life-changing chain of events, culminating in the birth of Jesus Christ, the Saviour. Her name is mentioned in the genealogy of the Lord Jesus in Matthew 2, she is one of just four women called by name in that list.

What about Naomi, who preferred to be called Mara, because the Lord had made her life very bitter? Did she, I wonder, ever long for another husband who would give her the security of marriage? It may well have been the case, but a second marriage did not materialize for her. Why was Ruth restored in that sense and not Naomi? These are the questions that sometimes plague our minds. We have certain (and often very specific) ideas or desires as to how things should happen. We feel we cannot survive without a spouse, we need to return to full health or a secure financial position if ever we are going to be happy again. However, more often than not, circumstances are not restored according to what we consider best.

Was Naomi's life second-best to what she had before? Was she disappointed? Ruth 4:16 and 17 make it clear that she shared abundantly in Ruth's blessing. In her grandson Obed, she received a new descendant who could restore and continue the family line which had been cruelly severed by the death of her sons. The neighbours who came to visit the mother and her newly born child congratulated Naomi and praised the Lord for what he had done for her (Ruth 4:14-16). They said that this child would renew

Naomi's life and sustain her in her old age and they mentioned, in passing, how much she was loved by her daughter-in-law (Ruth 4:15). Naomi could rejoice in being part of a family where the members were deeply bonded by their love for one another.

So, after profound sadness and uncertainty, there was ample reason again to rejoice and to be thankful. Herein I also see hands being filled by God. In his way and his time. We must never forget that we follow no one less than the Almighty One, he is in total control and doesn't ever let go of us. Rather, he travels before and with us as a faithful guide and friend, filling our empty hands with his loving kindness, blessing and grace. These facts should give us confidence and a deep sense of security.

Note

1.   It was part of the Law and therefore also of the Jewish culture that a widow would find refuge with her husband's next of kin. It was his duty to take over the deceased husband's land and marry the widow. The children from that marriage were to continue the name of the deceased (read Deut. 25:5-10). Ruth 4:1-10 refers to this custom. Verse 5 indicates that this arrangement wasn't always attractive to the kinsman-redeemer in question.

4
Growing While Under Pressure

In the previous chapters we looked at Ruth and Naomi who faced things bigger than themselves, things they couldn't change or reverse simply because they were beyond human control. When we now consider Joseph, we look at adversity of a very different nature. This man, son of Jacob and Rachel, had at least three major 'pit experiences' in his life and in each of these, people played a significant, negative role.

What are the situations where other people are responsible for our pain? We can think of redundancy, a growing problem in our technological age where many people lose their jobs because they have become superfluous or 'too old'. We can also think of situations where people are victims of a criminal act or of an accident caused by someone else. Or what about the woman who is deceived or left by her husband, the children who are being abused or who grow up in single parent families because of the divorce of their parents? There are many ways in which people can harm or damage one another. There are those, who have been infected with the AIDS virus through negligence with a blood transfusion, and there are others whose lives are made miserable by an addicted child or alcoholic spouse. There are countless examples of how people are hurt or let down by others. It is obvious that we can be left standing empty-handed because of what someone else did to us.

Having said that, it is also important to recognize that it is not always the case that another person is unequivocally to blame for our misery or pain. Once we consider ourselves a victim, we are quick to point to someone else and accuse them of doing us harm. Mostly, however, it isn't that simple. When difficulties and hurt occur in the area of relationships, the causes are often manifold and complex. Sometimes we ourselves contributed to what happened, which isn't an easy thing to admit! When we feel deeply hurt and offended, the mere thought of us maybe being a party to the events can be quite threatening and painful; it will need courage to look at things honestly and to consider the possibility that we may be at fault too. Our sincerity and openness, however, will help us as we seek to solve our problems and come to terms with our pain.

Pain that occurs within the context of human relationships is very different from pain that is caused by events that are beyond our control. In the latter case many or even most of our questions will remain unanswered and we will have to find a way to accept those things that cannot be changed. But the cases where someone else and/or we ourselves are to blame for what happened, require a different course of action. Here *forgiveness* will be a key factor in our coming to terms with things and in bringing about a change for the better as well as in our own healing process. Just as was the case with Ruth, it is in taking refuge with God, or in 'coming to hide under God's wings', that we will be set free to acquire the right attitude in the given circumstances.

In this and the next chapter we will concentrate on Joseph, a young man who at least three times in his life, was left empty-handed. His first traumatic experience was no doubt the cruel separation, at the age of seventeen, from all that was familiar to him. Favouritism in the family was one of the major factors that made his brothers decide to dispose of him and sell him to a passing caravan of Ishmaelites. From that first heart-rending moment of total bewilderment, we follow Joseph to Egypt where he was thrown into prison after years of faithful service to his master. This was the result of the fierce anger of a woman who didn't get what she wanted. Joseph himself was innocent. And finally whilst in prison, there was a third big disappointment when he was forgotten by someone he had set his hopes on for his release. Three pit experiences over a period of thirteen years and then Joseph was appointed second-in-command by the Pharaoh of Egypt. As we consider these painful experiences in Joseph's life, we must admit that we can hardly imagine that such things could ever fit in with God's plans, let alone be engineered by him! When negative events come our way and we are being humiliated or let down as Joseph was, it is more natural for us to question our circumstances and to rise up, seeking justice and a turn for the better, than to want to see God's hand in these things. Joseph's story, however, reveals that God may have some big surprises in store for us!

We all have our own mental conception of how things should happen. But the reality is often completely different. We have seen earlier that God does restore and heal, but not always according to our plan. What matters in the first place to him is *us* rather than our specific situation. God's way of restoration is that he moulds us through events and circumstances into the people that he has in mind. He wants us to become more and more like his Son, people after his own image and purpose. In fact, throughout the Bible the emphasis is on our holiness rather than on our happiness! This is a sobering thought but once we grasp the value and magnitude of this truth, we will be more able to let go rather than to waste our energy in fighting against our circumstances. God never wastes our sorrows, but uses or even sends them for our spiritual growth and sanctification. Sometimes empty hands are necessary in order to make that growth possible or deepen our relationship with God. Often we need to reach the end of our tether and feel deeply and utterly helpless before we can let go, thus 'creating' the best possible conditions for God to do his work in us. We sometimes reach that point of complete surrender only through deep valleys and pain that strip us of our human securities, our steady income, our solid marriage, our good health or promising career. We sincerely believe that we are dependent upon God but we are deeply shattered when all the things that we took for granted in our lives start to crumble or even vanish. It is then that we realise that a large part of our certainty and security was based on those things rather than on God. Maybe that is why at times they are removed from us.

Joseph

Joseph came from a secure and sheltered home with parents who doted on him. Later on, he had a favoured position in the house of his master. He lost it all. I am sure that he wondered why these negative things happened and how in the world he should continue. Yet, time and time again rather than despairing, he was able to pick up the pieces and carry on, even when there seemed to be no hope. When finally he was given the position of prime minister of Egypt, we see the fruit of the years of adversity: Joseph came out of prison, a man pruned and shaped by God. What is more, he was released to arrive at the place that the Lord had prepared for him. God had worked out his plans in and with him, right through many incomprehensible and bewildering experiences and events. That very fact may encourage us to trust God in all perplexities of life. Our circumstances are totally secure in his hands.

In this chapter we look primarily at the events described in Genesis 37, 39 and 40, although now and again I refer to additional Bible passages which I shall mention specifically.

Favouritism within the family

Joseph's family was a complex one, consisting of a father, four mothers and a number of children who were fully or half related to one another. An amalgamated family like his isn't uncommon in our day and age in as far as parents may raise children that have a different father or mother. The complicating factor in Joseph's family, however, was that all four mothers of Jacob's children were present, which made a perfect setting for jealousy and tension.

Joseph was one of those people who seem to be born with a silver spoon in their mouths; he was the fulfilment of both his parents' dreams. In the years preceding his birth, his mother witnessed her own sister and the two concubines of her husband bearing one child after another whilst she herself remained barren. This deeply affected her and caused strain and friction between her and her husband (e.g. Gen. 30:1-2). When she finally conceived and Joseph arrived (Jacob's eleventh son!), he was welcomed as a first-born son and instantly became the most favourite and favoured one. We read in Genesis 37:3 that Israel (Jacob) loved Joseph more than any of his other sons, 'because he had been born to him in his old age'. What is more, Joseph was 'well-built and handsome' (Gen. 39:6). What more could one wish for? He was given a richly ornamental robe, a gesture that signified that Jacob gave him the rights of the first-born; it should have been given to the eldest son (Gen. 37:3).

It is quite extraordinary that Joseph's parents Rachel and Jacob fell into the trap of favouring one child over the others. They each had their own negative experiences in that area. Rachel and her sister Leah were lifelong rivals and Jacob had had a similar experience with his twin brother Esau, who was the elder one and his father's favourite because of his manliness. Jacob, a more homely type, was his mother's favourite (see Gen. 25:27,28), a fact which led to a dreadful course of events. It appears that

Rebekah's attitude was a determining factor as Jacob's character was developing, he found it easy to cheat in order to get his way. We read in Genesis 25:29-34 that Jacob first bought his brother's birthright and later stole his father's blessing from Esau by deceit. The latter was his mother's advice, given in the name of the Lord (Gen. 27:1-29)! Sometimes we go to great lengths in our striving to obtain what we consider most desirable or most valuable. How much damage we cause in doing that! Jacob had to flee in order to escape his brother's revenge and consequently the family fell apart. His parents recommended that he go to his uncle Laban, his mother's brother, whose two daughters he eventually married. Rachel, the younger one, was his beloved wife whereas the elder sister Leah was unloved by Jacob.

It is quite possible and not unusual that we find it sometimes easier to get on with one person than with another, it happens within our own families. We don't want any favouritism and yet we might click more with one child than with the other and before long we start making comparisons: 'Look at your sister, why can't you..?' or 'Why does your room always have to be the messiest one?' Such words can hurt and worse, wound. How does a child feel when his brother or sister is loved more, when all the attention seems to go to the others who apparently do better? It is a hurt that one may feel for years, even well into adulthood. It is quite paralysing when you have always had to listen to how your brother or sister was more intelligent or could play the piano better, was such good company and so well-behaved and helpful, did so well at school. Years later the child in us can still experience and struggle with the emotions he felt then, can still think, 'I am ugly' or 'I'm useless'. It can work like a self-fulfilling prophecy where we bring these things about in our own lives; we fail in our studies, job or relationships and time and time again that old feeling wells up within us: 'See, nothing ever turns out right for me, I am just no good'. It isn't, however, only the less favoured child that suffers, a favoured child can also suffer from what they experience. They may come to believe that it is natural for them always to be in the limelight and to always succeed. These things have a bearing on one's character; a favoured child may turn into someone who isn't easy to get on with, they may make life quite difficult not just for others but also for themselves. They may find it extremely difficult or impossible to cope with disappointment or failure, let alone accept these negative things. This was the case with Rachel, Joseph's mother.

Three pit experiences

a) Betrayed by those near to him

In the midst of all the complexities of that large mixed family, the Lord revealed himself to Joseph in two dreams (Genesis 37:5-10), a fact both remarkable and moving as it shows that God isn't held back by negative circumstances or issues. Sometimes we think that he will pass us by, simply because things in our families or personal lives aren't the way they should be. We assume that God can only use supermen, which makes us uninteresting to him as we don't fit into that category. There are umpteen people much more suitable (and certainly holier!) than we are. Such reasoning stems from a limited human perspective; it is not God's way of thinking! He seeks us out in spite of our shortcomings and failures and he intervenes in the most unlikely situations.

At this point in history, God had Joseph in mind to play a prominent part in his great plan of salvation. Majestic things were about to happen, things far beyond human comprehension or imagination. Joseph's dreams were a first indication of this, yet, rather than working out positively – as we assume God's guidance should – the first visible result of these dreams was negative. For to Joseph's brothers, who already hated him because of his position as their father's favourite, this was the last straw (Gen. 37:4-5).

Their much detested brother now had the nerve to present them with dreams in which he was lording it over them and requiring them to bow down before him. Weren't they already doing that, wasn't he the little king in the family anyway? Embittered and enraged, they decided to get rid of him. And so at age seventeen, Joseph was thrown into a pit like a worthless nobody. (The NIV speaks of a 'cistern', but as I find that word somewhat alien, I prefer to use 'pit' as in the RSV translation.)[1]

When Joseph for the very first time in his life found himself standing empty-handed, a great and godly plan for him was probably the last thing on his mind, all that he registered and all that mattered was the here and now which looked quite grim. It is hard to look beyond our pits! When we are unpleasantly surprised by negative events and everything seems to work against us, we usually feel that something has gone very wrong and we certainly don't view our situation positively, let alone as God's wonderful way with us! How important it is that we learn to change our way of thinking in order to be open to discern God's hand, even when we are disappointed and hurt. The very fact of God's sovereignty and goodness implies that negative things in our lives never are a class apart, nor are they ever beyond God. Our knowing that God is able to make things work together for good may strengthen our trust and guide us in our response and attitude to that which is painful. Paul puts it like this in his letter to the Romans: 'be transformed by the renewing of your mind. Then you will be able to test and approve what God's will is – his good, pleasing and perfect will' (Romans 12:2). The transformation or the renewing of our mind and attitudes is a learning process, we need thorough training in order to achieve that. Joseph's training happened to start in a most improbable place, a pit. There were a few more pits yet to follow.

When Joseph landed at the bottom of the pit, his life was shaken to its foundations. It is quite significant that his brothers had removed his beautiful robe, which had coloured his life and stood for his exalted position. Joseph, once the privileged son, had in a matter of minutes become a nobody, he had lost his position as well as the security and freedom that went with it. He was sold to a passing caravan of Ishmaelites en route to Egypt and carried away to an unknown country. Once the most prominent amongst his siblings, he was now a mere slave. Cruelly cut off from his familiar surroundings and beloved family, he faced a twofold grief: he had ceased to be somebody and had lost the people he loved and belonged to.

How does one react in such a situation? The answer is simple: Joseph reacted like any human being would. We read later on in Genesis 42:21 that he pleaded with his brothers to spare his life. He sought mercy and help with his own people, but his cries fell on deaf ears. Maybe Joseph thought of each one of his brothers, placing his hope on one after the other. But they let him down. Even those who are very close to us can disappoint and desert us.

b) Unfairly treated: Punished for a deed of integrity
After the Ishmaelites had sold Joseph to the royal household of the Pharaoh of Egypt, he managed to work his way up to another prominent position as the right-hand man of Potiphar, the captain of the royal guard. But then, at the very stage when he had acquired some sort of rehabilitation, he found himself empty-handed once again. The setting of that second big drama in his life is described in Genesis 39 where we read how the wife of his boss attempted to seduce him, not just once, but persistently over a period of time (verse 10). When Joseph refused time and time again to respond to her advances, she took the matter into her own hands and tried to force him to give in to her desires. When alone with him in the house, she grabbed hold of Joseph, who fled from her, leaving her holding his garment in her hands. Later on she

used that garment to bear witness against Joseph, blaming him for trying to seduce her.

Joseph's attitude in this absurd situation is quite remarkable as it testifies to the fact that he had grown in integrity. The erstwhile spoilt adolescent, who certainly did not dislike his privileged position in the family, would now not be seduced into doing wrong. Certainly what he did was far from easy. To consistently keep resisting the advances of Pharaoh's wife probably became increasingly difficult. People are very vulnerable in the area of sex. Vulnerability, however, doesn't automatically imply that we need to give in to temptation. The Lord God says to Cain in Genesis 4:7 '... sin is crouching at your door; it desires to have you, but you must master it'. Joseph did what God said here: no compromise, no sin, only God's way. He didn't want to betray Potiphar's trust in him nor did he want to sin against God (Gen. 39:9). Here we see 1 Corinthians 6:18 in practice: 'Flee from sexual immorality'. Indeed, Joseph had to literally flee in order to escape from sin.

Another remarkable thing is that this was the second time that Joseph lost his position as well as the garment that went with it. It was part of the servant-lord relationship of that time that Potiphar – who might have known better, and probably did – chose to believe his wife's account of what happened. He dropped Joseph like a stone even though he enjoyed his full trust and had never abused it. There was no consultation, no hearing, Joseph simply didn't have any rights and was thrown into prison without mercy (Gen39:20). Once again he experienced the shock of being cut off from that which had become familiar to him. Once again he lost his rank (and cloak) and all the human securities and conveniences that were part and parcel of it. People had again disappointed him, but this time the situation differed from the earlier one in that he was treated unjustly, for in no way was he guilty. For the second time he was thrown back on himself and consequently on his God. It would not be the last time!

c) Forgotten by someone he counted on

In prison Joseph managed again to win favour with his boss, who soon let him run all the day-to-day affairs. Things seemed to go reasonably well for him, but there was another disappointment lying in the lurch. Now coming to Genesis 40, we are told how Joseph came into contact with two prominent fellow prisoners and was able to interpret their dreams. He then asked the cupbearer, who was about to be released from prison, to remember him once he would be back in office and to put in a good word for him with Pharaoh (verse 14). Verse 23 tells us that 'The chief cupbearer, however, did not remember Joseph; he forgot him'. The following verse (Gen. 41:1) reveals that this good man's memory didn't just fail him for a week or so but for all of two years, which is a very long time when you have set your hopes on a speedy release.

Here we witness the third time that Joseph was deeply disappointed in people – first his own brothers molested and sold him, then Potiphar, whom he had served faithfully, treated him badly; and finally he was forgotten by the cupbearer. By now he should have learnt that people aren't reliable, or rather, that it is better and wiser to put your trust in God! Psalm 118 states very clearly that 'It is better to take refuge in the Lord, than to trust in man' (verse 8). David, whose life we shall look at later on in this book, says in Psalm 40:4 'Blessed is the man who makes the Lord his trust'. He himself discovered this truth in the deep valleys in his life.

To be forgotten for two whole years by someone you trusted and set your hopes on is an extremely painful experience. How did Joseph cope all this time, fluctuating between hope and despair? How did it affect him when it dawned on him that he could be so totally unimportant to someone else that he wasn't given any thought? Meanwhile the cupbearer was very busy getting on with his own life. He had been rehabilitated, he counted again and, as happens often in such circumstances, he easily forgot what was behind him.

Again, here is a situation of empty-handedness that isn't alien to us. It hurts when you are forgotten or when you appear to be unimportant to someone else. It hurts when other people are so occupied with themselves and their own things that they pass by your need without even noticing it or simply forget it. They don't mean it badly, these things just happen, but it hurts very deeply. I wonder, did Joseph, in his disappointment and disillusionment, ever doubt God's goodness? Did he ever ask the Lord to remind the cupbearer of his request to remember him before Pharaoh? Did he give up hope?

Where was God?

One lesson that stands out throughout Joseph's story is the discovery that we cannot ever conceive of God's ways in the lives of his children. We often have preconceived ideas about the ingredients that are needed for a happy life and tend to expect that God uses only merry ones – sunshine, no clouds – in the lives of his children. If that is our assumption, we are bound to be in for some bewilderment, as Joseph's experience shows! His life began auspiciously, yet instead of continuing positively for him, what followed was a series of pits and disillusionments. Where ever was God when so many things went wrong?

It is both fascinating and moving to see time and time again in the story of Joseph, not only that the Lord was present in his life, but that he was *actively* present and that there was a godly pattern and plan behind these incomprehensible events. They were in fact God's design, which started to unfold in the pit. A pit is the imagery of a place or moment of darkness where we have reached the end of our tether. Whilst in our experience it is our lowest point or even a dead end where nothing and no one can help us, to

God it is potentially the very place where we meet him face to face. It may sound contradictory because our emotions often tell us the exact opposite: we don't only feel deserted by people but also by the Lord and can't imagine that he is present. To us there is nothing potentially precious going on, rather, we wonder how God could ever allow such negative circumstances. He, however, often uses our wilderness-experiences to draw us to himself.

Once, I witnessed people digging out an old castle well which, legend had it, was at least 160 metres deep. Rigging was put up and a courageous man was strapped to the pulley and then let down armed with hosepipes, buckets and a pickaxe. At regular intervals a signal came from down below, after which he was hoisted up again and had the opportunity to catch his breath. It was obvious that digging out that well would have been a very dangerous undertaking without reliable safety measures. The walls of the well were extremely slippery and there was no way of telling how deep the water was. Slipping and falling could mean death by drowning.

While reading Genesis 37:24 I was reminded of this scene. The eleven words contained in this verse underline the great truth of God's presence in the pit that Joseph was thrown into. We read: 'Now the cistern was empty; there was no water in it'. These words are proof of God's endless love and care for Joseph at a moment when He may not have been very tangible to him. God was there and his eyes were fixed on Joseph. He made sure that there wasn't any water or deep mud in the pit, so that Joseph wouldn't perish. Joseph, in his distress, probably didn't give a thought to this detail. Sometimes we find ourselves in such a depth of misery that we are unable to see a light at the end of the tunnel. But the fact that we are unaware of God's presence doesn't mean that he isn't there! It is just that our eyes aren't attuned to him! When I asked the man who was digging out the ancient castle well, how dark it was deep down, he said something quite poignant: 'It is pitch-dark, but when you look up you see light'.

The pit may have seemed a dead end to Joseph, but to God it was a starting-point that marked a new beginning. Rather than a place of perishing, it was a crossroads. As such, it was a dramatic turning-point which paved the way for new things. Egypt was the target; here Joseph, after a long journey, became part of Pharaoh's royal household. He arrived as a slave, just seventeen years old and unfamiliar with the country, its culture and its language. He was unfamiliar also with the experience of being a slave.

What did Joseph notice of God's presence and care for him whilst he was a slave in Pharaoh's household and later on when he was a prisoner? We are told that in both situations he was given so much grace that he was given a prominent position. Of course his success can be ascribed to the way he behaved and possibly also to the fact that he was young enough to still be optimistic and able to get on with things. But ultimately his success wasn't due to him, but to God only. We read in Genesis 39:2 'The Lord was with Joseph and he prospered' and in verse 3 'that the Lord gave him success in everything he did'. We read similar words in verses 21-23. They remind me of Psalm 1:1-3 with its description of a man who is 'like a tree planted by streams of water, which yields its fruit in season and whose leaf does not wither. Whatever he does prospers'. The man of Psalm 1 is someone –and here we have the conditions for 'prospering' – 'who does not walk in the counsel of the wicked or stand in the way of sinners or sit in the seat of mockers. But his delight is in the law of the Lord, and on his law he meditates day and night'. It almost seems like a magical formula ensuring success; as long as we love and obey the Lord God, nothing will go wrong for us. Unfortunately it doesn't work that way, time and time again we discover that God's interpretation of prospering and success is quite different to ours! His purpose is our spiritual growth, including our growing strong in the face of temptation.

We saw earlier how Joseph responded when he was harassed by Potiphar's wife. God was also present then; it is obvious from the fact that Joseph stood firm during that very difficult period of persistent sexual temptation. As a young adult in a foreign country, where his God wasn't served and in the same house as the woman who threw herself at him day after day, wouldn't adultery and unfaithfulness have been more natural than persevering in chastity? How easy it is, in a godless environment, without the encouragement and moral support of fellow believers, to adapt and to stray. But Joseph was of a different opinion. He didn't want to jeopardise his relationship with the Lord. God was more important to him than attractive and tempting things. Apparently God's presence had become so precious to him that he wanted to hold on to that, cost what it may. And God in his grace held on to him! This is how Joseph 'prospered', by growing into a man of God.

It was in prison that God's grace enabled Joseph, no doubt often himself distressed, to be sensitive to others and reach out to them. Disappointment can make us turn in on ourselves and feel so defeated that we are no longer able to see beyond our own situation and pain. This was not the case with Joseph. In Genesis 40:6, 7 we read that he noticed that something was bothering two fellow prisoners and he encouraged them to share their worries with him: 'Why are your faces so sad today?' When they told him that they had a dream that no one was able to interpret, Joseph's answer was that of a godly man: 'Do not interpretations belong to God? Tell me your dreams' (verse 8). He was actually saying: 'This is a matter of *God* so tell *me*', implying that he wasn't relying on his own wisdom but, as a servant of God, he was willing to be a channel for the Lord.

God was with Joseph and yet... when Joseph had come in contact with Pharaoh's cupbearer and had asked him to put in a good word for him with Pharaoh, this man forgot all about Joseph. New hope had been dawning, only to be crushed. Joseph's attempt to take his fate in his own hands was futile. But this disappointment was necessary for God to show Joseph that he was in control. It seems that his relying on people was yet another 'walking stick' that God had to remove from Joseph in order to make him realise where his ultimate support and security lay. Where people sometimes forget us, the Lord is totally faithful and therefore totally reliable. Being holy and perfect, he cannot ever be unfaithful as that would be contrary to his very nature. Therefore, the psalmist says in Psalm 146:3-6:

> Do not put your trust in princes, in mortal men, who cannot save. When their spirit departs, they return to the ground; on that very day their plans come to nothing. Blessed is he whose help is the God of Jacob, whose hope is in the Lord his God, the Maker of heaven and earth, the sea, and everything in them –the Lord, who remains faithful forever.

God was with Joseph even when it appeared that he was totally abandoned and forgotten in prison. He gave Pharaoh dreams that no one could interpret (we have now arrived at Genesis 41). Dreams again! And now we see lots of things falling into place. The cupbearer remembered Joseph who was then summoned to interpret Pharaoh's dreams. When, with God's help, he was able to do so, he was given the highest and most powerful position imaginable: Pharaoh put him in charge over all of Egypt. A poignant detail here is that Joseph was given a new garment ('robes of fine linen') as well as a gold chain around his neck and Pharaoh's signet ring (Gen. 41:42). The garment was very different from the one his father had made for him in the past or from the one that went with his function as top assistant to the captain of the guard of Pharaoh. This garment was fit for a man of God, who had been prepared and equipped by him and judged suitable for a special task. Joseph, by his own merit or deeds, could never have 'earned' or engineered this formidable position and mandate, the interpretation of dreams was God's doing. Also Joseph's promotion, as well as his preparation for it, was God's doing.

God's time for Joseph had come and we witness the culmination of perfect planning. Even the two years of 'unnecessary' waiting in prison due to human negligence were part of it and certainly no mistake! They were needed for Joseph's training as well as for the situation in Egypt to reach the point where Joseph was needed to perform a task that no one else could handle. When Joseph had seen these two years out, the seven years of plenty in Egypt were just beginning, years that would be followed by seven years of hunger. At this precise moment someone was needed to organise things, to take precautionary measures for the seven lean years in order to save the country – and in fact more than just that one country and people – from perishing in what would be a disastrous famine. Who was more fit for that momentous task than Joseph, who had just finished thirteen years of training? Twice in those years he had occupied a managerial position – with Potiphar as well as in prison. Furthermore, he had learnt to cope with disappointment, temptation and loneliness. Through all those things he had learnt to put his trust in God and in no one else. Finally, after thirteen years, Joseph had reached his destiny and had come to the very place and task that God had in store for him.

God has the overall picture

Having God's Word, we are able to view Joseph's life in its totality. We realise that God orchestrated all the situations and events in

Joseph's life, down to the smallest and even painful details. Just as Joseph ended up in Egypt as a result of the negative dealings of his brothers, so it was through the evil actions of Potiphar's wife that he landed in prison and specifically in that section where God wanted him in order to meet the chief cupbearer, who would later remember him and be instrumental in his release and subsequent promotion.

Joseph's history can encourage us when we consider our own lives. Events that seem to be chance happenings or set-backs can have their place in God's plan, they need not be seen or felt as meaningless or purely negative! God is able to make crooked ways straight and he can even use them to teach us valuable lessons that we may not learn otherwise. We are taught to trust God's presence not only in life's ups but even more so in life's downs. When we are disappointed in people or run into difficulties caused by others, it isn't true to say that things are out of control. Even when people stand in the way, God continues to work out his plans for and with us. Acts 7:9 and 10 underline this in the case of Joseph: 'Because the patriarchs were jealous of Joseph, they sold him as a slave into Egypt. But God was with him and rescued him from all his troubles. He gave Joseph wisdom'. When in distress and at the end of our tether, let us remember these two words: *But* God!

Obedience can be costly

At the end of this chapter I want to return to that one experience of suffering which was a direct result of Joseph's faithfulness to God, his imprisonment after he refused to give in to sexual temptation. It shows that *it is possible to stand empty-handed as a result of our obedience to God.* This is often more difficult to understand or accept than other kinds of pain we experience. Yet the Bible tells us that we should not be surprised when we suffer for God's sake (1 Pet. 4:12-16). It happened both in Old and New Testament times and it still happens today. In many countries Christians are viewed unfavourably and face persecution or oppression from hostile governments. Even in Western Europe they can face difficulties or be subjected to harassment. There may not be actual cases of physical torture or murder, the pressure is often more subtle and has to do with gross unfairness, comparable to what Joseph faced when he chose to be faithful to God as well as to his human boss and was punished for it by people (Genesis 39). His dismissal and imprisonment were wrong and unjust.

Just as wrong and unjust as is the situation where a nurse is dismissed because she refuses on religious grounds, to assist in the operating theatre where a foetus is being aborted, or where a businessman is less successful because he has decided to be honest in financial affairs. He sees his colleagues, who think nothing of tax evasion or of producing 'alternative financial reports', promoted whilst he is passed by. There is also the pressure that young people who stand firm for Christian morals experience. It is 'uncool' to not want sex outside of marriage or to refuse to experiment with drugs or alcohol and so they are ridiculed by their peers. There are many varieties of pressure that Christians can be subjected to. It can in effect be very costly to obey Christ, on an ethical, business, sexual or other level and it can leave us, humanly speaking, empty-handed.

When Paul, in his second letter to Timothy, writes about the persecutions and suffering that he has had to endure, he says:'In fact, everyone who wants to live a godly life in Christ Jesus will be persecuted' (2 Tim. 3:12). Peter also writes about this:

> But how is it to your credit if you receive a beating for doing wrong and endure it? But if you suffer for doing good and you endure it, this is commendable before God. To this you were called, because Christ suffered for you,

leaving you an example, that you should follow in his steps. 'He committed no sin, and no deceit was found in his mouth.' When they hurled their insults at him, he did not retaliate; when he suffered, he made no threats. Instead, he entrusted himself to him who judges justly (1 Pet. 2:20-23).

Peter points to the Lord Jesus as the supreme example of true godliness and obedience to God. His uncompromising steadfastness led not only to his being rejected, by friends and enemies alike, but also to great suffering and even death. The Lord Jesus could have made life easier for himself by allowing people to crown him as king or by becoming a political leader or by retiring to live a quiet life in some remote village. But he chose instead to be obedient to his heavenly Father. The writer of the epistle to the Hebrews says of Jesus: 'Although he was a son, he learned obedience from what he suffered' (Heb. 5:8).

It is significant that Joseph, who is considered to be a type of the Lord Jesus, as far as we know also did not threaten or become abusive when he was treated unfairly because of his obedience to God. I mentioned earlier that there is no evidence (in Gen. 39:16-20) that he was ever given the chance to tell Potiphar his side of the story. We read that he was thrown into prison and that there he was somehow able to do what came his way. He showed such a positive attitude that he was given a responsible position. To me that is proof of the fact that Joseph, up against all odds, was growing in wisdom and godliness. Obedience to God or godliness can be an attitude that is acquired through suffering. The natural, human response to gross injustice is rather one of protest or retaliation; we want to justify ourselves and feel a need to hit back. God's way, however, often is the lowest or meekest one – and in that the deepest – and it produces good fruit! We see it in Joseph and that testifies to the fact that he had learned to hide with God and that there he was meeting things more powerful than the negative things he was experiencing (see Gen.39:21a).

Note

1. A cistern was a reservoir for storing water, which was collected from rainfall or from a spring. J.C. Whitcomb, Jr., Professor of Old Testament, tells us in an article in the *New Bible Dictionary* (IVP, 1966), that these cisterns were usually pear-shaped with a small opening at the top, which could be sealed to prevent accidents and unauthorized use. There were private as well as public cisterns. Actually Joseph wasn't the only one who was thrown into a pit, the prophet Jeremiah had the same misfortune. The cistern he was thrown into also had no water in it, but only mud which Jeremiah sank down into. The prophet would have starved to death if he hadn't been hauled up (Jer.38).

5
Pruned By God

Did Joseph know what it meant to hide with God? We aren't told specifically, but there is ample reason to believe he did. There are several indications of his growing walk with God. We see it in his attitude during the years of his unwanted exile in Egypt, in Potiphar's house as well as in prison. We see it as he came out of prison, a mature man of God. It looks as if in thirteen years, all that he had always taken for granted, all that he had been leaning on was taken away from him. As Joseph literally lost garment after garment, the Lord was gently peeling off layer after layer of self-sufficiency and circumstantial as well as people support. He did so until Joseph stood naked and helpless before his heavenly Father. During the last two years in prison God trusted Joseph with silence; there was no help forthcoming from the cupbearer on whom he was counting. After that man's release, Joseph was probably living initially on cloud nine, expecting his own release and rehabilitation to come any moment. It didn't come. When that dawned on him, he must have realised that there was nothing else he could do and no one left to help him. He was alone –a perfect setting for self-pity and bitterness or for a deep meeting with God! Adversity can make us or break us. When we are placed in God's hands, it makes us into people who will seek God more intensely and who are increasingly satisfied with what they find in him. Losing everything can mean gaining all good things. This, I think, was Joseph's experience and it is the subject of this chapter.

Did Joseph know that precious ongoing communication with God that is an integral part of hiding in him? Again I can say I think he did. But a personal relationship with God isn't something that is instantly acquired, it requires a learning process, a letting go of all things that we count or lean on in order to gain him. We know that in that first moment of distress, when Joseph was thrown into the pit, he pleaded with his brothers to have mercy on him. As he was led away by the Ishmaelites, he probably kept looking back, hoping that his brothers would relent and still come to his rescue. I can imagine how, in those moments he also sought God, crying out to him for help. But abiding in God is more than praying for help when things go wrong, it is ongoing communication. Our contact and conversation with God grow in frequency and depth when other sources of help or support disappear. We learn best to wait for God's intervention when all resources have been used up. We abandon ourselves to him when there is nothing and no one else left to lean on. Sometimes God puts us through the discipline of utter darkness and despair to teach us to heed him, not just occasionally but in an ongoing friendship with ongoing communication and absolute dependence. Again, this is what Joseph experienced.

Having arrived at Genesis 41 (Joseph's release from prison), in this chapter we will look at the story as it continues to unfold up to and including Genesis 48.

Joseph released and exalted

When Joseph was summoned from prison and brought before Pharaoh, four things strike me about him, all of which have to do with empty hands being filled by God. I mention them below in no deliberate order:

A man prepared for his God-given task

When Joseph, at the age of thirty, was given the highest imaginable position in Egypt as Pharaoh's right-hand man, he had come to the very place that God had prepared for him and he could not have landed a better job. Was Joseph a man to earn his living as a shepherd or sheep farmer, continually out in the fields, toughened and weather beaten through constant exposure to the outdoor elements? Was what Jacob had had in mind for his son indeed a position in the family's sheep rearing business? It seems obvious – but the Lord had his own unique plans for him. Joseph was to get a high position, not in farming, but behind a desk. His practical training for that particular job included two apprenticeships as a slave and a prisoner where he learnt things that he certainly would not have learnt had he continued in the protected and carefree position of the favourite son in Jacob's extended family. In Pharaoh's court he learnt to serve rather than to be served and rather than being shielded from difficulties, he was exposed to trials and forced to deal with difficult matters such as temptation, disappointment and loneliness. As a slave, he also learnt to be concerned about other people rather than just about himself. Joseph neither looked nor asked for these periods of training. There must have been countless moments when he wondered about the purpose of his experiences. Many times he was forced to do things he didn't want to do and more than once he was disappointed and discouraged. But during all those thirteen years he was, so to speak, a student at the Divine Academy of the Lord God and followed courses that had been carefully selected as preparation for a very special task. When, finally, Pharaoh put Joseph 'in charge of the whole land of Egypt' (see Genesis 41:41-45), he had arrived at the best imaginable place for him, he had reached his destination for that particular period of his life.

A changed person, a man of God

When Joseph came out of prison to take upon himself the task of prime minister of Egypt, he was fit for this assignment, having become a man of God. Let us look at the things that make that apparent.

a) He was a man in whom the Spirit of God dwelt
What was it that qualified Joseph for the responsibility of governing a country that was heading for a severe seven-year famine? His training and previous experience, important though they were, weren't decisive. It was something of a completely different order which made Joseph competent to fulfil his new task. Pharaoh put it into words when he said in Genesis 41:38 – 'Can we find anyone like this man, one in whom is the Spirit of God?' He underlined that again in verse 39 when he attributed Joseph's discernment and wisdom to God.

Joseph had been pruned and moulded into a mature and godly man. The favoured and maybe somewhat opinionated adolescent had become a wise man who had made room for God. In spite of all the knowledge and experience he had gained in the previous years, he acknowledged his total dependence upon the Lord. Therefore the co-management of the vast country of Egypt was in safe hands with him.

b) He was a man comforted by God
A person who is led by the Holy Spirit is developing spiritual eyes which make him view things from a different angle. When Joseph had two sons by his Egyptian wife Asenath, he called them Manasseh and Ephraim. Manasseh sounds like and may be derived from the Hebrew for 'forget'. Genesis 41:51 says Joseph called his firstborn Manasseh 'because God has made me forget all my trouble and all my father's household'. Ephraim sounds like the

Hebrew for 'twice fruitful'. Genesis 41:52 recounts that Joseph said about his name: 'It is because God has made me fruitful in the land of my suffering'. The meaning of these names points to the psychological distance Joseph had acquired from his native country; here we are actually allowed a deep, and so far rare, insight into his inner life. He wasn't traumatised by his negative experiences, the torture of his forced and heart-rending removal from his parental home and native country and the misery he endured in Egypt had become overshadowed by the joy of God's presence and blessings in Joseph's life. Despite the fact that there were many bewildering moments and painful things that he didn't understand, Joseph was able to discern God's hand in his life and was thus comforted. Healing had taken place which had enabled him to forget and had thus created room for joy in his heart. When a person has received comfort, it is usually coupled with a new perspective of his present circumstances.

c) He was a gentle and merciful man

When the famine, foretold by God in Pharaoh's dreams, affected not only Egypt but 'the whole world' (as far as it was known then), Joseph's father Jacob and his sons also felt the pinch and Jacob sent his ten elder sons to Egypt in order to buy grain. Only the youngest one, Benjamin, stayed at home. We have now arrived at Genesis 42 where we are told of that first meeting since years between Joseph and his brothers, a moment of great mercy.

We read that, although Joseph recognized his brothers immediately, they did not recognize him. Humanly speaking the hour of truth had arrived and Joseph was presented with a brilliant opportunity to avenge himself and make his brothers pay for what they did to him years ago. Revenge and retribution are quite human characteristics. They are more natural to us than unconditional love and forgiveness. In all honesty, we often feel that revenge or anger are right and totally justified in a given situation.

Therefore I can understand Joseph's initial response to his brothers; he was quite sharp, he tested them and even had them locked up for three days, accusing them of using Egypt for their own advantage and of being spies. Maybe his attitude was the result of his deep emotions during that moment. However, he also wanted to test his brothers in order to see where they stood and how they felt. But he didn't intend to harm them, he wanted to act justly and wished to spare their lives, a positive attitude which was the fruit of his walk with the Lord ('I fear God', verse 18).

We witness the moment when Joseph's brothers, maybe for the first time ever, realised what they had done to him. They spoke from Joseph's perspective when they said to each other (in verse 21): 'Surely we are being punished because of our brother. We saw how distressed he was when he pleaded with us for his life, but we would not listen.' They linked what was now happening to them in Egypt with what they did to Joseph in the past. Their words made Joseph realise that there was indeed one brother, Reuben, who had stood up for him all those years ago when he was in such great distress: 'Didn't I tell you not to sin against the boy?' (verse 22). The mood of the discussion reveals that they still remembered the events in detail. They may have 'forgotten' or repressed things for a while, but here in Egypt all the feelings returned vehemently. Actually all those years they had lived with their father, who mourned the loss of his beloved son, so they hadn't really been able to avoid the confrontation with their evil deed and their lie about Joseph's death. The wrongdoings of people will continue to haunt and pursue them, until they are solved.

Joseph was deeply moved when he heard his brothers acknowledge the grief and pain he suffered so many years ago. One of the most difficult things in broken relationships is the lack of understanding about the pain that has been caused. Here, however, in a tight corner themselves, Joseph's brothers remembered his distress and maybe, realising the cruelty of their deed, regretted it. 'Maybe', because we cannot look into the hearts of Joseph's brothers. In any case, at this moment they were anxious and feared for their lives.

Joseph may have looked and spoken like an Egyptian, but he was able to follow his brothers' dispute, since it was in his mother tongue. He was deeply moved by it; in verse 24 we read that he turned away and wept. Then he provided them with an abundance of food and also gave them money for the journey back to Canaan. But Simeon had to stay behind as security for his younger brother Benjamin, whom Joseph wished to see face to face. He did indeed come with his brothers on their second journey to Egypt, which brings us to Genesis 43. We are told that on that occasion Joseph blessed his younger full brother and then had to withdraw, because 'he was deeply moved at the sight of his brother, and he looked for a place to weep' (verse 30). Apparently, in those times it was also embarrassing for a man to show his tears.

I cannot fathom the emotions Joseph experienced in that period between the first and second encounter with his brothers. The fact that he initially accused them falsely and made them journey back home, with all the risks involved in those days, indicates that Joseph needed some time to work things through in order to reach the point where he could love his brothers unreservedly. When they returned, however, he showered them with good things, showing that he still carried his brothers in his heart. In spite of all that they had done to him, he was still graciously capable of blessing them. But the encounter was deeply emotional for him; when Joseph, after having tested them one more time (Gen.44), finally made himself known to them, he was unable to hide his tears. We read in Genesis 45:2 that he started to weep so loudly 'that the Egyptians heard him, and Pharaoh's household heard about it'.

In that revealing moment where Joseph made himself known to his brothers and they were horrified, he encountered them with an attitude of unconditional love. He bade them to come close

(Gen.45:4), he comforted them ('do not be distressed and do not be angry with yourselves', verse 5) and invited them with all their children and grandchildren and possessions, their flocks, herds and whatever else, to come and live close to him ('Otherwise you and your household and all who belong to you will become destitute', verse 11). Whereas before his heart may have been filled with grief, disappointment or anger, these things had now made room for warm forgiveness and generous love. He asked his brothers to return to their father's house in order to fetch their relatives and live-stock and then we read in verse 15: 'And he kissed all his brothers and wept over them'. Later on he saw them off with rich provisions for the journey and vehicles for their father, wives and children. His farewell words are telling: 'Don't quarrel on the way'(verse 24); there had been enough tension when they were young and it had affected all of them.

Joseph's love for his brothers who had caused him so much grief was profound. This is forgiveness with a capital 'F'! Sometimes we say that we have forgiven someone because it is, after all, what is expected from a child of God, but here we are witnessing abundant forgiveness. Joseph's attitude enabled him to put his arms around his offenders and to welcome them full-heartedly. What we see here is the incredible gentleness and generosity of a man who didn't need to avenge himself any more, or to get to the bottom of the matter to put the blame where it belonged. He didn't even feel the desire to tell his brothers what he thought of them. This is Romans 12:17 in practice: 'Do not repay anyone evil for evil. Be careful to do what is right in the eyes of everybody'. I think we can only manage to do so if we have found refuge with God and have come to know his unconditional love and comfort in our hearts. When we are ourselves 'people of grace' – that is those who have received and come to know God's grace – we are able to be merciful to others. When we know what it means to be safely kept in God's love, we have room for others and are able to offer them safety.

Joseph's mercy towards his brothers was unconditional; they never actually asked him directly to forgive them. When they did ask for it in Genesis 50 (from verse 15 onwards), it was after they had already lived fifty years in Egypt and they asked on their father's behalf. Jacob had meanwhile died and they feared that Joseph might now have second thoughts and would still want to pay them back for what they did. Anxiously, they offered their service (verse 18, 'We are your slaves'). It seems that even after all those years, they were still afraid and felt that they needed to win Joseph's favour. But they asked for something that Joseph had already given them unconditionally many years ago. In fact for over half a century they had lived and enjoyed life by the grace of Joseph. Their attitude revealed their heart, but Joseph remained steadfast in his dealing with them: he reassured them and spoke 'kindly to them'(verse 21).

Joseph, in his offer of grace, again is a characterisation of the Lord Jesus, whereas we, like Joseph's brothers, sometimes doubt God's unconditional offer of ample grace through Jesus Christ. We who are invited to live by grace, in reality often live with some doubt as to the truth of it. We live and act as if we still need to deserve or earn God's favour, we do not dare to accept the grace he freely offers us, we do not dare to believe in it. We, who are invited to find refuge in God's grace and come to rest under the wings of the Almighty, often continue our restless search for these very things that have already been provided.

d)He was a man able to discern God's ways
When, in Genesis 45, Joseph made himself known to his brothers, his words (in verse 5) reveal his great generosity and particularly his discernment as to God's dealings: 'And now, do not be distressed and do not be angry with yourselves for selling me

here, because it was to save lives that God sent me ahead of you'.

It is interesting to read Genesis 50:20 alongside this verse: '*You* intended to harm me, but *God* intended it for good to accomplish what is now being done, the saving of many lives'. Joseph was saying that, where they intended to harm him, God turned their evil deed to good. In saying this, Joseph wasn't focusing on his own profit or well-being in that he himself hadn't perished, but on that of his brothers and of many others with them who would be saved. But there is the other side as well. Paul says in Romans 8:28: 'And we know that in all things God works for the good of those who love him, who have been called according to his purpose'. These words should not be separated from what follows in verse 29: 'For those God foreknew he also predestined to be conformed to the likeness of his Son'. The apostle Paul makes it clear that God's dealings concern not only a broader or general purpose but also a very personal purpose, namely the shaping or moulding of the man or woman involved. He or she will reach his or her destination in becoming a man or woman after God's heart, and bearing the likeness of his Son.

As we have already seen, Joseph's life resembles that of the Son, Jesus Christ, in more than one respect. The Lord Jesus was humiliated; the Son of the King became a humble servant. He went the lowest way and went that way in obedience, without complaining. He too was exalted, after his death and resurrection, and is able to save all those who come to him. Like Joseph, Jesus too lost his precious garment; the soldiers took it from him before he was nailed to the cross. But we must never forget that, contrary to Joseph, Jesus wasn't humbled but he humbled himself. He wasn't helpless but chose this way. Paul makes that clear in Philippians 2:6-11. He states that Jesus did not count equality with God a thing to be grasped but He made himself nothing, taking the very nature of a servant. All that, in order to save us.

e) He was a man who believed in God's sovereignty

Joseph was privileged to see God intervene in his life. He was allowed to see how the Lord gave a positive turn to the negative deeds of his brothers. But it goes even further than that — Joseph didn't just see that God could turn things around, he believed God actually orchestrated things! In Genesis 45:5-8 Joseph says that God himself sent him to Egypt 'to save lives' (verse 5) and 'to preserve for you a remnant on earth and to save your lives by a great deliverance' (verse 7). He concludes: 'So then, it was not you who sent me here, but God. He made me father to Pharaoh, lord of his entire household and ruler of all Egypt'. Joseph's brothers didn't know what they were doing when they sold him to a passing caravan, but it was the Lord God who sent that caravan along and then led it to Egypt and to Pharaoh's house.

God's sovereignty is again manifested as the story continues. Joseph was instrumental in the reuniting of his family. His leadership brought about a change. The family, that for different reasons used to be very divided, reunited itself for a joint future. They would share this future in the land that God had promised to Abraham, Isaac and Jacob. Joseph was also instrumental in saving his family from perishing in the famine: through him his brothers survived so that the twelve tribes of Israel were preserved.

There are a few other things that stand out in Joseph's life, of which I want to mention just two. The first is related to our view of happiness, the other to our attitude in situations where others harm us.

Our pursuit of happiness

One doesn't need to be a child psychologist to realise that the way Joseph was favoured by his parents, particularly Jacob, wasn't necessarily the best thing that could happen to him, in fact it could easily have become detrimental had God not intervened. His purpose and agenda for Joseph were quite different from that of Joseph's parents: He intended him to grow into a man of God and had a special task in mind for him. For that purpose Joseph needed discipline rather than sheltering and pampering. Overprotection may be comfortable for a while, but it is harmful rather than beneficial for its subject.

Here lies a significant lesson for parents. Often we have certain wishes or plans for our children which we presume will bring them happiness. What is it really that we are after? Do we want our children to become men and women of God and are we willing to accept God's ways of bringing that about? Or is it our main aim to provide our children with the best circumstances – a stable financial position, good health, stimulating relationships – and to protect them from problems? Can we accept that God's plans might have different 'ingredients', yet still be the best? Can we accept also a 'career' completely different from what we thought it should be like?

Our interpretation of happiness or fulfilment is a determining factor when it comes to our plans and goals. It would be a good exercise to ask ourselves regularly what exactly we are seeking and to hold our mind set up against the light of God's Word. We shall find that, in spite of our noble intentions, we are easily affected by the mood of the world around us and seek fulfilment in and through things that are at best relative and unreliable. God's idea of happiness, which is probably conveyed best by the biblical concept of *'blessedness'*, refers to things of a totally different order from our mental conception of it. He himself wants to be the source of our dreams and delight! It is not surprising, therefore, that when in the psalms we read: 'Blessed (most often a translation from the Hebrew *asrey* meaning happy') is the man, who...', this is often directly linked with *taking refuge in God*. The latter is the case in Psalm 34:8 and 40:4 where David says: 'Blessed is the man who takes refuge in him (the Lord)' and: 'Blessed is the man who makes the Lord his trust.' We saw earlier how this was Ruth's choice; she sought and found refuge under the wings of the Almighty (Ruth 2:12) and as a result, the woman we meet in the Book of Ruth is a 'happy' woman, despite her circumstances. It appears that hiding in God is conditional to our finding true and lasting fulfilment. He gives us an inner peace and stability that has the potential to prevent us from being thrown off balance. Joseph certainly testified to that truth.

In the Bible the word blessed isn't only linked with taking refuge, but also with *obedience* and *discipline* (sometimes called chastisement), they are often mentioned in one breath. In Psalm 94:12 for instance we read: 'Blessed is the man you discipline, O Lord'. It is usually hard for us to understand and accept that discipline can be a blessing, or even, that it can make us happy. Yet it is often through adversity – which is a form of discipline – that we grow in holiness, which means that we are learning to find our delight (or to be delighted!) in God. This is why God prunes us and this is why he led Joseph through many trials and tribulations. It was a form of discipline, which helped him to discover that his position before God was giving him more satisfaction than his position as a model slave, model prisoner or even prime minister of Egypt. I dare say that if that high political position had also been taken away from him, it wouldn't have thrown him the way his separation from his family did thirteen years earlier.

Had Joseph and his parents been able to choose and direct Joseph's future themselves, they probably would have chosen the obvious in their circumstances and time: Joseph would have stayed at home and would probably have been given a prominent position in the family sheep rearing business. God, however, removed him from his country and people, placing him in a distant and unique spot. The consequences were momentous: first, a prestigious position in Egypt that neither he nor his parents could have ever orchestrated; second, the rescue of the Egyptians and of God's people (including his own brother Judah, who was to be one of the ancestors of Jesus, see Matthew 1); and third, his own growth into a mature and balanced man of God.

The happiness that God desires to give his children is not related to a feeling or emotion that is brought about by fragile circumstances or a certain achievement. It is an inner state of peace and balance brought about by our position in Christ. As such it is stable and lasting and finding it is inextricably linked with our pursuit of God. Joseph's life shows how important it is that godly parents, in seeking the best for their children, commit them to the Lord, daring to let go of them in the sense that they allow God to upset their calculations and go his way with each individual. It is hard sometimes to release our own ideas or desires and to be open-minded when we pray for our children's future. But God desires that our prayers and aspirations for them become attuned to his will. When we see God's hand in and throughout Joseph's life, we are challenged to trust God more. It can help us to relax when all we can see in our child's life seems crooked or undesirable! Even when we feel disappointed and lose heart, we can continue trusting that God has his own unsearchable yet loving ways even with this child. Which goes for each one of us!

When others harm us

At least three times Joseph found himself in difficult circumstances through the deeds or negligence of others. What can we learn from him? What are we to do in comparable situations? It is crucial that we do not focus and remain focused on the event itself or on its cause or originators, but rather and increasingly on *our attitude* towards those who harmed us. We are likely to have feelings of bitterness, not just towards God, but certainly and probably sooner towards the man or woman who injured us. In fairness, a negative reaction isn't out of place and more often than not it is quite justifiable. But the question is what we do with our anger, whether we harbour or release it! Our desire for justice will sometimes get us entangled in bitter and prolonged legal proceedings that can continue for years, thus obstructing our leaving things behind and hindering a mental and emotional healing process. We need to carefully consider the value of getting to the bottom of things and seeing justice done to those who wronged us. Our anger can take root and grow into a poisonous tree, embittering our lives, which only intensifies the damage. When we have done what we should do without having been able to reach a satisfactory solution, we must learn to leave justice where it belongs, even if we feel people are getting away with their evil deeds! It may indeed seem like that but vengeance and revenge are not ours, they are God's business. Paul says in Romans 12:19: 'Do not take revenge, my friends, but leave room for God's wrath, for it is written: "It is mine to avenge; I will repay, says the Lord."' When this truth comes home to us, we are set free from persistent feelings of revenge or deep resentment.

Being open to our possible share in a negative situation that has arisen, as well as acknowledging our faults, is necessary but particularly difficult when we are deeply hurt. Our feelings and emotions can easily get in the way and hinder the process of an honest examination. Only when we have calmed down somewhat and have been able to gain some emotional distance from the situation can we be more reasonable and objective. But how do we reach that stage? One important step forward is when we learn to not keep going over , thus feeding our own feelings, but to seek the Lord with all those feelings. In the safe setting of our hiding with God, he will open our eyes to see things in the right perspective. David, in Psalm 139, asks God to search and test him and to see 'if there is any offensive way in me' (verses 23-24). He dares to be vulnerable and risk a painful answer, because he feels utterly safe with his heavenly Father. God provides a framework of security and unconditional love, which creates a spacious place of grace where we find room for ourselves but then also for the other person: it becomes possible for us to ask them to forgive *our* deeds, whereas before we were focusing on *their* guilt and were expecting them to beg us for our forgiveness! God's grace enhances our minds and hearts and his tenderness affects our feelings of anger and bitterness.

When Paul mentions the fruits of the Spirit in Galatians 5, the first he names is love, the very characteristic that I as a human being cannot produce let alone administer, especially to someone who has wronged me. I do not want to love my offender, I would rather hit them for what they have done to me, I desire to avenge myself. Those feelings, reasonable though they may seem, do not fit the principles of the Kingdom of God. Here natural tendencies collide with the principles and fruits of the Spirit of God. The latter aren't natural to me, but these godly fruits are available, because God has put the seeds for them within me by his Holy Spirit, as an option. When they are watered and fed they will grow, when they are neglected or pushed away they will wither. In other words, we can choose to learn to love, but we can also choose to leave it. The closer our walk with God, the simpler our choice will be. In fact don't just stay as close to him as possible, but remain *in* him (John 15:4). Then fruit will develop in your heart and life and there will be room for what seemed impossible: love, and *in* that love, forgiveness. It is only human and therefore natural that that moment will be preceded by many and deep moments of anger, bitterness and resentment. Let's beware and not allow these negative emotions to take root in our lives, for then we reach a dead end and run aground. There is nothing that Satan would like more, and he will jump at any opportunity to make us stumble and fall. We need to realize that only if we are able to let go of what is negative and destructive, only if we are able to forgive, can we really move on.

Joseph received many blows but, rather than giving up, he found his way in each new situation and moved on. This doesn't mean that Joseph never felt like giving his brothers or Potiphar or the cupbearer a piece of his mind, I think he probably did! But he never had the opportunity to do so. When he was thrown into the pit, he was at his brothers' mercy which wasn't exactly the right moment to tell them off! On the contrary, he had to humble himself and plead for mercy to have his life saved. He didn't have the chance to justify himself with Potiphar either; even though he had a high position, he was still a slave and as such had no rights whatsoever. When in prison the cupbearer forgot him, Joseph was in no position to lecture the man about that. After all, the cupbearer was released and therefore out of his reach.

Was Joseph the kind of man who would harbour feelings of revenge or resentment? I don't know, but it would have been absolutely futile in his situation. Such fretting would more likely have added to his suffering, in fact holding on to negative feelings will always hurt and harm us more deeply in the end. What is clear beyond any doubt is that Joseph did not get stuck in or paralysed by negative circumstances; time and time again he was able to move forward. It is also obvious that his character and attitude changed over the years – he learnt to live with the Lord and was freed from possible negative and destructive feelings and reactions, even whilst he suffered. In those years of training he probably got to know himself better and also became aware of his own shortcomings. The closer our walk with God, the stronger the light and the clearer the things that cannot bear light. Joseph hadn't been totally innocent and blameless in the conflict with his brothers, as a youngster he may well have boasted about or misused his favoured position in the family; he was a tell-tale, passing on nasty things about his brothers to their father (Gen.37:2). But thirteen years later he gave the very same brothers his very best!

Called to forgive

It is Jesus who summons us to forgive our fellow men. He knows by experience what that involves and what it costs. It cost him his life! The way in which he dealt with Peter who denied him three times is very moving. This denial by an intimate friend hurt him deeply, but was no reason for him to drop Peter. Jesus' love was totally unconditional; in no way did it depend upon Peter's reaction or behaviour. Peter couldn't undo or restore what he had done. Some things are irrevocable. Nevertheless, Jesus forgave him as we see later on and more than that! We read in Luke 22:31 and 32 that the Lord Jesus prayed for Peter that his faith wouldn't fail, that he wouldn't perish and that Satan would not get a hold on him. Jesus had the best in mind for Peter, despite everything.

We are often hurt in the context of a relationship and this very fact implies that the effects are far reaching as trust is broken and the relationship at least disturbed. The closer the relationship, the deeper the hurt will be. When the Lord Jesus was betrayed by Peter, it was a very dear friend who broke his promise of faithfulness. They had shared intimately, had closely walked and worked together. This makes the moment of Peter's denial dramatic and emotionally wounding. Luke says (in Luke 22:61-62) that the Lord Jesus turned around and looked at Peter and that Peter then went outside and cried bitter tears. Both parties suffered grief. But there was restoration; Jesus, the One who was betrayed, took the initiative to restore the relationship. In John 21 he appeared after his resurrection, at the Sea of Tiberias. There he met some people including Peter. By a coal fire on the beach Jesus asked him three times if he truly loved him. When Peter affirmed his love for Jesus three times, he was entrusted with a new task. It is interesting to note that these three affirmations were spoken by a coal fire after three denials which also took place by a coal fire. It is as if Jesus took Peter back to that painful moment when things went wrong, not to crush him, but to reveal to him his unconditional love and forgiveness. As Christians we can rest assured that these very things are also available to us and in fact so abundantly that we overflow. Having experienced God's forgiveness in our own hearts, we can ask his Holy Spirit to shed and transmit his love and forgiveness in our own relationships where healing and restoration are needed.

Are we willing to follow our Lord and to forgive in situations where we have been deeply hurt and where someone's words and deeds have harmed us? Are we willing to seek that forgiveness even in situations where we aren't sure that the other person is truly sorry and feels remorse? Is restoration so important to us that we are prepared to pay the highest price in order to make it possible? Or is it rather so that resentment and anger cause us to maintain our conflict or even nurse it? Let it suffice to say that forgiveness is necessary if we want to be free people (and if we want to free others from our judgement) and if we seek reconciliation and restoration. Often there is no room in our hearts for forgiveness. When we find refuge with the Lord, we find that he wants to touch our negative feelings, desiring to break down the walls of hurt and self-protection that we erected, in order to create new possibilities and room for forgiveness and love. Also here, it is true that when the Lord charges us to forgive, he also gives us room to learn to do precisely that. Just as Naomi was given space for her temporary bitterness, so we too are sometimes allowed space for our anger. God knows our helplessness and he meets us where we are. But we need to remember that the space he gives us is never meant as a passport to harbour and feed our negative feelings. God commissions us to forgive and we are to obey.

6
When Pain Continues

Leah

In this chapter we consider Leah, Jacob's wife and Rachel's sister, who also faced traumatic years of empty-handedness in her life. Unlike Naomi, Ruth and Joseph, however, we have no clear indication that her problem was ever solved or even that she was given something to alleviate the pain caused by her particular circumstances. She was someone who had to 'live by faith' without seeing her longings fulfilled. And yet God was as much with her as he was with the three people we looked at in the previous chapters. But for her there was no happy ending, at least as far as we know from what the book of Genesis tells us about her. Leah appears to have lived all her life in the shadow of her younger sister and was second best, both in her youth and in her marriage to Jacob. Her story is recorded in Genesis, starting in chapter 29.

It is via Rachel that Leah is first mentioned. Jacob, en route to his uncle Laban, met his cousin Rachel towards the end of his journey, when she came to water the sheep at a well where he was chatting with some shepherds. It must have been love at first sight for him, for just one month after that first encounter, he asked Laban (whose household he had meanwhile joined) for her hand in marriage. At this point we are informed (in Gen.29:16) about the existence of an elder daughter, Leah. She is described in verse

17 as a young woman with 'weak eyes', whereas it is said of her sister Rachel that she was 'lovely in form, and beautiful'. These descriptions suggest that Rachel was a rather striking girl, whereas her elder sister may have been a bit plain. It isn't completely clear what is meant by 'weak' eyes. The Hebrew word *rak* occurs eighteen times in the Old Testament. Twice it is translated as 'weak' as is the case here. *The Harper Collins Study Bible* suggests that it may have been a case of a cosmetic imperfection or a defect in her beauty, related to Leah's eyes. Whatever may have been the case, I imagine that Rachel was the kind of girl who automatically drew everybody's attention. Leah simply wasn't any match for her. That very fact can give one weak eyes! Not surprisingly Jacob fell for the pretty younger one and offered to work seven years for her father Laban in return for her. Genesis 29:20 states that his love for her was so strong that these years flew by for him. But Leah's situation remained unchanged – still in the background, nobody had turned up for her.

Did you ever stop and think what it must have meant to Leah to witness her cousin's growing love for her younger sister over a period of seven long years, whilst nobody ever came for her? Would Rachel have prided herself on it in front of her older sister? Did she have any consideration for Leah's pain? Whilst reading the story and getting to know Rachel (a little), I suspect she didn't. Rachel seems to have been mainly occupied with herself. It is my impression that Leah was a very lonely person.

When the seven years were over, Jacob's uncle had concocted a very deceitful plan. He didn't give Rachel to his nephew in marriage; he gave him Leah instead (Gen.29:23). Interestingly there is a notable parallel here. Jacob, who once cheated his own father by pretending to be his brother Esau, at Laban's house became the victim of a similar deed. The deceiver was himself deceived. So well-known is this event that it still plays a role in Jewish tradition today. It can happen at an orthodox wedding in the synagogue, that the bridegroom goes to his bride before the ceremony begins and raises the veil covering her face, as if to ascertain that she is indeed the one he intends to marry!

Leah must have had very mixed feelings about the role she had to play when Laban shoved her into Rachel's position. In doing so he forced his nephew to accept as his wife the elder sister whom he did not love. Leah knew very well that Jacob loved Rachel, but she may have hoped against hope that things would change. There is no indication that she had had a say in the matter; in a sense she was also a victim. Her future marriage was a lost cause even before it had begun. After the wedding night, Jacob was stunned and infuriated when he discovered that his bed partner wasn't his beautiful beloved Rachel but, instead, the older unattractive sister in whom he had no interest. The incident itself is quite perplexing to say the least: how is it ever possible that it wasn't until after the wedding night that Jacob realised that he had mistaken the one sister for the other? They must have served very good wine at the wedding feast and Laban probably had a good chuckle thinking his plan had worked! But Leah! She must have felt extremely hurt and humiliated. Her father forced her on to the man who loved her sister. If she had harboured any hope, however vague, of winning Jacob for herself, the events of the morning after her wedding night made it painfully clear that her hope wasn't realistic. Jacob was beside himself and went in great indignation to his father-in-law, who then had the nerve to suggest that he should first finish his bridal week with Leah after which Rachel would be given to him. Following that he was required to work another seven years for her (Gen.29:27).

I imagine that to Leah it was yet another deep humiliation to realise that Jacob had to first finish the bridal week with her, knowing very well that the actual bride and loved one had had to resign herself to waiting in the wings and was probably fuming with the same intense rage that Jacob was feeling. For Leah this experience of hurtful rejection must have confirmed and intensified her feelings of being second rate. The events will have given rise to a lot of gossip in the women's quarters!

Both rejection and the struggle to survive in a loveless marriage are situations that are familiar to us today. Many men and women are not loved by their partners. Many people admit that they feel desperately lonely and deserted in their marriage. Many – Christians and non-Christians alike – share the experience of a husband or wife who abandons them for someone else. How does a woman feel when her husband prefers someone else, when she is faced with rejection, unfaithfulness and desertion? How does one cope with the humiliation, pain and loneliness which, as in Leah's case, can last for years?

In Leah's day, as well as in ours, women stood empty-handed. Some rise up to their situation and do everything within their power to change things. This is what Leah did. For years she sought her happiness in the love and devotion of her husband, but she did not succeed. In Genesis 29 we see that she started to compete with her own sister by giving birth to several children. Did she hope that she could win her husband's love in that way? Judging by the meaning of the names of her children, it may well have been the case. Genesis 29:32-35 reports the births of her first four sons. Certainly in the names of the first three we can see Leah's longing to still win Jacob's love. Reuben (verse 32): 'the Lord has seen my misery. Surely my husband will love me now'; Simeon (verse 33): 'Because the Lord heard that I am not loved, he gave me this one too'; Levi (verse 34): 'Now at last my husband will become attached to me'. The name of the fourth son does not carry the same feeling. It is Judah (verse 35): 'This time I will praise the Lord'. It is noteworthy that it is this son who is later mentioned in the genealogy of the Lord Jesus, a fact which Leah couldn't have known then. Why then, did this fourth son get a name that is derived from the Hebrew verb 'to praise'? What reason did Leah have to praise God? Had her attitude changed, had God himself inspired her to name her son thus? Her situation hadn't changed, her longing for Jacob's love had not been fulfilled. In fact we see that Leah went on fighting for her husband's love, she wasn't prepared to give up. This is obvious by the name which she gave to her sixth son, Zebulun, at whose birth she said 'God has presented me with a precious gift. This time my husband will treat me with honour' (Genesis 30:20). She still sought Jacob's respect and love. Her sister seemed to have both whereas, as far as we know, Leah's love remained unrequited.

The intense and desperate struggle between the sisters is described in Genesis 29:31-30:24. When Leah had four sons and Rachel appeared to be infertile, Rachel got her maidservant Bilhah to join the battle. She became pregnant by Jacob and gave birth to one and later to another son. In Genesis 29:35b we read that Leah had now stopped bearing children. Her next move in the fight against her sister was to enlist her maidservant Zilpa, who then also had two children by Jacob. It looks as if Leah wasn't only fighting for her husband's love, she was also fighting against her sister. In their competition both were prepared to go to the extreme, there seemed to be no rules or boundaries. Leah went as far as 'hiring' her own husband from her rival. When Rachel wanted to have the mandrakes that Leah's son Reuben had found in the fields, Leah's first reaction was one of dismay: 'Wasn't it enough that you took away my husband? Will you take my son's mandrakes too?' Rachel then made a bizarre proposal to her sister. She suggested that in exchange for the mandrakes, Jacob could 'sleep with you tonight'. Leah accepted this bribe and that evening she went out to meet Jacob, telling him: 'You must sleep with me... I have hired you with my son's mandrakes.' We then read: 'So he slept with her that night'(Gen.30:14-17).

When Leah had intercourse with her own husband that night, she was again deeply humiliated, because she had to hire him from the woman he loved. During their wedding night Jacob assumed he was making love to her sister Rachel; now as he made love to Leah, he did so because he had been bought. She was his legal wife, but she had to ask him to sleep with her. How long did Leah keep trying to change her situation? She was, and remained, the unloved one. There was always rejection, both from her husband and from her sister.

It isn't clear whether only hatred and envy existed between Rachel and Leah or whether there was ever a moment when they got on better together. Rachel seems to have been a heartless, selfish woman without any consideration for anybody else. I get the impression that she was used to always getting her way, even if it meant having to put pressure on people or actually forcing them to meet her demands. When she seemed incapable of conceiving, she put the blame on her husband and went as far as saying to him: 'Give me children, or I'll die!' (Gen.30:1). That is one way of dealing with empty hands! The fact that her sister had been able to have Jacob's children obviously made her extremely jealous.

I wonder what troubled Rachel more, her childlessness or the fact that Leah had something that she didn't have. I am tempted to believe it was the latter, particularly when I read Rachel's words after her servant Bilhah had given birth to a second son: 'I have had a great struggle with my sister, and I have won' (Gen.30:8). These are the words of a spoilt woman, who would do anything within her power to get what she considered her right. Nevertheless, we must not forget that Rachel was also a victim. She was used to being the prettier of the two sisters, life had probably always gone smoothly for her. The fact that her father gave Leah and not her to Jacob in marriage, may well have been the first major set-back in her life. Later she had to face her infertility whilst witnessing the pregnancies of her sister and of the two maidservants. How vulnerable one feels in such a situation! Both Rachel and Leah were obsessed by that which they did not have and made their happiness dependant on it. Later on, God remembered Rachel's cries and opened her womb (Gen.30:22). Here we see God's infinite goodness, when, in spite of ourselves, he meets with us and blesses us.

As the story continues, there isn't any clear indication that Leah's situation ever changed for the better, even though she was given the honour of being buried in the family grave (see Genesis 49:31). When Rachel died after giving birth to Benjamin, on the journey from Bethel to Bethlehem, she was buried 'on the way' (Gen.35:19). I don't know if that fact reveals something of Jacob's feelings for Leah after having known her for a number of years. I can imagine that life with a spoilt woman like Rachel was far from easy, but we are never told that Jacob's attitude towards Leah changed. It seems that Leah, at least for the greater part of her life, remained the second choice and that she spent her married life with a husband who not only did not love her, but, even worse, who loved someone else. The fact that her rival was part of the same household and prominently present must have aggravated her even more.

What do we know of Leah's later years? We know that after twenty years, resentment and friction set in and Laban's attitude towards his son-in-law changed. Jacob was told by God to move away from Laban's house and return to the land of his fathers and his relatives (Gen.31:2-3). From verse 4 onwards we are told that Jacob consulted both Rachel and Leah, who, interestingly, were both negative about their father: 'Does he not regard us as foreigners? Not only has he sold us ...' (verse 15). The end result was the departure of the extended family and their livestock and this time Laban was deceived, for he was not informed about the move (verses 20-21).

In Genesis 32 Jacob sent messengers ahead of him to meet his brother Esau, whose anger he still feared, having fled from him years ago. When he learned, and later also saw, that Esau was on his way with four hundred men to meet him, he began making preparations for the confrontation. What he did is very telling with regard to the position of his wives and children. We read in Genesis 33 that Jacob divided his people, drawing them up in order of battle. He himself went ahead, then, of those following, he put in front the maidservants and their children. They were least important and would bear the brunt should there be a battle. Following them were Leah with her children and finally, safely in the rear guard, were Rachel and Joseph, the favourite wife and favourite son. Nothing had changed, they still had a preferential position.

Looking at the remaining story, we realise that Leah had yet to face a number of blows in her life. Her daughter Dina was raped (Gen.34:2), an event that led to murder and manslaughter instigated by her sons Simeon and Levi. Consequently the safety of the family was in jeopardy, a fact which didn't do any good to Jacob's relationship with Leah's boys (verse 30). We must not lose sight of the fact that, from the very moment that Rachel had given birth to Joseph, Leah's children had always been at a disadvantage. Joseph was indisputably Jacob's blue-eyed boy, which must have hurt his half-brothers and Leah. This open favouritism for one child must have caused yet more division within the family than the rivalry between the two sisters had already caused. On top of these family tensions Leah also witnessed Rachel's death and the disappearance of Joseph. Both events left their marks on Jacob and consequently on the family. We read in Genesis 37:35 that Jacob, after Joseph's presumed death, refused to be comforted. All his sons and daughters did their best to help him get over his grief, but they were unable to reach him in his distress. Seeing her children trying hard to comfort their father and realising they could never make up for the loss of their half-brother Joseph, must have been another painful experience for Leah, as well as for the sons who realised they too were second-best.

When pain continues

What does one do when pain and hurt continue? Let us consider five points:

a) Keep trusting the Lord — He sees us in our distress
In Genesis 29:30 we read that Jacob loved Rachel more than he loved Leah. Then, in the very next verse we read: 'When the Lord saw that Leah was not loved, he opened her womb, but Rachel was barren'(verse 31). When Leah 'hired' her own husband for a night from her sister, we read: 'God listened to Leah, and she became pregnant' (Gen.30:17). God saw and heard. In a situation where we are left completely on our own and feel totally rejected, God is there. He sees us and he hears us. He knows our misery and pain. The fact of his continuing presence and care should give us a confidence that remains steadfast in all circumstances, even at times when we feel forsaken and desolate. We are always in a position to seek him and to draw close to him.

b) Keep seeking the Lord — He desires to reveal himself.
What do we pray for when painful situations continue? Whatever the situation may be, at any time when we are hurt or distressed, we can always call on the Name of the Lord and give our cares to him. This truth isn't always a reality in our lives. We often find it easier to share our burdens with people than with the Lord. It is important that we learn to make it our habit to go to him. 'Do not be anxious about anything, but in everything, by prayer and petition, with thanksgiving, present your requests to God,' says Paul in Philippians 4:6. Our heavenly Father is involved in all the details of our lives and he longs for us to share all our troubles

with him. We can come to him with confidence and be open about everything with him, whether big or small. But there is more than this. We should not just present our cares to him but our very selves with them. Rather than delivering a parcel of burdens, we need to surrender ourselves. It is *me* coming to meet with God and this affects my burdens and my attitude to them. As we grow in our relationship with God, we will see a change in the order of things we pray for. Instead of seeking God's presence because of what he can do for us, we start seeking him because of who he is.

This change or shift in emphasis is a step in our discovery process of who God really is. Sometimes this doesn't happen until we stand empty-handed and it isn't until then that we discover the goodness of the Lord and the wonder of hiding in him and of expecting everything from him rather than relying on ourselves or other people. Trials and tragedies drive us into his arms and are a means of getting to know him more deeply. It results in a new sense of joy and adds a new dimension to our lives which might otherwise never have happened. John White, who has gone through great trials in his own family talks about this in his book, *Daring to Draw Near*[1]. He says:

> What you can always experience is a deepening relationship with him. For you may be sure that the pain has a purpose in your own life. It is divine surgery that, if you respond to it appropriately, will heal and correct defects in your Christian growth. But it is essential that you respond with trust in the mercy and goodness of God. No bitterness or rebellion must be permitted to cloud your vision of him even when he seems not to answer. Otherwise the pain designed to enrich and deepen your relationship with him might have the opposite effect as you allow yourself the luxuries of self-pity and doubt.

White later on adds:

> What I have gained through them (trials) in sheer treasure makes the suffering a trivial price to pay. I hate pain, but I would gladly undergo the same pain again to find more of the same treasure. ... I can certainly smile wonderingly at the harvest of joy I have reaped.

A few years ago I stood by a close friend during a period of prolonged illness that led to her death. Over the three years that she knew she had cancer, we prayed together and with other friends, for the miracle of healing. We shared moments together in tears of desperation, in grief and in fear of suffering. The suffering became a reality. She experienced increasing physical weakness and pain. One month before she died, we read Philippians 3, where Paul talks about how knowing Christ surpasses all things that seem to us like gain. Paul declares that 'gaining' Christ is worth everything to him. He says in verse 10: 'I want to know Christ and the power of his resurrection and the fellowship of sharing in his sufferings'. It was New Year's Eve and that night I stayed in the hospice with my friend. Around midnight some people came into her room. It was a very emotional moment, painful for some, because they weren't quite sure what good wishes to extend to someone who would soon die. I think that, despite all the questions that probably remained until the end of her life, we had actually read in Paul's letter to the Philippians what to wish for her: that she would know Christ more deeply. This is in fact what happened to her and it became very apparent. Her situation did not change in the sense that she was physically healed, but God became more and more precious to her. On the Sunday afternoon that she died, we prayed together and declared that she could finally leave her suffering behind. I assured her that the Lord was waiting for her with open arms and we spoke of going home to him, whom she knew and loved. When I look back on her progressive illness and suffering, I still do not understand why she had to go through it, but I can see how God gave her the joy of knowing him more intimately and how time and time again, he gave her the strength and grace to cope with it all. We have to learn to seek God, fully trusting him, instead of looking ahead and fixing our thoughts on what might happen tomorrow.

In his psalms, David repeatedly speaks about 'being satisfied', not just by life itself or through circumstances, but only by God. In Psalm 63:3-7 he says:

> Because your love is better than life, my lips will glorify you. I will praise you as long as I live, and in your name I will lift up my hands. My soul will be satisfied as with the richest of foods; with singing lips my mouth will praise you. On my bed I remember you: I think of you through the watches of the night. Because you are my help, I sing in the shadow of your wings.

These words are the fruit of David's walk with God. Through trials he discovered God's goodness, a characteristic that cannot be shaken or influenced by circumstances. Like David we may increasingly discover that God is worthy of our praise, irrespective of what happens around us. Even if a loveless marriage causes empty hands which are not filled with the love we long for, even if in sickness we don't receive healing, God can fill our hands with his comfort and loving kindness. Isaiah says about that: 'The Lord will guide you always; he will satisfy your needs *in* a sun-scorched land' (Isa. 58:11).

c) Learn to notice the flowers on your path
It is said that, when God shuts a door, he opens a window. Sometimes we concentrate so much on the closed door that we

do not notice the window. Did Leah ever know happiness; was she able to enjoy things? I think of what was given to her through her children. It was God who opened her womb and blessed her with offspring. Not everyone is given that; Rachel was barren initially. Leah, however, had six sons and a daughter. When Reuben found mandrakes in the fields, he brought them to his mother. I see in that lovely gesture God smiling kindly upon her and am sure that there were other similar moments of joy.

We need to develop an awareness for God's blessings and goodness in our lives. When we keep concentrating on things we lack or things that have been taken away from us, we fail to see what we do or can have. As long as Leah allowed Jacob's lack of love for her to be a determining factor in her life, ruling out any possibility of happiness, she was a pitiful person, because these circumstances didn't change.

There are numerous examples of continuing pain. Childlessness is one of them, as is remaining single or being handicapped. Joni Eareckson had to face and come to terms with the latter when she was only sixteen years old. A swimming accident left her paralysed. Now, confined to a wheelchair, she is a blessing to many people. She has developed impressive artistic gifts and has become an advocate for handicapped people, organising conferences and seminars, providing instruction and guidance, all aimed at stimulating full integration of the handicapped in society as well as in the church. She rightly feels that handicapped people should be given room to use their gifts and bless others through their lives. Joni is an example of someone who accepted her difficult circumstances and found the freedom to grow and develop. But there is more: through (and maybe even because of) her handicap, Joni has grown into a deeply spiritual woman. Pain and sadness did not deform her but formed her instead. These things were possible because, by God's grace, she was able to look beyond the closed door and notice the open window rather

than becoming imprisoned by her immediate circumstances.
Therein lies a very important lesson.

d) Endure suffering and know that God never wastes our pain
It is true to say that suffering can damage or even break a person,
but it is equally true that nothing can have a stronger formative
effect on us than the suffering we meet in our lives. When we
come to the Lord with our pain, we give him space to do his
work in us.

Suffering can produce a refining of our faith – it becomes
purer and grows stronger. To be tested in 'the furnace of affliction'
(Isa.48:10) can seem cruel or senseless, but it is aimed at our salvation
and spiritual growth. Distress or suffering can peel off the 'outside'
of our faith; mere form or frill doesn't survive the test of affliction.
People who have gone through severe suffering testify of their
faith being changed through tribulation: they have learned to
persevere and their relationship with God has developed in strength
as well as in depth. Suffering requires a lot from us, but we also
receive much grace to stand firm. It seems a contradiction, but is
in fact a wonderful truth: when we grow in our dependence upon
the Lord, we become stronger people.

Paul experienced a personal affliction that he describes as 'a
thorn in the flesh'. The fact that he never openly said what it was
that bothered him, gave rise to quite a bit of speculation regarding
its possible nature, one suggestion being that Paul was suffering
from an eye disease. Whatever the case may have been, he was
quite open about the fact that he wanted to be delivered from it
and he prayed accordingly. The situation, however, continued and
there was no relief from whatever was hindering him. But Paul
did get an answer from the Lord: 'My grace is sufficient for you,
for my power is made perfect in weakness.' Paul learned that
weakness or difficulties can bring forth good fruit. He comments
that he delights in weaknesses as well as in insults, hardships,

persecutions and difficulties, because through them he learns to know more of God's grace and power (2 Cor.12:7-10).

It isn't only our faith which is deepened and strengthened through suffering, but we ourselves are changed as well. Those who learn to surrender themselves to the Lord in times of distress often become gentle people. In their hiding with God they find that his consolation overshadows their anger and bitterness. They have found peace and rest in him, which makes their own search for a change in their situation of pain less urgent. Their happiness is no longer solely dependent upon being loved in their marriage, nor in having children or a marriage partner or good health. By God's grace they become people who are able to comfort others. They are better equipped to help others because of their own experiences; they are able to understand more deeply what suffering is and have learned to abandon easy answers, because they realise there aren't any. They have been comforted by the Lord himself and have come out enriched. It is good to read 2 Corinthians 1:3-5 in this context. For a child of God, suffering is not meaningless. Suffering, when placed in God's hands, brings forth good fruit. The 'loveliest' people are often those who know what it means to suffer.

e) Look beyond the here and now

There was a very large window that Leah probably never saw. It was a window to the future. Leah may have felt second-rate all of her life, but in God's eyes she was unique and part of a great heavenly plan. Leah's son Judah was to become one of the forefathers of the Lord Jesus. He is mentioned in the genealogy of the Lord Jesus in Matthew 1. As his mother, Leah was an instrument in God's plan of salvation, a link in the chain of lives and events that led to the birth of our Saviour.

In our studies we have seen how God guides individual lives and works out his plans through these lives, however varied and complex they may seem to us. This knowledge should encourage us to surrender ourselves completely to him and trust him for our own life. God can use our lives, including adversity, to bring about something, the effect of which can reach far beyond our own time and remain unknown to us. God isn't limited to human boundaries of time and space, he sees things from the perspective of eternity. We must hold on to that truth, even and especially, when things happen that are perplexing to us. We need to learn to trust him through thick and thin. It is easier to do that when things turn out well, but extremely difficult, when our pain continues and things do not change for the better or even become worse.

Sometimes we experience a peace that passes all understanding and know tranquillity in the midst of a severe storm. At other times we find anxiety washing over us in great waves. Sometimes we experience God's presence and sometimes we don't. At all times, we can go and hide with him; we need to learn to make him our place of refuge in all circumstances. We can only leave things where they belong, with God, knowing that his plans for our lives go far beyond what our human eyes and minds are capable of capturing. As we become more mature in our faith, we shall be more and more open to these things. Even whilst we continue to pray for a change in our situation, we may find we pray increasingly for God's way and his honour in the things that come to pass.

Note

1. John White, *Daring to Draw Near: People in Prayer Are People Open to God*. IVP, USA, 1977.

7

In Trouble as a Result of Our Calling

In this book, where we reflect on what it means to find refuge in God, there is another person we shouldn't miss, Ruth's great-grandson David, the shepherd-king. His life is recorded from 1 Samuel 16 to 1 Kings 2:11 (as well as for the greater part in 1 Chronicles 11-29). David was the youngest son of Jesse (of the tribe of Judah, one of Joseph's brothers) and he has a prominent place as ancestor and forerunner of the Lord Jesus Christ. Jesus referred to David when he said: 'I am the Root and the Offspring of David' (recorded by John in Rev.22:16). David is mentioned no fewer than fifty-eight times in the New Testament, including in the title 'Son of David' which is often given to Jesus.

David is known for his kingship as well as for his music and poetry. He is the author of seventy-three of the Biblical psalms. In these psalms he often speaks of his taking refuge in the Lord and of God as a hiding place or shelter, a refuge, rock, fortress and stronghold. David is in fact an outstanding example when we consider the meaning of taking refuge with God. Before we look at this more closely, however, let us first look at David's life in order to discover how taking refuge with God became a part of it, as well as to see what it entailed.

David

David, God's chosen, second king of Israel, found himself empty-handed more than once in his life. We saw earlier how such experiences throw us back on ourselves. Although mostly experienced as negative or undermining, our very helplessness can become a means through which we begin to discover, by grace, what it means to find a safe refuge with the Lord. This was what happened in David's life.

In this chapter we look at an initial period of numerous great difficulties in David's life. The problems he faced were directly related to his calling to be king over Israel, which indicates that the very fact of *a divine calling to a certain task can involve suffering*. The consequences of David's God-given destination to the throne were quite dramatic for at least two people: he was to replace King Saul and bypass Jonathan, the prince-royal. His suffering was caused by the former: when Saul began to realise that David was a serious competitor to the throne, he started to dislike his erstwhile favourite servant, an attitude that soon grew into intense hatred and led to David being ruthlessly persecuted for many years. In those years David's life was constantly threatened and a number of times he only escaped death by the skin of his teeth. The difficulties and distress that he experienced during this stage of his life are described in 1 Samuel from chapter 18 onwards. There are also a number of psalms which refer to these years of misery under King Saul.

Persecuted by King Saul

David's calling to become the second king of Israel was preceded by the inauguration of a first king, an event which was contrary to God's will, although it took place with his consent. In 1 Samuel 8 we are told that the people of Israel had reached the point where they were no longer satisfied with spiritual leadership from the by then old prophet Samuel and his two corrupt sons. They made it clear that they wanted a king, just like the other nations (verse 5). The Lord God responded to their request by saying that, in their wish to replace Samuel by a king, they were actually rejecting him (verse 7). But he nevertheless granted them their request and in 1 Samuel 10 Saul, a descendant of Benjamin, was anointed by the prophet Samuel to be the first king of Israel (verse 1). Saul's kingship, however, wasn't an overwhelming success; three times he was disobedient to God and finally he was rejected as a king (1 Sam.15:26,28).

In 1 Samuel 16, the prophet Samuel was sent by the Lord God to Jesse and there it was revealed who was to be the next king over Israel: Jesse's youngest son, David, who at that moment was a shepherd; he is described as a boy with 'a fine appearance and handsome features' (verse 12). Such was his position in the family that they forgot all about him when Samuel asked to see all of Jesse's sons. Yet he, the youngest and least prominent, was the very one that God wanted! In verse 13 we read that Samuel anointed David to be king. This information is followed by a very important announcement: ' from that day on the Spirit of the Lord came upon David in power.' The poignant detail here is that Saul experienced the reverse, we read in verse 14: 'Now the Spirit of the Lord had departed from Saul, and an evil spirit from the Lord tormented him'. It was this very fact that actually led to Saul's first acquaintance with David. In an attempt to find relief from Saul's terrifying moods expressed in bouts of depression and aggression, David was summoned to play music on his harp, which had a positive effect on Saul; it made him feel better and caused the evil spirit to depart from him (verse 23). Not surprisingly, we read in verse 21 that Saul took a great liking to David and in verse 22 that he was pleased with him.

Everything seemed to go like clockwork for David: he was a popular guest at the king's court; he became Saul's armour-bearer and when he also defeated the much dreaded enemy, the Philistine giant Goliath (described in 1 Samuel 17), he had reached the pinnacle of fame and seemed to have made it. In 1 Samuel 18, King Saul invited David to move into the palace (verse 2), but shortly after that, things changed as, in the wake of certain events, Saul's affection for David was found to be short-lived. When David won victory after victory and became the favourite of the people, Saul became jealous. Twice, he attempted to kill David with his spear. When he didn't succeed, he tried to get rid of his rival in a different way: he sent him off to fight in an extremely perilous battle against the Philistines where he was almost sure David would perish. But – David survived.

From 1 Samuel 19 we read of Saul's further attempts on David's life. It was the onset of a long and difficult period where David had to run for his life almost constantly. No place was safe for long, time and time again he had to hide and then move on again and whoever came to his aid was cruelly punished (1 Sam.22:6-19). Even Saul's son, Jonathan was confronted with his father's rage because of his loyalty to David. He narrowly escaped death when his father also attempted to kill him (1 Sam.20:33).

Imagine being called by God to a tremendous task and then finding yourself ruthlessly persecuted by people! It must have been a bewildering and extremely undermining experience. I am absolutely sure that poor David struggled with heaps of questions. Following the auspicious start of having been elected by God himself to become king, after his anointing by the prophet Samuel and his privileged position at the royal court, he suddenly found himself to be a man on the run. It seems as if the once promising circumstances had been totally reversed and turned against him. David wasn't sure of his life any longer – a perplexing experience. No wonder he asked Jonathan during his flight from Naioth at Ramah: 'What have I done? What is my crime? How have I wronged your father, that he is trying to take my life?' (1 Sam. 20:1). It was a cry from the heart of an exhausted and desperate man, who had to keep moving on to avoid being discovered, hiding in caves and strongholds in the hills, while Saul and his men continuously hunted him down (e.g. 1 Sam.23:14,23). *David was someone called by God who, consequently and humanly speaking, was left emptyhanded.*

How did David react?

How did David handle that extremely perilous situation of insecurity and desertion? In the first place he did the obvious thing in trying to escape from Saul and save his life. David wasn't passive and did not give up, he was constantly alert and on the run. In other words, he took responsibility for himself and did what he could to guarantee his own safety. In doing so he sets an example, for it is a fact that when we are left empty-handed, there are things that just need to be done. Sometimes, when we feel lonely and deserted, we may just give up and allow our circumstances to overtake us. Sometimes we turn bitter against God. David probably was as tempted as we sometimes are to give up when under great stress, but he didn't. He knew a whole range of feelings, as is apparent from the psalms. Often he cried out to God, in utter desperation and probably feeling at the end of his tether. However, with tenacity he kept moving from place to place and continued to communicate with his God.

It is crystal clear from many of David's psalms that in his dialogue with the Lord he was honest about his feelings. In Psalm 18, his song of thanksgiving after his deliverance from his enemies and Saul, he looks back to the distressing situations that had plagued him. From what he says it is clear that he not only took responsibility for himself by doing all he could to save his life, but on top of that he also called for God's help. We read in verse 6: 'I cried to my God for help'. Now this is something we can identify with! Distress drives us to our knees; when we are hard-pressed or in danger we call or cry out to God. For many of us our prayers are never more sincere and more urgent than at such moments. For some people, these are the only times they pray. Yet our seeking God in our distress can also be a natural reaction that belongs to being a child of God. When a child is afraid, he will automatically call for his mother or father, because he knows and trusts them. The same goes for David; his prayers weren't isolated panic-prayers, they were part of his relationship and ongoing communication with his heavenly Father. He was a man to whom praying was much like breathing; it was an essential and indispensable element of his life. Sharing his heart with the Lord was a natural thing to do; he dared to be honest and real about his feelings and emotions. David's prayers included thanksgiving, worship, confession of sins and intercession. There was, however, also room to express the hard questions, his feelings of helplessness and his inability to understand. Prayer, to David, was the logical consequence of his intimate bond with his heavenly Father. When here, in verse 7, he cries out to his God, it is no more than a natural reaction of a child that seeks the protection of his Father.

In verses 1-3 David sums up who God is. He calls him his strength, his rock, his fortress, his deliverer, his shield, his horn of salvation and his stronghold and he adds 'in whom I take refuge'. What does this really mean, when one is surrounded by danger and not sure whether one will still be alive the next day? Does our taking refuge in God guarantee our safety or survival? And is it God who is protecting us, when in fact we ourselves are employing various strategies to escape our enemy? When we are absolutely worn out but cannot permit ourselves any rest because we have to keep alert, is God our refuge then? Is he tangibly present like a shield around us or is it rather a case of feeling totally abandoned to fate, completely alone and deserted? How can taking refuge in the Lord be a reality in such circumstances?

Just as God's presence in our life is no guarantee for (whatever we consider as) prosperity and success, nor is taking refuge in God a guarantee of survival, or a safeguard from difficulties and distress. We all know of situations where people of great faith were or are struck by what seems to be a disaster or 'ill-fate'. The question is what this suffering does to us and also how it affects our trust in God.

It is true to say that our emotions tend to interpret suffering or difficulties as 'God is absent'. In our black and white thinking we view being delivered or cured of a disease as positive and therefore as proof of God's presence, whereas persisting problems or dying from an illness are regarded as negative and, as such, as a sign of God's absence. We thank God for his grace and intervention in the first situation, but are at a loss about the latter. Is God still present even then? How would David have dealt with that? On top of the world over his military victories and down in the dumps while fleeing from Saul? In the earlier days fully convinced of God's presence and intervention, but later not so sure of it any more? Is it possible that in moments of great danger and extreme tiredness he doubted God's presence and control over his life? Were there moments when he perhaps even doubted God's goodness and faithfulness?

In Psalm 18, David gives us an insight into how he felt at that perilous phase in his life. He describes in vivid language what he went through and experienced under King Saul's persecution: 'The cords of death entangled me; the torrents of destruction overwhelmed me. The cords of the grave coiled around me; the snares of death confronted me. In my distress...' (verses 4-6). David's feelings of despair and anxiety are quite understandable and he did acknowledge them. His words are those of a hunted man, a man in fear of his life. But note, he didn't leave it there! In

David's prayers there is room for lamentations, for uttering distress, anxiety and grief. There is also room to talk about being hurt and disappointed by God's silence. However, even whilst doing that, David always also expressed his belief in God's faithfulness, loving kindness and justice. True, at times David had to exhort his own soul to put his trust in God –as for instance in Psalm 43:5 – but he stated repeatedly that he took refuge in God and that his only hope was in him.

We see this happening in Psalm 59, which refers to the events described in 1 Samuel 19:11. David escaped after Saul made an attempt on his life by trying to pin him to the wall with his spear (verse 10). After David had fled, Saul had David's house encircled by his men who had been given orders to kill him the following morning. In the light of the reality of this overwhelming oppression, described in detail by David, verses 16 and 17 are very significant: 'But I will sing of your strength, in the morning I will sing of your love; for you are my fortress, my refuge in times of trouble. O my strength, I sing praise to you; you, O God, are my fortress, my loving God.' David didn't rely on himself; when he counted on being rescued it was only because of God's faithfulness and goodness, which he had experienced before. He remembered, that is, held on to these truths about God and underlined them. In his memory he had created memorial stones in order to remind himself of God's good deeds. He knew who and how God is and he kept those facts foremost in his mind, especially at times when he was left empty-handed.

Tokens of God's presence

In 1 Samuel 18, the chapter in which Saul's bloodthirsty hatred towards David is so graphically described, we read three times a short sentence which we also noted in Joseph's story: 'The Lord was with him' (verses 12, 14, 28). How was that apparent with David, how would he have known? Let me mention a few things:

a) Prosperity

The words 'The Lord was with him' are obviously related to David's military successes and his growing popularity. In verse 14 we read: 'In everything he did he had great success, because the Lord was with him' and in verse 16: 'All Israel and Judah loved David because he led them in their campaigns.' Even Saul couldn't help but recognise that God was with David: 'When Saul realised that the Lord was with David' (verse 28). It frightened him and he hated David because of his success.

b) Protection

David wasn't only blessed by the Lord in his military career, he was also blessed in that God protected him. While being persecuted by King Saul, David faced direct as well as indirect assaults on his life, but time and time again the Lord spared him. In 1 Samuel 23:14 we read: 'Day after day Saul searched for him, but God did not give David into his hands.' These words convey God's omnipotence and faithfulness, which are apparent in different situations when David miraculously escaped from Saul. 1 Samuel 23 from verse 25 mentions such an occasion: had Saul not been called away and had he not been forced to call off his manhunt for David, he would humanly speaking not have been able to escape.

c) God heard and answered

God's intervention, time and time again wasn't just a sign of his presence and faithfulness, it also proved that he heard and answered David's cries for help. In Psalm 18:6-17 David says: 'From his temple he heard my voice; my cry came before him, into his ears' (God heard); 'He parted the heavens and came down... he shot arrows and scattered the enemies, great bolts of lightning and routed them' (God answered and intervened in the strategy of the enemy); 'He reached down from on high and took hold of me; he drew me out of deep waters. He rescued me from my powerful enemy...' (God answered and saved David). God heard and answered, but do note, not always before things got really bad, but often *in* deep waters!

d) Support in friendship

There was a fourth token of God's presence in David's life: in his moment of great need, he was given two people to stand by him, people who loved and supported him (see 1 Sam.18). It is ironic that both of them were children of King Saul. His son Jonathan had a deep love for David and the two of them made a friendship pact that would stand the proof of time (verses 1,3). Saul's daughter Michal, David's wife, also loved David (verses 20,28) and she too protected his life. The loyalty of these two people must have been a tremendous comfort to David. I see in their presence a sign and reflection of God's love. At times he gives us people who are very close and stick by us through thick and thin, thus communicating his love and faithfulness. This is in fact what Ruth did with Naomi; she was a faithful companion and support during her mother-in-law's bitter days of grief.

To us who read these things with hindsight, it is obvious that God was present in David's life. But how did David himself look at his circumstances? Saul remained a lifelong enemy (1 Sam. 18:29); loneliness, frustration and fear must have been familiar companions to David. As a hunted man there wasn't time or energy to do much more than simply concentrate on the next escape strategy, which would then surely be followed by others. There was the prospect of becoming the next king of Israel, but the years leading up to that milestone aren't to be envied! Yet something miraculous happened that, as it were, surpassed all discomfort and distress.

e) God put David 'in a spacious place'

There is something that exceeds deliverance and being saved, it is of a higher value; God gives us room in our anxiety. David says in Psalm 18:18-19: 'but the Lord was my support. He brought me out into a spacious place' and in verse 36 he says: 'You broaden the path beneath me'.

Let's go to Psalm 31, which speaks of this same concept of space in verse 8: 'You... have set my feet in a spacious place.' This psalm, a prayer in distress, starts off with the words 'In you, O Lord, I have taken refuge; let me never be put to shame' (verse 1). David continues: 'be my rock of refuge, a strong fortress to save me. Since you are my rock and my fortress' (verses 2 and 3).

David is dealing with a basic principle here that, literally, gives space. When we take refuge in God and surrender to him, we shall know inexplicable peace and rest. The fact that we belong to him provides us with a sense of security that surpasses human need or hardship. It doesn't imply that when or as long as we rest in God, we shall never know moments of pain, sorrow or anxiety. We shall, however, experience a basic security which is built on solid rock. It will provide us with a firm foothold when life's storms are raging around us. The knowledge of God's everlasting arms underneath us (Deut.33:27) prevents the bottom from dropping out of our lives. Therefore, 'my ankles do not turn over', as David puts it in Psalm 18:36.

The person who is standing in God's 'spacious place' knows the reality which goes beyond our reality on earth. The here and now can oppress and depress us, but there is the awareness of a higher plane, hidden to those who do not know God, but revealed to his children. It enables us to live differently, because we know of a deeper dimension and a wider perspective.

The basic principle of standing in a spacious place, is that of having our eyes fixed on the Lord and holding on to who he is. Time and time again David states: 'God...is a shield for all who take refuge in him. For who is God besides the Lord? And who is the Rock except our God?' (Ps.18:30-32). The result of focusing on God is a growing trust in him. This will make us more stable and less vulnerable.

What is the reason that we so often feel cornered rather than free and 'in a spacious place'? J.B. Phillips in his book, *Your God is Too Small*[1], suggests that the trouble with many people today is that they have not found a God big enough for their needs. They may look for him, but find him inadequate. The blame for this never lies with God, but rather with our view of him. People have different conceptions of what God is like. Some may stem from childhood ideas of him and these can be so persistent that it may be difficult to develop and hold an adequate idea of God in later years. Sometimes our concept of God is conditioned by a particular Christian upbringing or associated with certain experiences, past or present. Negative experiences can be so powerful that they interfere with a biblical view of God. He may thus become a god of disappointment or a god of cruelty or a spoilsport. When this is our view, we are clearly oppressed and hampered rather than set free in a spacious place. As we grow in faith we must learn to do away with such habits of the past.

It is not just our own inadequate view of God that can hamper us, it is very possible that our idea of God is in fact biblical, but gets blocked or blurred because we allow past or present negative circumstances to stand in the way. They are so prominently in view that we are, as it were, unable to look through or beyond them. Overwhelmed by the greatness of our problems God seems small and becomes in our minds and hearts a powerless, distant being, even though we know better. Actually it is a matter of priorities! When our eyes are, in the first instance, focusing upon our difficulties, then our view of God is obstructed. The problems are literally mounting up between us and him; they loom large and oversized before our eyes. Seen from that point, God has shrunk to powerless proportions. When, however, we focus upon him first, we realise that he is the great mountain, he is the steady rock of ages and the difficulties are placed and seen in the right perspective: they are smaller and certainly less powerful than he.

When we are with the Lord, we are standing in a spacious place; but when we focus on our problems, we feel cornered. That is why praise and thanksgiving are so crucial and why they ought to come before our prayers of intercession for ourselves as well as for others. It is simple: when we look to God first and remember and confess who he is, then we get things into the right perspective and see what's what! That was always David's aim and we see him practising this principle in his psalm prayers. Here lies the secret to his growing confidence in God, even when all odds were against him and the danger he faced seemed to be overwhelming. By focusing on God, David placed himself in a spacious place, that of God's love, grace and goodness. This is the background of his moving words in Psalm 31:22: 'the Lord showed his wonderful love to me when I was in a besieged city'.

f) David tasted God's goodness

We move on to Psalm 34, also written by David during the period he had to flee from Saul. In this psalm we read that tremendous statement: 'Taste and see that the Lord is good; blessed is the man who takes refuge in him,' (verse 8). Then, in verses 17 and 18 he says: 'The righteous cry out, and the Lord hears them; he delivers them from all their troubles. The Lord is close to the broken-hearted and saves those who are crushed in spirit.'

The experience of God's goodness exceeds everything else and is independent of our circumstances. David praised God's goodness whilst he himself was surrounded by problems. He discovered or 'tasted' it, not because he was delivered, but because he met God personally as he sought refuge with him. There he discovered God's endless love and goodness and that in itself was sufficient for him, actually *it was all he needed*. He says in Psalm 63:1-3:

> O God, you are my God, earnestly I seek you; my soul thirsts for you, my body longs for you, in a dry and weary land where there is no water. I have seen you in the sanctuary and beheld your power and glory. *Because your love is better than life, my lips will glorify you.*

God desires to demonstrate his goodness and loveliness to us. Sometimes he uses wilderness experiences or situations of empty hands to create in us a deep longing for himself so that we will seek him and come to discover who he is. This in itself will fill our hands and hearts!

We see this principle clearly stated in the book of Hosea. Israel was going through a time of religious pluralism and worship of the god Baal. God desired to restore his relationship with his chosen people and said (in Hos.2:14): 'Therefore I am now going to allure her; I will lead her into the desert and speak tenderly to her.' The desert is a symbol to barrenness. When we have come to the end of ourselves, we have reached the place where God can and does seek a deep encounter with us.

Sometimes there is no rescue from difficulties as was the case with David despite God's interventions. The misery of Saul's hatred and persecution continued for years and was followed by yet another problematic situation. Sometimes our prayers are not answered in the way we would like. There may, however, be an unexpected answer, in which we find that we have been satisfied in a different way – a deeper and more precious relationship with the Lord. The prophet Habakkuk has the following to say about that:

> Though the fig-tree does not bud and there are no grapes
> on the vines, though the olive crop fails and the fields
> produce no food, though there are no sheep in the pen
> and no cattle in the stalls, yet I will rejoice in the Lord, I will
> be joyful in God my Saviour. The Sovereign Lord is my
> strength; he makes my feet like the feet of a deer, he enables
> me to go on the heights. (Hab.3:17-19)

In other words: when my expectations have not been met and when 'success' is not forthcoming, I will yet rejoice because my joy and peace are not dependent upon the things I would like to see happen, but only on God's goodness. He puts me in a spacious place and on the heights and he makes my feet like the feet of a deer. This is something completely different from going through painful circumstances with lead in my shoes and bowed down under my arduous burden! Remarkably, we find the same words of 'light-footedness' and heights in David's song of thanksgiving in 2 Samuel 22:34 and Psalm 18:33 which brings us back to the situation around King Saul.

It is worthwhile to ascertain which psalms refer to the period in which David was fleeing from King Saul and then to read those psalms with that in mind. Psalm 57 is an example of this. In my Dutch Bible it is entitled: 'Calm (in the sense of unperturbed) with God in the midst of danger' and subsequently we read the words 'When he had fled from Saul into the cave'. The psalm refers to the events described in 1 Samuel 22:1 and 24:3-24. Looking at some of the words in Psalm 57, there seems to be a contradiction: David had a steadfast heart and praised God whilst he was in the midst of trouble. His calm had to do with taking refuge, not so much in the cave into which he had fled, but in his hiding in God! Firstly he stated his position: 'Have mercy on me, O God, have mercy on me, for in you my soul takes refuge. I will take refuge in the shadow of your wings until the disaster has passed' (verse 1), then he stated the fruit of his hiding in God: 'My heart is steadfast, O God, my heart is steadfast; I will sing and make music ... For great is your love, reaching to the heavens; your faithfulness reaches to the skies' (verses 7,10).

At a certain moment the danger had not only become less acute, but what is more, things had taken a favourable turn for David: he was hiding with his men deep inside the cave, when Saul chose that very cave to relieve himself! Initially an extremely hazardous moment for David, he suddenly realised that Saul's fate now rested in his hands as the king was defenceless. But even though the opportunity to have done with his persecutor was presented so openly to David, he spared the king's life. It seems that in finding refuge with God we are given 'space' not just for ourselves, but also with regard to others, meaning that revenge or retribution aren't what we are automatically after; we are free to decide otherwise. Later Saul put that into words when he said to David: 'The Lord gave me into your hands, but you did not kill me' (1 Sam. 24:18).

This event, described in 1 Samuel 24, seemed initially to be a turning point in David's circumstances. When King Saul realised that David wasn't intending to harm him, he said: 'You are more righteous than I. You have treated me well, but I have treated you badly.... May the Lord reward you well for the way you treated me today.' After saying this, he made David swear to him that he would protect Saul's descendants as well as his name (verses 17-22). It looked like an agreement, but the promise was one-sided, for in 1 Samuel 26 Saul was again persecuting David, this time in the desert, and David again spared Saul's life. Then David asked Saul: 'Why is my lord pursuing his servant? What have I done, and what wrong am I guilty of?' (verse 18) and Saul made a promise: 'I have sinned. Come back, David my son... I will not try to harm you again. Surely I have acted like a fool and have erred greatly' (verse 21). It was a fine promise, but David had lost his trust in

Saul and escaped to the land of the Philistines. There, freed at last from Saul's persecution, he finally found rest (1 Sam. 27:4).

Continuing to trust

How does one keep trusting when God's promises are not being fulfilled? God gave David unmistakable promises concerning his future task. He was even anointed king by the prophet Samuel. In practice, however, things not only didn't seem to be working out, but they seemed to go against everything that was promised. Such events give rise to despondency rather than hope.

We saw how David dealt with his situation. True enough, when he was on the run from Saul, he was sometimes close to despair, but he still kept holding on to God. In his anguish and distress he kept referring to what he knew about God: he *is* a refuge, he *is* a rock, he *is* the Holy One. David continued to trust in the God who is faithful to his promises. Faced with the visible, he chose to focus on the invisible that would take shape in God's time. The writer of the epistle to the Hebrews says about that (Heb.11:1): 'Now faith is being sure of what we hope for and certain of what we do not see.. When later on in that same chapter people are listed who in their lives had witnessed of their faith, we note David is mentioned as one of them (in verse 32). He is in the good company of quite a few people who had to hold on to God's promises for years whilst never getting beyond only seeing the things promised and welcoming them from a distance (verse 13). When reading Hebrews 11, we come across words like 'By faith Abraham' and 'Abraham [2] considered him faithful who had made the promise' (verse 11), 'Abraham who had received the promises' (verse 17); Moses 'was looking ahead ... he persevered because he saw him who is invisible' (verses 26,27). Time and time again it is echoed: 'By faith...'! The recital of the acts of faith does not, however, omit the great difficulties that went with that faith, they are openly and honestly mentioned – destitution, persecution and ill-treatment. People were severely tested, many perished, but in their faithful endurance they received strength (verse 34) and their faith was strengthened.

David kept looking for ways to escape Saul's blood lust. In doing so he obeyed God's plans for him. He could also have chosen a different path, the one of least resistance. He could have given up on his future kingship and God's calling and retreated somewhere where subsequently he would have passed into oblivion. Instead, he continued on that difficult path that he himself had not chosen and in doing so showed his steadfastness and faithfulness to his calling. He did not allow obstacles or hardship to distract or finish him.

God is faithful to his children and he is faithful to his plans and promises. For that reason and with that in mind David could be sure that his dreadful situation of being pursued was not without purpose and that it wouldn't destroy him. He could continue to look forward to the fulfilment of those promises with regard to his kingship over Israel. Furthermore, in his particular circumstances he got to know the Lord better and learnt what it meant to find refuge in him. It was a training school of dependence and trust, things that he would need badly during the next phase in his life.

Notes

1   J.B. Phillips, *Your God is too small*. Epworth Press, London
2   The Greek text mentions Sarah, which the RSV does too, whilst the NIV allows her a footnote!

8
Giving in to Temptation

David

Having looked in the previous chapter at the years when David was persecuted by King Saul, we will now consider the next phase in his life, where he landed again in difficulties. This time David owed his trouble to himself, it was a consequence of his sin. For this can happen too: *we can find ourselves empty-handed as a result of our own actions*. That in itself is painful enough, but what was even more dramatic in David's situation, is that his sin occurred at a time when he was both extremely successful and deeply committed to the Lord. The latter was the fruit of the previous years of continual harassment by King Saul; David had learnt to lean upon the Lord and to depend solely upon him. The psalms which he wrote during that time reveal how precious and dear God had become to him. But when, following Saul's death, David had finally become king of Israel, the unimaginable happened: he, God's chosen king, committed adultery. This incident, described in 2 Samuel 11 is an outstanding example of a rash deed that has momentous consequences.

What went on before

After years of distress and peril, David saw God's promises

fulfilled in his life: his kingship was realised. Immediately following the death of his predecessor King Saul, David was anointed king over the house of Judah by his fellow tribesmen (2 Sam. 2:4). Subsequently he settled in Hebron where he ruled for seven and a half years. During the first two and a half years, David still faced unrest as there was a civil war going on between his men and Saul's old supporters, who had made Saul's son Ish-Bosheth king. Following the death of this man as well as of his right-hand man Abner, the organised opposition against David came to an end and he was anointed king over the twelve tribes of Israel (these events are described in 2 Samuel 3-5:5). Shortly afterwards David took up residence in Jerusalem from where he reigned for thirty-three years. In 2 Samuel 5:4-5 the following is said about this period: 'David was thirty years old when he became king, and he reigned for forty years. In Hebron he reigned over Judah seven years and six months, and in Jerusalem he reigned over all Israel and Judah for thirty-three years.' We are now considering the period from David's taking up residence in Jerusalem until the moment of his sin, described in 2 Samuel 5:5-10.

David was a very able leader of Israel; militarily speaking he was almost unbeatable and gained victory upon victory, but he was successful in quite a few other areas as well: a palace was built, roads were constructed and trade routes established. Meanwhile David's private circumstances had changed considerably; following his move to Jerusalem, his family had expanded with new wives and concubines as well as more sons and daughters (2 Sam.5:13). It was a fruitful and rich time in many ways, including spiritually. In 2 Samuel 6 we are informed of the fact that David brought the ark of God back to Jerusalem and placed it in a tent that had been specially constructed for that purpose. David had a close relationship with the Lord, who, through his prophet Nathan, made him great promises for the future (2 Sam.7). Summing it all up, one could say that this phase of David's life was a high time, socially, politically and spiritually. Let us consider several things that stood out regarding his relationship with the Lord:

a) David recognised and acknowledged God's intervention
David was conscious of God's deeds in his life and also of what he owed to God (2 Sam. 5:12 'And David knew that the Lord had established him as king over Israel and had exalted his kingdom'). Later he confirmed this in his prayer of thanksgiving in 2 Samuel 7:18-29, where he shows great awe and reverence for his God.

b) David relied on God
It is apparent that David had an intimate relationship with God and that even in his own position of authority, he was deeply dependent upon his heavenly King. He consulted the Lord, asking him how to act in certain situations and he acknowledged his counsel (note for instance 2 Sam. 5:19,23-24). In 2 Samuel 5:25 we read that David obeyed God unconditionally: 'So David did as the Lord commanded him'.

c) David put God first in his life
Even in his prestigious position as king of Israel, David seemed to be more concerned about pleasing God than about what his subjects thought of him. In 2 Samuel 6 we read how the ark of the Lord was transferred to Jerusalem, an event accompanied by sacrifices (verses 13,17) and dancing, shouts of joy and the sound of trumpets (verses 14-15). When David's wife Michal despised her husband for his boisterous, enthusiastic behaviour – he was leaping and dancing before the Lord, verse 16 – David stated that he was prepared to behave in an undignified manner before the Lord and to be 'humiliated in my own eyes' (verse 22). He was actually saying:

'I don't mind making a fool of myself in my worship of the Lord God.'

d) David was overcome by God's far-reaching promises

In 2 Samuel 7, we are presented with an impressive list of the most wondrous and far-reaching promises that the Lord made to David, by the mouth of his prophet Nathan (verses 1-17).

The promises related to Israel (they would get a home of their own and would no longer be disturbed by their enemies) as well as to David's son, Solomon, whose kingdom would be established and who was to build God's house. God himself would be his father and 'my love will never be taken away from him' (verse 15). There was also a promise with regard to David's house and his kingdom: 'Your house and your kingdom shall endure forever before me; your throne shall be established for ever' (verse 16). In this whole list of promises, look at the moving words spoken by God in verses 8 and 9: 'I took you from the pasture and from following the flock to be ruler over my people Israel. I have been with you wherever you have gone'. When David responded in his prayer of thanksgiving, he said among other things: 'Who am I, O Sovereign Lord, and what is my family, that you have brought me this far?' (verse 18) and 'For the sake of your word and according to your will, you have done this great thing. How great are you, O Sovereign Lord! There is no-one like you and there is no God but you' (verses 21-22).

The promises made to David would reach further than he could have ever fathomed; they refer and point to *the* Son of David, Jesus Christ, who is the ultimate fulfilment of all that is being foretold here. The shepherd-king David was the forerunner of the Great Shepherd-king, who tends very different sheep from the ones David cared for and whose Kingdom stands forever. One remark in David's prayer of thanksgiving seems to suggest that he did have an inkling of these greater things to come: 'you have also spoken about the *future* of the house of your servant'(verse 19). The RSV translation says: 'Thou hast spoken also of thy servant's house for a great while to come, and hast shown me future generations'. At times the Lord gives his servants spiritual insight and eyes to see further than they naturally are able to!

Vulnerable at unexpected moments

But then comes 2 Samuel 11, the chapter about David and Bathsheba, a black mark in the history of the king. The consequences of the one event described there make it clear beyond any doubt that *one can find oneself empty-handed through one's own fault.* We are familiar with the event and what provoked it; the king enjoyed a cool evening on the roof of his palace – not at all unusual in Eastern countries – and from that high vantage point he spotted a beautiful woman bathing. He didn't think twice, he enquired about her and had her summoned, a disastrous move which led to adultery and murder.

Temptations often come when we least expect them. Here they came at a time of a spiritual high, which is not exceptional; it happened even to Jesus at the onset of his ministry on earth (see Luke 4), when he returned 'full of the Holy Spirit' from the river Jordan where he was baptised and where his sonship was confirmed by the Holy Spirit in a miraculous way. In Luke 4 we read how, immediately following those tremendous events, Jesus was being severely tempted for forty days by the devil in the desert; it is as if Satan had been lying in wait for that very moment! Poignant detail here is that the Holy Spirit had led Jesus to the desert for the final act in his time of preparation for his work on earth. Here he was to undergo severe testing by Satan. When Jesus did not blink and proved no prey for his opponent, demonstrating instead unswerving obedience to his heavenly Father, he was fit to return to Galilee. We read: 'Jesus returned to Galilee in the power of the Spirit' (verse 14).

The temptations that Jesus was exposed to in the desert were meant to undermine and discredit his sonship. He was being challenged to abuse his divine power, to reach his goals in this world by submitting to the devil instead of to God and to question his Father's love. The areas where Satan attempted to make Jesus stumble are related to power and possessions and to his relationship with and particularly obedience to the Lord God, all of them areas where we are also vulnerable and often slip. But Jesus, during those forty desert days, showed steadfast and uncompromising obedience to the Father. Unswerving, he repeatedly appealed to God's Word: 'It is written...', thus showing that obedience to God is indissolubly linked with knowing, loving and holding on to his Word and to God himself. This is underlined in Psalm 119:2-3 where we read: 'Blessed are they who keep his statutes and seek him with all their heart. They do nothing wrong; they walk in his ways.'

We must realise that temptation is part of life and part of the strategy of God's opponent, the devil, who is a living reality wanting to separate us from God. But there is hope! Jesus' victory over Satan's temptation in the desert, at the onset of his ministry, was made complete about three years later, when he didn't waver on his way to the cross and his death but remained loyal and obedient to God to the very end. His total victory over Satan makes Christ into a High Priest who can give us strength when we are tempted. Hebrews 4:15-16 tell us:

> For we do not have a high priest who is unable to sympathise with our weaknesses, but we have one who has been tempted in every way, just as we are – yet was without sin. Let us then approach the throne of grace with confidence, so that we may receive mercy and find grace to help us in our time of need.

In Hebrews 2:18 we read: 'Because he himself suffered when he was tempted, he is able to help those who are being tempted.' The devil may be alive and well and temptations may be very real, but the grace and help that are offered to us in the Lord Jesus are just as real and much more powerful! Jesus is more than an example of a man who lived a good life; he is God's Son, who conquered death and who, since his resurrection from the dead is seated at the right hand of God. When we pray, we do more than just express our feelings or unburden ourselves of worries or fears. We lay our concerns and cares at the feet of the living God, who doesn't content himself with just listening as we pour out our hearts before him; he reaches out and supports and strengthens us so that we can carry on with perseverance. Where Satan considers temptation as a means to bring us down, God can use it for our good!

Sexual temptation

When David fell for Bathsheba's beauty and his own lust, he fell prey to one of three main temptations that people face: money, sex and power. These realities have the potential to be either a great blessing or to become a deep curse in someone's life. Provided they are used wisely and well, they can be a source of great blessing and joy, for ourselves as well as for others. Yet somehow, money, sex and power are the very things that we do not control well and tend to use incorrectly. In fact, if we aren't alert, they will control and manipulate us and can become more important and urgent than God himself. Misuse of these gifts can separate man from the Giver of them.

The ones who seem to understand this very well are those who belong to God's opponent, Satan: in their striving to destroy the Church of Jesus Christ, the church of Satan has devised an extremely clever strategy, in that they concentrate on prayer for sexual sin amongst Christian leaders as well as for the breakdown of Christian marriages. In doing so the Satanists are focusing on the very areas where we are particularly susceptible and vulnerable. I don't suppose their strategy was thought out by people, it is so clever in its evilness that it must have been inspired by Satan himself. The horrible thing is that it works, for adultery is a fact, also amongst Christians and Christian leaders. Its consequences are heart-breaking, not just for those directly involved, but also for God's Name and work that are thus being dishonoured. The world is very smart and quick to spot television pastors who are more deeply committed to their own material empire than to God's Kingdom and they are also quick to uncover sexual sin amongst spiritual leaders.

What should we learn from that? Firstly that we need to be more realistic and face up to the fact of temptation, also among those we look up to because they are prominent and strong spiritual leaders. Let us follow the example of the church of Satan and become radically dedicated to prayer. In doing so let us pray with urgency for the purity and steadfastness of our spiritual and church leaders and offer up intercessory prayer for those who carry responsibilities within a church or missionary organisation, for those who are on a council or committee or in a position of leadership, as well as for those who are in the limelight as speakers or who are active in pastoral work. We often think these people have 'made it' and have as it were become immune to the ordinary problems which 'normal' people face. We take their ministry and service to the church more or less for granted and don't give much thought to the fact that their marriage could suffer because they are so heavily involved in Christian ministry. These people are in a lonely and vulnerable position and need the protection of prayer and support. We are quick to judge when things have gone wrong, but we need to examine ourselves and consider whether we too might be guilty because we have neglected them in our prayers and care.

Here, then, is another lesson we can draw from David's story: no one is immune to sin; each one of us will at times be tempted to exchange our fellowship with the Lord for something that is very attractive and appealing but nevertheless wrong. David shows that this can happen when we least expect it, including at those times when we are close to the Lord and spiritually speaking on a mountain top. Paul says in his first letter to the Corinthians: 'So, if you think you are standing firm, be careful that you don't fall!' (1 Cor.10:12). His words are spoken in the context of a passage about the Israelites, who in the desert 'were all under the cloud, …. all passed through the sea. They were all baptised into Moses in the cloud and in the sea, they all ate the same spiritual food and drank the same spiritual drink; for they drank from the spiritual rock that accompanied them, and that rock was Christ' (verses 1-4). The circumstances of these people were supreme, God was very near and yet there was sin amongst them and the majority of them did not follow God. Paul then says in verse 6: 'Now these things occurred as examples, to keep us from setting our hearts on evil things as they did.' Following this crucial remark, Paul makes specific mention of a number of things, including sexual immorality.

At the moment of his sin David was a great and mighty man, as king he was elevated above his people. He was also a man of God, his kingship had been destined and confirmed by the Lord.

He was highly successful and respected, people looked up to him. Added up, these facts make for loneliness and vulnerability.

What do we see and look at?

The mere fact that David's eyes fell on Bathsheba wasn't sinful, although it was a moment laden with potential temptation. This became a reality when David allowed his eyes to rest on Bathsheba; it was then that temptation came into the picture. When David's eyes weren't averted but remained fixed on this woman, the setting became the perfect soil for lust to grow. By thus looking at her, David was actually already taking possession of her. That is where he crossed the line and where sin, misery and death began.

What we witness here is a practical outworking of a principle that John, in his first letter, calls 'the lust of human eyes'. We see something, and our seeing is converted into wanting. To John that desire is linked to 'the cravings of sinful man' and 'the boasting of what he has and does'. These three things are not 'from the Father but from the world' (1 John 2:16). The RSV puts it like this: 'the lust of the flesh and the lust of the eyes and the pride of life, is not of the Father, but is of the world'. It is important that we recognise that 'the sinful man' here doesn't apply to sexual sin only; seen in its context it points to the seeking of self or to concentrating on one's own wishes and desires rather than on the things of the Spirit. Paul pursues the matter in Galatians 5:13-26, where he says that there are many cravings and works of the flesh, among them adultery and impurity. But there are also many fruits of the Spirit, among them self-control. Faithfulness and love are also mentioned as fruits of the Spirit; in the context of potential adultery they are as crucial as self-control, in fact the three are interrelated. It is obvious that faithfulness and love towards God, one's own partner and toward the other person involved, are very important in the decision to control oneself and resist temptation to commit sexual sin.

The Lord Jesus speaks in plain terms about these matters. He says that whoever looks at a woman lustfully has already committed adultery with her in his heart. He also says that it is better to gouge out the eye that would cause you to sin and to throw it away than to end up in hell (Matt. 5:27-29; read this side by side with 18:9). James is also quite outspoken when he talks about the cause of temptations. He writes in his letter: 'but each one is tempted when, by his own evil desire, he is dragged away and enticed. Then, after desire has conceived, it gives birth to sin and sin, when it is full-grown, gives birth to death' (Jas.1:14-15). He adds, in verse 16: 'Don't be deceived, my dear brothers.' In other words: Don't fool yourselves!

Somewhere between the desire rising up and the desire being full-grown, lies a moment of decisive choice. Like Joseph, I can flee from sin, by a decision of the will. Or, like David, I can take a step forward by lingering awhile. This is also a decision of the will, even though we usually like to feel that we couldn't help ourselves, but were overcome by things. If we are tempted to find excuses for our behaviour and emphasise our helplessness, we need to read Genesis 4:7 again, where God spoke clear language to Cain about temptation: 'Sin is crouching at your door, it desires to have you, but you must master it.'

I remember one occasion where it became very clear how our eyes can get used to looking at the wrong things from a very young age onwards. A friend of mine, a secondary school teacher, was on a week-long field trip with a group of twelve-year-old pupils. One day he found a group of giggling girls, drooling over the most blatant sex magazines. He was deeply shocked but even more so when he realised that his colleagues thought nothing of it, in fact they were humoured. Hubert, however, discerned that this so-called harmless pastime could well carry in itself a potential habituation to perversity. This young teacher had the courage to stand up and tell the children and his colleagues how he felt about it in a special meeting that evening. 'If you fill your eyes and thoughts with sex and get used to perversities, you will soon start experimenting with these very things and some of you girls may have a first abortion at fifteen or sixteen,' he said. 'By the time you are nineteen or twenty, you will have lost the ability to form a pure and meaningful relationship and the wonder of sexuality will have been deeply violated, you have distorted something beautiful that God intended to be a blessing in the context of marriage.'

Was Hubert exaggerating, making a mountain of a molehill? I don't think he was, in fact his uncompromising attitude was the fruit of his walk with God; he needed to speak out against what was evil. The fact that, out of all of the staff he was the only one who held and stood up for this conviction, shows how easily we get used to and tolerate things that are contrary to what God holds out before us. We know for instance that when our children spend hours watching television, they are likely to hear a lot of bad language and will see countless acts of crime, immorality and perversity, yet we let them. It may at times be convenient for us that they are out of the way and occupied, but they are exposed to things that will affect them, polluting their minds and souls. Similarly, we adults can damage ourselves by things we allow our eyes to watch, see and read. Purity in thought and deed is closely linked with purity of the eyes!

Hubert's evening had an interesting ending. After throwing three magazines he had confiscated that afternoon into the open fire that they were sitting around, he asked the pupils to go to their rooms and collect any sex magazines that were left and to hand them to him. He offered to refund the purchase price out of his own pocket. More than twenty magazines turned up which cost him about £35. After burning these, a deed which was applauded spontaneously by the pupils, one boy remarked: 'That wasn't clever of you to offer money for it, look what it cost you!' His teacher's response was very profound: 'I only paid £35 for a few magazines, but God paid for all our sins by sacrificing his own Son!'

It strikes me that David, who let his eye fall and rest on Bathsheba, in his prayer for forgiveness and deliverance in Psalm 25, says that his eyes are ever on the Lord, 'for only he will release my feet from the snare' (verse 15). Although it is not completely clear which situation David is talking about here, we do know he said these things in the context of asking for forgiveness for the sins of his youth and for his rebellious ways (verse 7). By mentioning both his eyes and his feet, he clearly links what we see or look at with what we do.

It seems simple. If we keep our eyes fixed only on the Lord, if we fear only him and walk with him, we won't sin. We know by experience that unfortunately it doesn't always work like this, but rather goes as John describes: 'If we claim to be without sin, we deceive ourselves and the truth is not in us' (1 John 1:8). The bad news is that we regularly exchange our fellowship with God for a walk in the darkness; sin is a fact in each person's life. The good news, however, is that by God's grace we are invited to return over and over again to the security of our place of refuge which is God. There we can confess our sins and meet his faithfulness and justice and we shall be forgiven and purified from all unrighteousness (1 John 1:9).

An eye for abundance

One of the most tragic things in the story of David's sin is that he had received so much. His hands were filled and there was nothing else he needed. This is in fact what the Lord said to David through Nathan: 'I anointed you king over Israel, and I delivered you from the hand of Saul ... I gave you the house of Israel and Judah. And if all this had been too little, I would have given you even more' (2 Sam. 12:7-8). These words of God are based on an overwhelming truth: he who has made us and knows us through and through (a truth that was fully endorsed by David in Psalm 139), knows what we need and what is good for us. Because he is a God of love, we can know for sure that he would not want to withhold good from us, but rather takes pleasure in blessing us abundantly.

David acknowledges these things, when in his prayer of thanksgiving in 2 Samuel 7, he says: 'Who am I, O Sovereign Lord ... that you have brought me this far? And as if this were not enough in your sight, O Sovereign Lord, you have also ...' (verses 18-19). He doesn't just say it there, but over and over again and particularly in his psalms which are pure songs of praise about God's goodness.

How can a child of God reach the point where he feels he is lacking something? Two reasons stand out. The first one is that we often concentrate on what we do not have. By looking in that wrong and negative direction we fail to see what we do have! King David left his palace where everything his heart desired was at his disposal and from the roof he cast his eye and let it gaze upon the very thing that was not his, a woman who belonged to somebody else. The next thing was that he felt he needed her to complete his happiness. The same thing happened with Adam and Eve who had everything their heart desired and needed, but wished to have the very one thing that wasn't theirs and that God had forbidden, the fruit from the tree of life. What they started has become a bad habit: we are focusing on the wrong things in order to be satisfied, but as long as we do that we shall not be satisfied in the deepest level of our being.

A second reason why we think we lack something is that, we so often concentrate on negative things in our lives, that we are unable to discern what good things the Lord has given us.

True, negative things can be painfully present and we have, earlier on in this book, looked at several of these. It would be inhuman to deny or ignore the reality of the pain of divorce, unemployment, a handicap or serious illness, of sexual abuse or strained relationships. Sometimes we seem to be tempted to do so; in our effort to cheer up those who mourn over a loss, we advise people to ignore their pain and say rash things like: 'Just look at what you do still have.' This is well-meant advice, but nevertheless hard to digest and cheap comfort when what is needed primarily is care and understanding. The Lord himself will, in his time, open our eyes to make us see his blessings, even in painful situations. We will find out that this blessing is found first and foremost in his presence; when we grow in our personal walk with him, we will begin to discover the full scale of his goodness to us. Then we will be able to say with David: 'The Lord is my shepherd, I shall lack nothing' (Ps. 23:1). Ezekiel 34 also speaks of abundance in blessing in God's 'shepherd-words': 'For this is what the Sovereign Lord says... I will tend them (my sheep) in a *good pasture*, and the mountain heights of Israel will be their grazing land. There they will lie down in *good grazing land*, and there they will feed in a *rich pasture*' (verses 11-14). It is obvious that the shepherd is looking for the best for his sheep, they get all the good they need and are given the best of care. 'I myself will tend my sheep and make them lie down... I will search for the lost and bring back the strays. I will bind up the injured and strengthen the weak' (verses 15-16).

When, in John 10, Jesus is speaking about himself as the good shepherd, he promises his followers 'life to the full' (verse 10), or 'life abundantly' (RSV translation). The word 'full' is the translation of the Greek word *perissos*, which occurs six times in the New Testament in the form that we see here in John 10:10. Study of the context in which the word *perissos* is used brings us to six totally different situations and consequently also six different translations. When comparing the different words, there is a common factor in that they are all superlatives and used often in comparison to something of a lesser magnitude or value. It concerns a *privilege* that one has over another, something that *exceeds* something else, an experience that is *superior*, something *extraordinary*, something that is *needed above* everything else and finally something that is *abundant (or 'to the full')*. This is what God offers his children. Once we grasp hold of the potential and impact of that abundance, our lives will be turned over and flow over.

We can, however, only do so in and through Christ as the promise of fullness cannot be separated from him. He, who is the giver of these things, is himself the biggest and most extravagant gift that God could ever give us; in him we have all the riches and fullness that we could ever desire. It is a wealth, totally different from what the media portrays and offers us in material glitter and glamour. These things can be nice for a while, but they will never satisfy us. We need to have our eyes opened to discover real abundance and we need to meet Jesus to get access to it. Paul says in Philippians 4:19: 'My God will meet all your needs according to the glorious riches in Jesus Christ.' When we desire to know true and everlasting riches and abundance and be satisfied to the core of our being, we need to seek God's presence and find refuge with him in and through Jesus Christ. There we shall find rest and will no longer need to chase after other means of fulfilment. We will find that the Lord himself satisfies us and gives us an abundance of good things to enjoy. It is a tragedy that experience shows that even as Christians we often keep seeking new and different means of satisfaction rather than learning to draw everything from him who is the very source of life abundant.

9

Suffering from the Consequences of Our Sins

The consequences of David's adultery were immense. The Lord told him (through the prophet Nathan, see 2 Sam 12:10-14) what he was to expect in mainly two areas of his life, politics and family. The sword would never depart from his house; there would always be fighting and unrest. Furthermore God would bring calamity upon David, rising up from within his own family and the son born from his liaison with Bathsheba would die. Sure enough, a whole string of negative and painful events was set into motion and it would be a good many years before there was a turn of events, coinciding with Solomon's succession to the throne. The first son of David and Bathsheba did indeed die (2 Sam. 12:15-18), later on David's son Absalom organised a powerful conspiracy against his father, for which he enlisted the men of Israel and consequently David had to flee for the second time in his life (2 Sam. 15). During his absence, ten concubines who had stayed behind to take care of the palace (2 Sam. 15:16) were publicly raped by Absalom on the same roof from where David had first spotted Bathsheba (2 Sam. 16:21-23). Following David's return they were confined to live in the palace as widows (2 Sam.20:3).

David himself was harassed during his flight by a certain Shimei and his men (a descendant of Saul, 2 Sam 16:5-14). When David returned to Jerusalem after Absalom's death, division as well as rebellion continued (2 Samuel 20). In 2 Samuel 21 we read about a three-year famine which was taking place and there is the report of renewed fighting between the Philistines and Israel. By then David was exhausted and it was decided that he would no longer be actively involved in battle. Finally, in the first chapter of the book of Kings, David, now well advanced in years, was struggling with his health. Even then, the problems hadn't ended and a serious attempt was made to thwart Solomon's ascension to the throne.

It is obvious that David went through a great deal of misery in the years following his adultery with Bathsheba. His life testifies to the fact that, even after having received forgiveness from God and having made a new start, the consequences of wrong deeds continued to fester for a long time and cause ever-widening ripples in the water. *This is how we can be left empty-handed as a result of our own actions.*

Some years ago a well-known Christian leader committed the same misdemeanour as David – he had an affair. When, after a certain time, the matter came to light within a small circle of people, he and his girlfriend owned up, acknowledged their guilt and repented. They terminated their relationship. Following that, in and by God's grace, the man's wife and children were able to forgive him and they began working on rebuilding the marriage and family relationships. The man was able to continue his ministry in God's Kingdom, and life was resumed as well as possible. I deliberately say 'as well as possible', because one of the fruits of the sin of adultery is a deep fragility and vulnerability in relationships even years after repentance and forgiveness have taken place. In this particular case things went well for a number of years, until one of the 'trusted friends', who at the time had been informed of the situation, let his tongue run away with him and talked about the affair. As a result, a scandal suddenly started circulating, just when the marital relationship had become more stable again. Sadly, the news spread, giving rise to a torrential stream of stories and fantasies, which soon became larger than life, threatening the reputation of the Christian ministry this man was involved in. He decided to resign in order to prevent God's work and Name being dishonoured. It was extremely painful for all the parties involved and once again the family struggled with the consequences of a deed which took place years before and had been dealt with.

Blessing in distress

David's liaison with Bathsheba followed him for the rest of his life. Ever since that disastrous event, he was, in many ways, left empty-handed. But did his hands actually remain empty after the Bathsheba affair? Is that how God punishes his people? Here we touch upon the question of forgiveness and restoration, things that are available in God, whereas people tend to be quick to condemn, slow to forgive and unable to forget. We feel that if someone has made a mistake, they will have to pay for it. If someone harmed us, we certainly don't wish them the best, it is a more natural reaction to wish to see them punished and suffering for their deeds. We may not say it out loud, but when we are deeply hurt, we are tempted to feel our offender can 'Go to hell!' When it comes down to it, we aren't very forgiving, nor are we able to forget.

How different it is with the Lord! Even when we sin, he does not withhold his goodness from us. David, who deeply dishonoured and hurt God himself, found his hands filled again, despite the brokenness which resulted from his sin. The Lord indeed kept blessing David, not by completely restoring his situation or his relationships, but in other ways:

a) God forgave David

However great our sin is – as a matter of fact the Lord never talks of 'greater' or 'smaller' sins; in his eyes sin is sin – God, in his grace, is always prepared to forgive us when we repent. We read in 2 Samuel 12:13 how King David said to the prophet Nathan: 'I have sinned against the Lord', whereupon Nathan said: 'The Lord has taken away your sin'. David came back to the issue in Psalm 32, a psalm dealing with God's blessing which follows our confession of sins. In verse 5 he says: 'I acknowledged my sin to you and did not cover up my iniquity. I said, "I will confess my transgressions to the Lord" – and you forgave the guilt of my sin.' In verse 1 of the same psalm, we find the words that are later quoted by Paul in his letter to the Romans (Rom. 4:7-8): 'Blessed are they whose transgressions are forgiven, whose sins are covered. Blessed is the man whose sin the Lord will never count against him.'

God's forgiveness is based on his grace alone, implying that our good behaviour or good intentions do not influence his attitude towards us. What God requires of us is that we truly repent and believe in the atoning death of Christ on the cross for our sin and in his resurrection. Whoever comes to God in Christ will receive unconditional and complete forgiveness. In Psalm 103 David praises the Lord for his grace and speaks of him as One, who 'forgives all your sins...who redeems your life from the pit' (verses 3-4). The moment a sin has been named and confessed and then forgiven by the Lord, that sin has vanished from his eyes and been forever erased. 'As far as the east is from the west, so far has he removed our transgressions from us' (verse 12). One cannot possibly imagine a distance further than the distance between east and west. This is how far God's compassion goes, it is the compassion that a father has on his children (verse 13). Our heavenly Father doesn't only offer us forgiveness, but on top of that, all good things: '(He) crowns me with love and compassion. He satisfies my desires with good things' (verses 4-5). Here is, once again, a truth, the full depth of which will only become clear to us when we take refuge in the Lord God and allow his compassion to become true to and in our hearts.

God's grace frees us from our guilt and at the same time delivers us from our shame about ourselves. It makes us into free people; our relationship with the Lord has been restored and the door to an intimate walk with him is again wide open. Where sin should lead to the sinner's death, the sinner who has repented and been forgiven by God's grace, can go on and *live.*

b) God did not forsake David

In spite of his sin, David again experienced God's presence and intervention in his life. God did not leave or drop him, his hand remained outstretched over David's life. Even in all the distress that flowed from David's sin, the Lord was near; his mercy was visible in the fact that David's life and kingship were saved and yet again, military victories realized. When David's son Absalom aspired to the throne of his father, he was unable to succeed, despite his good plans and many followers. One of them was David's advisor Ahithophel, who chose to follow Absalom in his conspiracy against his father. His false counsel was meant to bring David down, but was instead magnificently frustrated by the Lord (2 Sam.17:14b). Immediately following this event, David won a great military victory, which led to his return to Jerusalem. When in 2 Samuel 23 the names and deeds of 'David's heroes' are listed, we read twice that '*the Lord* brought about a great victory that day' (verses 10,12). David was aware of these things and it is clear from his words in 2 Samuel 24:14, that God's presence had become very precious to him: 'Let us fall into the hands of the Lord, for his mercy is great; but do not let me fall into the hands of men.'

c) God remained faithful to his promises

There was also the blessing of David's son Solomon (from his marriage to Bathsheba), promised by God in 2 Samuel 7:12-16. It is said of him that 'the Lord loved him' (2 Samuel 12:24) and he was to succeed David as king. Solomon became renowned for his beauty, wisdom and greatness and he is the one who built God's temple. His story is described from 1 Kings 1 – where Solomon ascends to the throne – onwards.

d) God granted David wisdom

Finally we consider the blessing of wisdom. Just prior to his death, David called his son Solomon and gave him the wisest advice that one can give a fellow man. His words of farewell to his son (who meanwhile had become king) are recorded in 1 Kings 2:3-4: 'observe what the Lord your God requires: Walk in his ways and keep his decrees and commands, his laws and requirements, as written in the Law of Moses, so that you may prosper in all you do and wherever you go'. These are the wise words of a man who, in his own life, failed in the very things he advised his son to do and who suffered the consequences of his disobedience to God. He had learned this lesson the hard way, but it had brought forth the fruit of wisdom. Whilst uttering these words, David probably felt the pain of his own helplessness in the past. Yet at the same time he could speak with hope and confidence because he knew of God's forgiveness and restoration. He was also certain of God being faithful to his promises as well as to his children, despite their shortcomings and failures.

Looking at these various blessings, I think we can conclude that God filled David's empty hands again; he tasted God's mercy and grace and knew of his presence. But even though his sin had been erased, the consequences or traces of it remained like scars.

When we ourselves are the cause of our pain

The story of the adultery of David and Bathsheba demonstrates how misery and pain can be the result of our own actions and how there can be a connection between our sins and negative things that happen to us. In the Bible we meet many people who brought disaster upon themselves, both in the Old and New Testament. John 4 describes an encounter which the Lord Jesus had with a woman at Jacob's well in Sychar in Samaria. She had been involved in a series of relationships and was now living with her sixth partner. But, exciting though it may seem, her life-style hadn't brought her happiness. When she asked Jesus to give her living water to quench her thirst, she was actually speaking of an inner emptiness (verse 15). She was, in other words, suffering from her own sinful, frivolous life-style. It appears, from her conversation with Jesus, that she was looking forward to the coming of the Messiah. She didn't yet know what it meant to be redeemed and to be a child of God. In offering her living water Jesus was saying to her that he could satisfy her inner thirst. He didn't say, however, that drinking of this living water guarantees a carefree existence.

Christians remain vulnerable to temptation and we are never exempt from pain that we have brought upon ourselves through our own mistakes. When we cross over the God-given boundaries and disobey him, we harm and hurt ourselves as well as others. Despite being warned, we set our eyes and hearts on the very things that God has marked as 'forbidden territory' and burn our fingers. It began with Adam and Eve who were richly blessed, they were given a perfect world to live in as well as a complete and whole relationship with God and with each other. Instead of enjoying what had been amply provided, they wanted that little extra, which was the very thing outside their reach. When they gave in to their desire, they suddenly found themselves outside the

Garden and imperfections had appeared in their lives and relationship with one another. They, who had received an abundance of possibilities and promises from God, found themselves standing outside the gate with empty hands.

Acknowledging our sins

When life becomes unpleasant as a result of our own misbehaviour, we are usually well aware of our own part in these events. Generally speaking we know the difference between right and wrong, but sometimes we do something against our better judgement, whereas at other times we make a deliberate choice to do what is wrong. The consequences of our wrongdoing are not always immediately obvious, which gives us a chance to fool ourselves by maintaining that what we did was wrong but not hideously wrong, it could have been a lot worse. We can shut our eyes to the truth, like the child I was once playing hide and seek with. He assumed he was invisible as long as he kept his eyes closed! We sometimes feel tempted to act the same way – as long as we don't open our eyes, we can imagine things don't exist or didn't happen. Of course, it doesn't work that way; we give evidence of spiritual maturity when we have the courage to face up to the truth and own up to our shortcomings and sins. That moment is the beginning of a solution of what may have become a very negative and complex situation.

The Lord points out our sins to us

What about circumstances where we ourselves are unwilling to face the facts? After David had committed adultery with Bathsheba and she became pregnant, he frantically tried to get himself out of his tight corner and cover up his deed. When this didn't work the way he had planned, the very next thing he did was to have

Bathsheba's husband killed. Then he sent for her to come and live in his house; she became his wife and gave birth to their son. It seems as though David had it all sorted out quite well. It required some drastic measures and organisation, but that wasn't a problem in his position as king. He also didn't need to be afraid that anyone would dare to take him to task because his status gave him a certain immunity. So it seems! But God cannot tolerate sin in the lives of his children and he will reveal to us that which is wrong. We read in 2 Samuel 11:27: 'But the thing David had done displeased the Lord' and then, in the next verse, in 2 Samuel 12:1: 'The Lord sent Nathan to David'. Via God's prophet there was a consultation behind closed doors about David's deed and its consequences. David needed to understand that his trespassing had brought suffering upon people and that he had also dishonoured God's Name. But that wasn't all – his sin had damaged his relationship with the Lord. In the light of these things it was virtually impossible for David to continue as if nothing had happened, the consequence of sin is death. It was by God's grace that he was shown the truth. However painful, the confrontation with our sins will be our gain ultimately.

We are not only quick to cover up our sins, we are also quite smart in finding excuses for what we did. In today's culture we tend to view a criminal as the product and victim of their dysfunctional childhood; they couldn't help what they did as others enticed them; we ourselves were helpless as we were overtaken by sin. All these things may carry some truth in them, yet sin remains sin, irrespective of the circumstances. We can come up with reasons to palliate or smooth over our conduct, but God will not 'measure', minimise or excuse evil, it is not a matter of proportions, it is the very fact of sin that is so abominable and intolerable to a holy God. And he holds us responsible.

The Bible often reminds us that sin can contaminate God's holiness in that it blemishes his Name. The Lord says in 2 Samuel

12:14 that David's deeds made God's enemies 'show utter contempt'. The core of David's transgression, though, was his disobedience: he had despised God's Word and God himself (2 Sam. 12:9-10).

I said earlier that it was by an act of grace that God pointed out David's sin to him. In the New Testament we see the same thing happen in and through Jesus Christ, who, himself being the Light, brings sin to light. Going back to his encounter with the woman at the well in John 4, we remember that she mentioned her thirst. Jesus, continuing his conversation with her along this line, talked with her about the fact that she had lived with five men and was now living with a sixth man who wasn't her husband. Fearing a disclosure of her personal circumstances, she very quickly changed the subject by asking Jesus where people should worship God – this question was a big issue in which Jews and Samaritans differed in opinion. The woman probably did know better, but simply could not face a confrontation with the truth about herself. Yet that was exactly what happened when she met Jesus and it is still the same today: whoever comes into his presence, comes to stand in the light; the shadows or darkness in our lives are being unveiled and revealed. Fellowship with God and walking in darkness are incompatible, for holiness and unholiness cannot go together (see 1 John 1:6). Therefore, when we meet the Lord Jesus and sincerely wish to follow him, sin will be disclosed.

a) God's Word speaks to us

In giving us his Ten Commandments, God has provided us with basic rules for living. We must not be content with them being inscribed on stone tablets, but we must etch them on our hearts, implying that we must come to love them as we love the Lord himself. The author of Psalm 119, which is an ode to God's law, says: 'You are my portion, O Lord; I have promised to obey your words' (verse 57) and 'Your statutes are wonderful; therefore I obey them' (verse 129). Obedience to God's Word is inseparably linked with a deep love of God. One could even say that the genuineness or depth of our love of God will be visible in the way we treat his Word. When we love God's Word and get immersed in it, we shall not only come to know it more deeply, but we shall find that we come to know and love the Lord of the Word more deeply too. As we read and study God's Word, we discover who he is and what his will is. In doing so we gain insight into good and evil and may find the Word speaking to us directly regarding our own sin and challenging us to radical obedience.

b) Our conscience pricks us

Clearly different factors can block a mature, responsible attitude towards our sins. It is fortunate that we have been given a conscience to remind us of wrong or even, to accuse us. But this doesn't happen automatically, a conscience needs to be developed. When we walk with the Lord and his work of grace goes on within us, our conscience will become increasingly sensitive as it becomes attuned with the Holy Spirit. Consequently our ability to hear 'the voice within' will increase. Dr. Jim Packer says:

> The quickening of conscience is a mark of Christian growth, without it our Christian life would be deficient. Put the other way around, one could say that an insensitive conscience is an index of spiritual immaturity.

It is interesting to look at Psalm 32 where David speaks about the joy of forgiveness. He indicates that whilst he kept silent about his sins, God's hand was heavy upon him. Verses 3 and 4 speak of the deep conflict one can feel when sin is not confessed. David's initial impulse was to stifle his guilt by banishing it to the subconscious, but then it seeped out in symptoms of physical distress. He was trying to silence his conscience, but the Lord in his goodness, kept bothering him. In verse 5 he says: 'Then I acknowledged my sin to you and did not cover up my iniquity'. The result of this is that he found forgiveness and consequently joy and gladness in the Lord (verse 11). It is important to realise that our conscience can prompt us and speak to us, but it can also be quieted or repressed or even corrupted so that it can no longer function properly. Paul says in his letter to Titus that there are people who claim to know God, while being disobedient to him in their lives. Both their minds and consciences are corrupted (Titus 1:15-16).

c) Our suffering may (or may not) be the writing on the wall

Sometimes it is the very pain, caused by our own misbehaviour, that makes us recognize where we went wrong. In the parable of the prodigal son in Luke 15, we meet a young man, who demands his share of the inheritance and after having received it, leaves his parental home to travel to a far-off country. Away from home, he starts to live it up until his finances run out and he begins to feel the pain of hunger and poverty. Having started off with all that his heart desired, he ends up being a swineherd and reaches the point where he is so hungry that he is willing to eat the pig food. But he isn't allowed even that. Then he 'comes to his senses' (verse 17), he discovers that he himself has caused his misery. His moment of insight comes when he feels the pain in the circumstances of hunger and loneliness. Sometimes heart-searching and insight are brought about by our feeling the discomfort of our sins.

d) God's Holy Spirit speaks clearly

Having looked at the Lord himself and his Word, as well as at our conscience and suffering as means through which we can come to see the part we ourselves have played in bringing about our suffering, let's not forget God's Holy Spirit, God's supreme voice within us. He prompts us regarding our disobedience. He pricks our conscience and challenges our thoughts; he makes our hearts restless and reminds us of God's Word and speaks to us through people. He does all these things (and many more) to keep us close to the Father and to instigate our love for the Lord Jesus. His very presence in us implies that we are not alone! We were given the Holy Spirit, God with us and God in us!

There is new life after forgiveness!

When Nathan spoke to David, he said (in 2 Sam.12:13): 'The Lord has taken away your sin. You are not going to die.' These words are very significant, because they imply that death is the logical outcome of our sin. Realising that makes us see how immensely merciful God was in sending Nathan to David, not with the commission to tell him that he was going to die, but rather to save him. By telling David a story, God graciously allowed him to discover for himself what he had done and what the consequences of his deed were. He was thus given the opportunity to come to his senses, confess his sin and ask for God's forgiveness. When God deals with us, we are not locked up, but rather placed into a spacious place where we come to life again.

Sometimes a person, after having received God's forgiveness, continues to struggle with feelings of guilt and can't stop condemning himself for what he has done. It is important to realise that even when forgiveness has taken place, the devil will keep doing his utmost to sow doubt and undermine our faith. One of his tactics is a subtle but persistent reminder of things we have already confessed and which have already been dealt with. He will continue to accuse us repeatedly and in doing so attempts to make us question and doubt our salvation and relationship with the Lord. In his attempts to separate us from the Lord, Satan doesn't hesitate to get hold of our emotions and feelings and feed them, thus causing us to feel weighed down by things that God has already removed from us. Consequently unnecessary suffering is put upon us. We need to be well aware of that and must firmly stand on God's Word and promises in order to withstand the evil one.

I once met a woman, who had had an abortion over forty years ago. At that time, almost crushed by confusion and stress around her unwanted pregnancy, she couldn't see another way out than to have her unborn child aborted. Years later she became deeply troubled by what had happened and sought professional help. Whilst working through the abortion and the events around it, she experienced overwhelming feelings of grief and guilt. She confessed these things to the Lord and asked him to forgive her, and her heavy burden was lifted off her shoulders. But even afterwards, each time she happened to hear about an unwanted pregnancy or about someone who had an abortion, her heart still tightened and it was as if she saw herself terminating her own pregnancy all over again. Each time, she was plagued by acute feelings of guilt. Could it be God speaking to her, wasn't her forgiveness real? It *was* real and the issue had been dealt with sufficiently, but this woman was unable to forgive herself and so she kept dragging her own guilt along, whereas God had removed it from her.

I remember one of Corrie ten Boom's favourite stories, which she used to illustrate the completeness of God's forgiveness. She said that God throws our sins into a deep lake where a notice has been put up, saying: 'No fishing!' It is useless to dig up the past; God's forgiveness is complete which means that we can carry on living with a clean slate. It is a great shame that we sometimes fall into the trap of rewriting what has already been erased! In doing so we rise to Satan's bait, and listen to his whispers, thus violating God's plans for us. For he says in Isaiah 1:18: 'Come now, let us reason together ... Though your sins are like scarlet, they shall be as white as snow; though they are red as crimson, they shall be like wool.' After we have repented and been forgiven, we can put on a sweater of pure white, soft wool. Dirty blotches can and will appear on it when our unrighteousness has again rubbed off on us, but each time that happens it can be cleaned again and it is impossible for old stains to reappear. In the same manner, God continually cleanses us when our soul is blemished by our sin. We must tenaciously hold on to this truth and must never allow old stains to be reintroduced. When God has acquitted us, we don't need to condemn ourselves any more. Even though we are confronted with and grieve over the past, it should never burden us and shouldn't ever dominate our thoughts or bind us in any way. Jesus came to set us free!

How good it is to know that in our moments of suffering which we ourselves have caused, we can stand on the promise of God's forgiveness and carry on without the heavy yoke of condemnation. How good that, even as sinners, we may again and again seek refuge under the wings of the Lord and be washed clean. How good it is to also know that even though we continue to suffer from the after-effects of our wrong deeds, we can in that very situation receive God's comfort and strength. And how merciful that after repentance and forgiveness, God sees us as new again. After all the things that had gone wrong with David, he is still mentioned in Acts 13:22 as a man after God's own heart. That stands, it wasn't left out in the New Testament because David had failed to live up to God's standards; God saw the man who, in spite of all his weaknesses, kept seeking him and longed to become what God already saw in him: a man of God!

Part 2

Part 3

10
Hiding in Friendship

Once while abroad I had to suddenly undergo two operations. During that difficult time away from home I received a letter from a friend that became very precious to me. One of the things she said was: 'How I would love to be with you now, not necessarily to say anything, but to be in God's presence together.'

I was reminded of Ruth who, I assume, said little or nothing as she accompanied Naomi on the journey from the land of Moab back to Bethlehem. Her mere presence was sufficient; because she herself knew what it meant to hide in God, she was able to be a companion and a hiding-place for her mother-in-law. I was also reminded of the bereaved mother's experience of friendship in the period following the death of her son (page 50). In those days of mourning several friends disappeared, leaving only a few people who stood by her and her family. They communicated comfort by being near and faithful without actually speaking much. Those friends who were able to be both present and silent became extremely precious to her and her family. They were in fact messengers of the Lord himself, serving as visual aids of his nearness.

The one sentence in the letter that I received communicated the same thing. Its message was stronger and deeper than what we usually get on get-well cards which are easily bought. Their message is often superficial or comical and is meant to make us laugh and forget our troubles. My friend, however, communicated something else: 'I want to bring you before God and I would love to experience and share his presence and nearness with you' or 'At this time of pain I want to hide with you in God'. She wished me God's nearness but also offered me human closeness through hiding in him together.

David and Jonathan: Friendship at its best

Friendships that are God-centred are the best and most valuable friendships we can have. I think God uses human friends to give us a glimpse of what he offers us in perfection in our relationship with him. Some aspects of human friendships reflect spiritual truths. Think of David who had a close and intimate bond with Jonathan, the son of King Saul. At times of great distress and uncertainty David was able to find refuge in Jonathan. But the two friends also hid in God together and the one strengthened the other's faith. This is how relationships between godly people can have a spiritual dimension. Through all his experiences, David became a man who had learned to hide with the Lord. His friendship with Jonathan was definitely instrumental in learning that. There is a great potential in believers being closely united in friendship.

When David was persecuted by King Saul, Jonathan was solidly behind him. His faithfulness was incredible. When David was in hiding, Jonathan went out to find him and informed him about the murderous plans of his father. He was totally dedicated to protecting David. This is quite remarkable, because David was actually his rival as he was called to become Israel's next king. This calling involved not only taking King Saul's place but also passing over Jonathan – the prince royal. Jonathan was aware of this but he stepped back in order to clear the way for David, the one who was chosen by God to succeed King Saul. In this friendship God came first just as he had been first from the very beginning when

David and Jonathan met. Their meeting wasn't concocted by people, but was God's design. We read about that moment in 1 Samuel 18:1. After David's triumph over the Philistine champion Goliath, he was brought before Saul by Abner, commander of the army. Jonathan was present at that moment and it was then that their friendship began. The Bible says 'After David had finished talking with Saul, Jonathan became one in spirit with David, and he loved him as himself'.

Love and oneness
The words 'Jonathan became one in spirit with David' are radical and dramatic. Two people who didn't know each other were instantly and radically united and knitted together, heart and soul. David, the simple shepherd boy, had entered the king's service and household because of his musical talents, later he became one of his armour-bearers (1 Sam.16:14-23). Jonathan was the prince royal. When they met and became instant friends, the differences in background, education, experience and also any possible rivalry disappeared. Their unity in thought, heart and spirit culminated into more than a standard friendship. These two young men were godly people and the 'one in spirit' that they experienced meant more than sharing mutual interests, it had a deep spiritual meaning: they shared their faith in the same God and were united and bonded together by him.

Dutch people, and I am one of them, don't easily talk about 'loving one another' in friendship. We tend to cover up our deeper feelings. It is acceptable to love your partner or children, but friends you *like*. This isn't, however, what God's Word holds before us. Jesus calls his disciples to love one another as he himself has loved us (John 15:12). When looking at the letters of Paul, who certainly wasn't a 'soft' kind of man, we discover how real and important his feelings of love for his friends were. It is fascinating to look at his letters with that in mind. Note his greetings at the beginning and the end where the words love and loving are prominent. Look at his letter to Titus where in his farewell he says 'Greet those who love us in the faith' (Titus 3:15). In 1 Corinthians 15:58 he says 'Therefore my dear brothers'; in 16:24 'My love to all of you in Christ Jesus'. He addresses his letter to Philemon with the following words 'To Philemon our dear friend...' (Philemon 1). Peter in turn, in his letter calls his readers to 'have sincere love for your brothers' and adds 'love one another deeply, from the heart' (1 Pet.1:22).

I am convinced that Christians, being united in Christ, can love each other deeply. But I am also convinced that we may only know one or two such God-given friendships as David and Jonathan knew. Just one or two, if that at all. It is impossible to arrange or organise them, they are a gift from God. These are the kind of friendships where one heart touches the other and where it is possible to find refuge in one another. In such friendships we are comforted and refreshed, built up and strengthened in our faith. They are spiritual friendships and it is as such that I mention them in a book where we consider what it means to hide in God. For these special friendships play a significant role in that they point to him as well as exemplify what love and bonding mean.

Gordon Aeschliman says in his book *Cages of Pain, Healing for Disillusioned Christians* [1] that 'the church is best understood in the context of truest friendships. Church is not primarily a structure or organisation... rather at its heart it is people who in relation to each other are a visible illustration of the family of God'. Aeschliman is blessed with a few friends whom he truly loves and who truly love him. He speaks about a mystical meeting point comparable to the bond between husband and wife. He says:

There are a few human beings with whom I am in love. ... We have been wrapped together in the tenderness of the Holy Spirit, regarding the other as higher than ourselves, as precious treasure. We bring to each other the comfort that Christ intended the family to give; we encourage, exhort, honour, forgive, enjoy and struggle. Dignity reigns between. Yes, you could say that we have seen Jesus in the other and we adore his creation.

Aeschliman continues:

I hope this does not sound too much like a mushy story. It is a love story...We have picked each other up from the gutter many times, we have applied salve to the wounds, we have nursed to the early hours of the morning, we have prayed desperately for the other's survival, we have entered into the other's hell and have emerged together singed by the scorching flames. And why not? Is this not love, to lay down one's life for a brother or sister? Thank God for the friend who loves at all times.

David and Jonathan made a covenant with each other and they affirmed it regularly. It is mentioned for the first time in 1 Samuel 18:3: 'And Jonathan made a covenant with David because he loved him as himself.' It is significant that the word used here for covenant is the same word that God uses for his covenant with his people. In their friendship and faithfulness towards one another David and Jonathan show us something of the meaning of God's covenant. We know that people aren't capable of faithfulness, as God has intended it and indeed we are often deeply disappointed in our human relationships, in marriage and in close friendships. Christians aren't immune to failure and disappointment. But we may, in Christ, keep striving for the best and the highest, and we rob ourselves of something good if we allow the disappointments and hurts that we have encountered in human relationships to reign over us and to control the level of our friendships. The example of David and Jonathan's friendship may encourage us. These two men belong to those whom Aeschliman describes as people who are in love with one another. They are among the few in our world who have this mystical meeting point, this intimate relationship that can be compared to the mystical bond between spouses. The basis of their closeness lies in their love relationship with God.

Faithfulness and responsibility

Jonathan's faithfulness towards David was far-reaching. He sacrificed his own comfortable life as prince royal. He took great risks for David's sake and persevered even in very tricky situations. The consequences of his faithfulness were outrageous, his own father attempted to kill him because of his loyalty to his friend, who, in his father's eyes, had become an enemy (1 Sam.20:33). Here we see the words of Jesus put into practice 'Greater love has no-one than this, that one lay down his life for his friends' (John 15:13).

Faithfulness is costly. In this early period it was particularly costly for Jonathan. There are phases in friendships where one may need to be stronger than the other and of him, the stronger one, is asked a specific dedication or action. When Naomi and Ruth travelled from the land of Moab back to Bethlehem, Ruth was the stronger one who accompanied her bitter, negative mother-in-law. When David needed Jonathan, he was available. Later it was the other way around. After Jonathan died, David (who was then king) checked if there were any living relatives of his friend Jonathan. He asked (in 2 Sam. 9:1): 'Is there anyone still left of the house of Saul to whom I can show kindness for Jonathan's sake?' He repeated his question in verse 3 with greater urgency 'Is there no-one still left of the house of Saul to whom I can show God's kindness?' When he heard that one of Jonathan's sons was still alive, a boy who was crippled in an accident (see 2

Sam. 4:4), he took him in and provided for him as if he were his own son (2 Sam. 9:6-7,11-12). This example of faithfulness in friendship reminds me of what Jesus asked his close friend John ('the disciple whom he loved', John 19:26) to do for him, when he was dying on the cross. He asked John to take care of his mother. We read in John 19:27 that his friend didn't hesitate one moment. 'From that time on, this disciple took her into his home.' What we see here is a practical, far-reaching commitment and responsibility. Good friends can count on each other.

Such a bond in friendship is deeply comforting and enriching. It is good to know that God wants to give us friendships where we taste something of unconditional love and oneness, faithfulness and responsibility, even though there will be disappointments at times. What makes these friendships so precious and valuable is that they show us something of God's character. I truly believe that we may pray for the blessing of such covenants in our lives here on earth and when the Lord grants them to us, they must be handled with the utmost care and sensitivity.

Sometimes friends disappear. Many people see their circle of friends diminishing in times of illness or grief, when unemployment continues or when there are serious problems with the children or in the marriage. People who disappear don't necessarily do so because they don't care, but more often because they feel helpless and don't know what to say or how to handle the other person's situation or grief. Sometimes people stay away because they are impatient and unable to appreciate or understand their friend's attitude or behaviour and the time he or she requires to work things through. They give well-meant advice, but if it isn't acted on, they feel unappreciated, insulted or even rejected. On some occasions the grieving person may himself push his friends away in bitterness and anger. How important it is that we learn to be faithful through a kaleidoscope of circumstances. It means above all things that we are and stay close, that we are available and faithful in prayer.

Paul says in his second letter to Timothy 'You know that everyone in the province of Asia has deserted me, including Phygelus and Hermogenes'. He continues 'May the Lord show mercy to the household of Onesiphorus, because he often refreshed me and was not ashamed of my chains. On the contrary, when he was in Rome, he searched hard for me until he found me' (2 Tim.1:15-17). Onesiphorus was to Paul a true friend in the Lord and somebody who was true to his name (bringer of profit). When Paul was a prisoner in Rome, he did all he could to trace him and then visit him. Sadly, he was the only one. All the other Asian Christians had chosen the easier way, they deserted Paul when he was in distress. Onesiphorus, however, wasn't ashamed of Paul's imprisonment. His friendship remained during difficult times. That is how he could be an oasis for Paul and as such was used by God as an illustration of his faithfulness.

God-centredness

When we look at Jonathan and David it is clear that faith in the Lord was the focal point of their friendship. 1 Samuel 23:16 says: 'Jonathan helped (David) to find strength in God.' A Dutch translation puts it like this 'Jonathan strengthened David's faith in God.' We find the same words repeated elsewhere and they express the secret of the stable unity between these two men. Jonathan and David were interdependent; their own personal relationship with God kept their friendship in balance and protected them from becoming unhealthily dependent on each other.

Jonathan was used by God as an instrument to strengthen David's faith. As well as protecting David and being a place of refuge to him, he was also pointing David towards God, the ultimate place of refuge. The fruit of David's times with Jonathan is seen in 1 Samuel 30:6. This verse describes the moment when his life was in danger and he was in great distress. It says 'David was greatly distressed because the men were talking of stoning him...' How did he react in that situation? The same verse tells us: 'But David found strength in the Lord his God.' He had learned an important lesson through Jonathan's faithfulness and had been stimulated in his own faith by his friend. We are sometimes given people whom we can lean on, but we must beware lest they stand in the way of our learning to rely upon the Lord. It must become natural to us to turn instinctively to him rather than cry out to our friends for help.

There is another moment which testifies of the fact that God came first in the friendship between David and Jonathan. Look at Jonathan's words in 1 Samuel 23:17 'You shall be king over Israel, and I will be second to you'. Humanly speaking, Jonathan was destined to be his father's successor, he was to become king. But he stepped back, creating room for David because he acknowledged the fact that God had certain plans for his friend. He knew the consequences of his attitude: his own future would change dramatically. But he wanted God's plans with David to be fulfilled even though it was extremely costly for him. Can you imagine what it costs to say to someone: 'You take my position, I'll step down'? It is true to say that Jonathan made a massive sacrifice. But good friends want the best for each other and godly people want God's purposes to be fulfilled not just in their own but also in the other person's life.

A place of refuge for each other

I think that the times when David and Jonathan were together were like soothing balm for David's soul. Their meetings were moments of peace and tranquillity in times of great anguish and fear. In the psalms David often expresses profound feelings of being deserted by people and by God. But Jonathan always stood by him and protected him where and when he could. He was a refuge and hiding-place for David, he also stood up and pleaded for him before his father. It is true to say that people can thus find security and safety in friendship. We learn in our close relationships what faithfulness and trustworthiness mean. We can uphold one another in prayer. As we find refuge with one another we can taste something of what hiding in God means. These things that we may experience to some degree in human friendships are to be found in perfection with him through Christ: he pleads for us, he loves us unconditionally and he keeps and protects us. His faithfulness and love are never -ending.

Our finding refuge with our friends implies daring to be vulnerable and daring to say that we need the other person. It means we trust the other person with our naked soul. We are confident that he is faithful in praying for us. A friend isn't, however, always and immediately available. Jonathan wasn't always able to be at David's disposal. In friendship, however, availability exists *in principle*. Friends may count on each other's help where possible and appropriate. They may *always* count on prayer. All these things are reciprocal, for in friendship we give and take, in healthy interdependence and faithfulness.

Intimacy and openness
Even though it isn't mentioned specifically, I think it is fair to say that David and Jonathan shared their innermost feelings with each other. They had the kind of relationship and bond which allowed them to open up and be vulnerable. They dared to 'let go' and communicate without pretence, they wept together (1 Sam. 20:41).

How many of our friends know and seek us in our vulnerability? How willing are we to share our pain and how many invite us to do so and tell them how we really feel? Who are the ones who encourage openness and honesty? Who is willing to listen to our pain and grief? Not everybody can cope with 'weakness' or emotions. When we meet people and ask: 'How are you?' we don't expect them to elaborate on what is going on in their lives, particularly if they have a sad story to tell. If they do open up about things that aren't going well, we get a bit of a shock. We aren't really prepared to hear much more than the standard answer to the standard question. We expect the usual 'I'm fine, thanks'. If someone has the courage to go deeper than the surface and to tell us about their problems, we often feel embarrassed and tend to make some neutral comment after which we try to disappear as soon as we can. Why? Because we don't quite know how to handle someone else's troubles or pain. It is much easier to handle 'I'm fine' than 'I'm not fine'. Good friends, however, invite each other to be open about what's happening in their lives and how they feel about it. Factual information about a situation isn't sufficient, we want to know the heart of the other person and only when we are able to look into each other's hearts can we truly be near.

David and Jonathan were bosom friends and their friendship implied these things. What we know about their friendship is placed in the context of a certain period and situation. David was going through an extremely difficult time and in those particular circumstances Jonathan frequently, or most often, was the strong one who cheered him up, comforting him and strengthening his faith in God. In 1 Samuel 20, however, we see them weeping together, some people might say we see them sharing a moment of weakness. I personally consider this moment where they both broke down in tears a moment of strength and an affirmation of their deep unity. What actually happened was that David shared his grief over the fact that Saul kept chasing him. Jonathan initially found it hard to believe his friend, but he was nevertheless willing to help him. He soon found out what this meant for him personally. A day or so after he had been with David, Saul attempted to kill Jonathan because he was 'siding with the son of Jesse'. We read in 1 Samuel 20:34 that Jonathan got up from the table in fierce anger and didn't eat anything that day because 'he was grieved at his father's shameful treatment of David'. The next day he went out to his friend who was in hiding and (verse 41) 'they kissed each other and wept together – but David wept the most'. It is interesting that the RSV translation says 'they wept with one another, until David recovered himself'. Contrary to the NIV translation we get the impression from the RSV that David at this time was the stronger one who braced himself because they needed to go on. The Hebrew text, as it stands, isn't very clear and it seems that the translators are attempting to speculate on what the text actually said. Whatever happened, in friendship strength and weakness alternate and so we grow together in the reciprocal giving and taking.

Security is crucial here. It has to do with reliability. When a person is reliable, I can let go and don't need to hide things from them. It is safe to open my heart to them. Is it really? No, even with the best intentions it isn't always completely safe to confide in people. People aren't one hundred percent reliable and some risk remains. There may be circumstances in which we will be disappointed or even betrayed by close friends. To be truthful, we ourselves aren't always reliable! One of the basic things we need to learn is to keep silent. This requires a lot of practice and dedication! We need to suppress our desire to share with others what someone told us in confidence and be content to pass these things on to nobody else but the Lord, in prayer.

In all these things the friendship between Jonathan and David can be an example and challenge for us. This is how God intends friendship to be. This is the kind of friendship he himself offers us. David describes it in Psalm 25:14 when he speaks of the Lord confiding in those who fear him. 'Confiding in' speaks of intimacy. He, who called Abraham, Moses and Enoch his friends, comes again to us with the offer of his friendship in and through his Son Jesus, which we'll investigate in the next chapter.

Human friendships as a training school

In his book, *Prayer: The Transforming Friendship*, Dr. James Houston, founding member of Regent College in Vancouver, Canada says:

> There is a close connection between our need for richer
> human relationships and our need for intimacy with God.
> Each dimension (our relationship with people and with
> God) reinforces the other. We move from the horizontal
> dimension to the vertical, and from the vertical to the
> horizontal in a constant interaction of friendship and prayer,
> prayer and friendship. Each dimension deeply affects the
> other. If we find it hard to form lasting relationships with
> those we see around us, then we will find it very hard to
> relate in any depth to the God we cannot see [2].

It is a fact that some spiritual truths may be brought home or clarified by things we see here on earth. This is very much so when we think about our relationship with God. How can we ever understand friendship or relationship if we haven't experienced these things on a human level? How do we understand parenthood or fatherhood if we haven't seen or known it in our own lives, however incomplete? How do we know what it means to 'be covered with God's feathers' or to 'find refuge under his wings' (Ps. 91:4) if we haven't experienced such things on a human level, if we don't know what it means to be protected or held or cherished? Even if we haven't personally experienced these things, then perhaps we have seen them happening in nature. The imagery that God uses in his Word needs a human base or an example from nature in order for us to understand it. Sometimes God uses people to illustrate spiritual truths or to show us some aspects of his nature. Of course, our relational experiences on earth are incomplete and portray only a marred reflection of what the Lord means and want to give us in perfection. Yet this world and our friendships here on earth may be a training ground where we learn about love, faithfulness, reliability and finding refuge with someone. In the same way, our close (spiritual) friends may be instruments in our discovering some aspects of God's character.

Joyce, now in her mid-forties, grew up without a father from the age of about three. This is what she told me: 'My mother did her utmost to keep us children happy, we didn't lack love or attention. There was laughter, there were tears. We were, I suppose, a normal family. Yet throughout my life, I have struggled with what I call a half-nest-syndrome. The fact that my father was absent had left a gap in the foundation of our family nest; though positive, our family was incomplete. As a result I have always struggled with a basic insecurity. This has become a real obstacle to believing in unconditional love and faithfulness.' Joyce's story illustrates how important it is for a young child to know security. Psychologists generally agree that if for some reason a child doesn't experience and grasp this in his early years, it may trouble him for the rest of his life. I don't deny the reality of that nor of the fact that some people may later on in life need professional help to work through these issues. Yet I am grateful that Christians may look beyond that psychological truth and know that the Lord is able to act and heal beyond human thinking and expectations. We can choose to live with open minds and hands uplifted which means that we need to work at finding a balance between accepting reality as it is, whilst living in a different reality with God. There we find peace instead of uneasiness, rest instead of restlessness and wholeness instead of brokenness.

That other, godly reality may be made visible on a human level, through our friends. For Joyce the turning point came when one of her friends said to her: 'I love you just the way you are. It is impossible for you to earn or lose my friendship because it doesn't depend upon your behaviour.' Initially she found it hard to believe and then to keep believing it, but through the years it proved to be true. The experience of good and close friendships has helped her to learn to trust. And even more than that, friends have provided that basic security that she couldn't know and grasp earlier. They showed her what God's unconditional love means. In his grace, the Lord used human friendships to make her understand more of himself. This experience is quite formidable in its consequences, because it shows that we bear a deep responsibility towards one another. Our lives and actions bear weight. Christians are called to communicate something of God's love, faithfulness and goodness. God wants to use us in this way. Once we realise this, then it is only logical that we strive for the best in our friendships and cover them with prayer.

Prayer partners

Sometimes a deep friendship leads to a commitment to pray for each other, not just in private intercession for the other person, but in also praying together regularly. If the latter is the case people become prayer partners, which adds a deep spiritual dimension and special bond to friendship. It is my experience that prayer partners often are or become bosom friends, like David and Jonathan they become knitted together. Keywords in such a friendship are love, faithfulness, responsibility and transparency; and prayer, with its companion: dedication.

A prayer partner is a person of prayer, meaning that they themselves have developed a lifestyle that is saturated by prayer rather than sprinkled with it occasionally when a need arises. The faithful prayer of our prayer partner gives them insight into our situation or our thoughts and deeds that goes further than the information we give them. They will understand us more deeply and will seek God with us and on our behalf. They are not spectators, they are involved. They are out to seek God's ways for us and their commitment implies that we can expect that they will be honest and sincere with us. They may sometimes say the things that aren't easy to hear or accept and they don't always automatically agree with what we do or think, therefore they won't always say we are right , but they want to help us to follow the Lord in our lives – they want to strengthen our faith. They are deeply involved, yet also able to let go. There is accountability but never a claim.

People who have found a spiritual friend or a prayer partner will find that their lives are enriched and that they are stimulated in their walk with God. I am encouraged to see, that not just in my own country but in many other countries as well, people are rediscovering the value of friendship. In our western world it may be a reaction to the individualism that is so common in society. People are becoming more and more isolated in a world where communication is increasingly becoming 'computerized' and where the lifestyle is dominated by busyness and pressure. We need to revitalise friendship as a means of regaining our humanness. As Christians we also need to revitalize and strengthen our fellowship and relearn togetherness and commitment as a means to stimulate one another to seek God and to maintain his values and ways in a godless world.

The Church of Christ: A hiding-place on earth?

Statistics show that today there is an increasing number of single people. Their aloneness isn't just physical in that they don't have a partner. It is also, and maybe more importantly, emotional. They lack what most married people take for granted: 'a belonging together'. The longing to belong is something that most single people – whether unmarried, divorced or widowed – feel deeply. For them finding a bosom friend is often a more urgent need than it is for married people, even though they too may long for special friendships and find them enriching and necessary. Each person longs for someone close, someone they can share their heart with. This desire for emotional security and belonging is a normal and natural human need.

It is important to acknowledge that being human implies knowing of an existential loneliness irrespective of being married or single. It is part and parcel of our living in a broken world. When God created man, he gave him a partner because he saw that man wasn't happy on his own and needed a fellow-creature. It was an ideal situation and even more so because the relationship with God was at that time still perfect and whole. We have come a long way since then. Relationships between people have become incomplete and often distorted. But our longing for that fellow-creature, for someone near, hasn't disappeared. Yet, brokenness in creation and therefore also in human relationships is and remains a fact. We shall keep longing for that one person who matches us one hundred percent and who is able to understand our deepest feelings; we long for a perfect relationship, for a hiding place in a world where individualism reigns and people tend to increasingly fend just for themselves and so we shall know disappointments or we adapt and follow the trend of our day in selfish soloism. As Christians, however, we are called to be different, we are called to togetherness and interdependence. These are essential elements of the Church of Christ, in fact they should characterise the fellowship of believers, the way we interact and live should reflect that we are family. 1 Corinthians 12:12-31 speaks clearly about these things and strongly emphasises that God's children need one another and are not meant to live and function apart from each other. We are part of the Body of Christ and our belonging to each other (verses 15-16) exceeds boundaries of marital status, we all equally belong. It is interesting that this Bible passage precedes the chapter of love, a gift that we are asked to seek or even chase after.

l Corinthians 14:1 tells us to 'Follow the way of love'. When we love each other wholeheartedly, we cannot leave the other person out in the cold. Paul, who as far as we know was a single man himself (at least during his ministry), is quite outspoken and free in his calling on the help of others. He belongs to them and they to him.

In our day and age we need to relearn the art of togetherness in our families, but also in a wider sense as the Church of Christ. The Church is meant to be a hiding place on earth. We need to make room for one another – for the young and the old, for marrieds and singles. Sometimes we need to make sacrifices; making room for another person takes energy and takes up some of our own space. There are, however, also times when it is quite legitimate to protect our private space. Sometimes couples or families need some time alone for whatever reason and aren't able (for a time) to be as open to others as they would like to be. They may need to work on their marriage or they may need extra time for the children. Some ailments require a time of incubation in order to facilitate recovery. This medical truth may be applicable to other situations as well. But beware! Space and time for ourselves may turn into selfishness. We may enjoy our own world so much that we don't allow another person in or near because we feel he invades our privacy. Single people may be more vulnerable to develop such an attitude and cherish selfish freedom. When living alone, one does not automatically need to reckon with other people. We all are, however, part of the Body of Christ and being part of his family implies that room for another person is a principle. There is space for others, not only when it is easy and fits into our plans and schedules, but also when it is costly. This means that hospitality is the rule and a closed door the exception. The space meant isn't just physical, but it is primarily heart space. Once that is available, the practical implications will fall into place.

I have met several single people who say that they often feel second-or third-rate in the lives of their married friends. They are welcome as long as there isn't anything else or special going on. 'I always have to wait and see what plans have been made,' someone told me. 'I am never part of the plans. I have to somehow fit in.' She continued: 'It is much like queuing for a bus and always having to let others go first. It means you are bound to be a loser in a competition that isn't fair.' A young widow discovered that, single again, she was no longer automatically part of the activities of the couples that she and her husband knew together. A very different story is that of a young single woman who had to undergo a serious operation. Her married friends offered hospitality for the time she needed to convalesce. She spent half a year living with these people and their busy family of five with a sixth child on its way. The children moved up so that she could have a room of her own. Thus this woman found a safe and warm place during a time of illness and uncertainty. Many people said they admired the family that took her in, they themselves thought it was nothing special but the obvious thing to do. A similar thing happened when a young couple who were going through a difficult time found a temporary home with a single woman. They thought it would be for just a few weeks, but the weeks stretched into months. It meant some commotion and some major adjustments, but it worked.

These things should be in principle possible within God's family. Love is the keyword in the Body of Christ and mercy and hospitality should be an integral part of our lives. If things work the way they should, then we shall find this warmth and welcome in our local church and with each other. For that is how God means us to function, knitted and bonded together in love. His Church on earth is to be a hiding place where people can taste how good the Lord is and what it means to find refuge with him.

In order for this to become a reality, we need to pray that the community of the Church will be revitalised.

Notes

1.   Gordon Aeschliman, *Cages of Pain, Healing for Disillusioned Christians* Word Publishing, USA, 1972, all rights reserved. This quotation is used by permission of the publisher.
2.   Dr. James Houston, *Prayer: The Transforming Friendship* Lion Publishing, 1989.

11
Hiding in Friendship with the Lord Jesus

In the previous chapter I underlined the importance of friendships among believers; they can have a deep spiritual impact on each other's lives as they encourage one another in walking with the Lord and in seeking refuge with him. We saw that happening with David and Jonathan, where one strengthened the other's faith.

In this chapter I want to look at another friendship, the one with God. In doing so we turn to the Lord Jesus. In his life on earth he showed us what it means to walk with God and to know him as a friend. He encourages us to seek this friendship too and challenges us to a personal and intimate walk with his Father. He invites us to learn it through him; he is the one through whom a friendship with God can become a reality in our lives: in fact, it is only through him that we too can experience this. He, who once walked on this earth, has through his death and resurrection paved the way to reconciliation and fellowship with God and is now seated at his Father's right hand where he intercedes for us. Whoever comes to Christ and believes in him has free access to God. We may come home and walk into God's presence with a childlike confidence, there aren't any barriers. This is what Jesus told Thomas: 'I am the way and the truth and the life. No-one comes to the Father except through me' (John 14:6).

By his life on earth Jesus has shown us what it means to walk with God. Through his death and resurrection he has made it possible for us to do the same. But he has done even more than that. He has made the Father known: through and in Jesus we see who God is and what he is like. Whoever sees Jesus and gets to know him, sees the Father and gets to know the Father. This is also what Jesus told Thomas: 'If you really knew me, you would know my Father as well. From now on, you do know him and have seen him'(John 14:7). When Philip asked Jesus to show him and his friends the Father, Jesus replied as follows: 'Anyone who has seen me has seen the Father... Don't you believe that I am in the Father, and that the Father is in me?' As a Man, Jesus was the embodiment of the Father, the image of the invisible God (Col. 1:15).

To summarize, we can say that it is impossible to consider friendship with God isolated from his Son Jesus for three main reasons:

1) Jesus shows us God's character and heart; he reveals the Father to us;
2) Jesus shows us what it means to walk with God;
3) Jesus has paved the way to God through his death and resurrection.

Friendship with God

Let us look at how Jesus walked with God during his life on earth. What did that entail? What did it mean that God was his Father in the ups and downs of his life? What did it mean at times of success and at times when people, including his own good friends, disappointed him? And what did it mean at that one moment in his life when he was confronted with being forsaken by God? What did it mean for him to hide in God?

Seeing and Seeking

In Luke 2:41-52 we read how, at the Feast of Passover, a large crowd of Jewish people travelled to Jerusalem, among them Jesus and his parents. After the feast was over and people returned home Jesus wasn't in the crowd. Assuming that their young son was somewhere among the travellers, Joseph and Mary weren't immediately aware of the fact that he had stayed behind; it was only after a day of travelling that they started looking for him and realised he wasn't with them. They then returned to Jerusalem where they finally found him in the temple courts, 'sitting among the teachers, listening to them and asking them questions' (verse 46).

I can imagine the immense relief of Joseph and Mary when they saw their Son. I can also imagine that mixed in with that relief was some annoyance about his apparent indifference. Jesus didn't seem too concerned about his parents being worried about him. When his mother mentioned their anxiety he simply said: 'Didn't you know I had to be in my Father's house?' (verse 49).

These words bear momentous weight. Firstly, because they are the first words of Jesus that are registered in the Bible. Secondly, because they are quite unusual words for a twelve-year-old for whom, humanly speaking, it would have been much more natural to be absorbed by the festive crowd of people and thoroughly distracted by all that was going on. That was in fact what his parents had assumed. They thought he had been so preoccupied and taken by the general excitement that he had forgotten all about them.

His mother Mary said (in verse 48): 'Son, why have you treated us like this? Your father and I have been anxiously searching for you'. When Jesus explained his presence in the temple, we read in verse 50 that they didn't understand what he was saying. I find that very poignant. A little over thirteen years ago Mary had a personal encounter with the Angel of the Lord. He told her that she would bear a son and who this Son would be (Luke 1:26 ff). At that time she sincerely expressed her obedience to the Father, she was obviously someone who knew God and who had a deep faith in him. Now here in Jerusalem when this very Son told her that he must be in his Father's house, she didn't understand what he meant. She had just celebrated the Passover Feast, had been occupied with the things of God, but this she couldn't understand. What mattered most to her was that it was time to go home and Jesus needed to come along.

What is it that Jesus said? He very clearly expressed that his priorities were of a different order to those of his parents at that given moment. They were on their way home. He, however, had chosen to do something else: he wanted to concentrate on things relating to his heavenly Father and his earthly parents had to yield to these things.

The Greek text of Luke 2:49 is somewhat ambiguous. When we look at different Bible translations we find two main versions. One is the text mentioned above: 'I had to be in my Father's house'. Another much used translation reads 'I had to be about my Father's business (or affairs)'. In my own study of the text I have opted for a combination of the two translations. Each emphasises a different aspect of the same thing. When we want to get to know the Father we need to a) seek his presence, and we need to b) concern ourselves with his affairs. Looking at it in the context of the situation that Luke describes one could say we need to a) be in our Father's house or in his presence, and b) concern ourselves with his purposes which is to study, discuss and ponder his Word. We need to look at him (seeing) and we need to study his Word (seeking). These two things are, as it were, the two sides of a coin. A large part of it is done in private, or 'in hiding'.

It is significant that Jesus spoke about these crucial things in the temple. The temple was more than a meeting place, it symbolised the place where God was. This is where Jesus spoke about his priorities in life: fellowship with the Father and being occupied with the Father's affairs. One could also say: a walk and friendship with God in which seeking God's face and his nearness as well as studying the Word are central elements.

I have to be in my Father's house (seeing)

These words of Jesus are 'heart matter' and therefore deeply personal. He spoke about a deep-felt longing *to be with God* and to have fellowship with him. Jesus wasn't talking about things we need to do or about merely or mainly being occupied with the affairs of God. His words expressed a longing to sit at his Father's feet, to, as it were, hold his hand and feel his heart-beat. It is the same longing that David speaks about in Psalm 27:4-5:

> One thing I ask of the Lord, this is what I seek: that I may dwell in the house of the Lord all the days of my life, to gaze upon the beauty of the Lord and to seek him in his temple. For...he will keep me safe in his dwelling; he will hide me in the shelter of his tabernacle.

These are the words of someone who seeks and longs for an intimate relationship with the Lord. David's longing to be with him is so deep that he actually says that it is the *one* thing that he asks of God.

It is this very thing, seeking God's face or nearness, that ran through Jesus' life on earth like a continuous thread. It is worth a thorough study to look at the moments in which he made a conscious effort to retire in order to be alone or meet with his Father. It is, by the way, equally interesting to have a look at the moments when Jesus simply talked spontaneously with his Father, openly and totally uninhibited. It didn't matter whether there were many or a few people around, speaking with his Father was a natural thing for him. But the moments alone with the Father, away from other people, were both a necessity and a priority for Jesus. They were important enough for him to be worth the effort of withdrawing from people. That isn't always easy, particularly when one is always surrounded by others and has a full agenda! Jesus certainly did but he did not allow people or circumstances to overrule his times with God. It is Luke particularly who mentions the deliberate moments that Jesus spent with the Lord. In Luke 5:16 we read that Jesus often withdrew to lonely places to pray, in Luke 6:12 he went out into the hills and spent the night praying there. In Luke 9:18 we read that he was praying in private whilst his disciples were near him.

We see the same thing happening in Luke 11:1 where the disciples witnessed Jesus praying. That experience led to their asking him to teach them to pray. Obviously something about Jesus' praying touched them and made them want to experience it themselves. Sometimes Jesus took them along as was the case in Luke 9:28. There Peter, John and James were allowed to join him when he went 'up onto a mountain to pray'. They were present at a very special moment: they saw the Lord Jesus change before their very eyes and witnessed his meeting with Moses and Elijah. In Luke 22:39-46 we read about one of the most moving moments of Jesus' prayer life. On the Mount of Olives he asked his disciples to pray whilst he himself withdrew slightly from them ('about a stone's throw') in order to have a private word with his Father about his impending suffering. It was a deep and lonely struggle. When Jesus returned to his disciples he found them sleeping. He woke them and urged them to pray. It was a clear call to personal prayer.

For Jesus, his love relationship with God came before and went above all other things. It wasn't sufficient to talk about him or serve him; he needed to see his Father face to face. Again I think of David's words in Psalm 27, where he says that he wants to gaze upon the beauty of the Lord and seek him in his temple (verse 4). He speaks of secret and intimate things in words like 'He will hide me in the shelter of his tabernacle' or in the RSV translation 'He will conceal me under the cover of his tent'. A Dutch translation speaks of the 'secret things' of God's tabernacle. All these things point to the intimacy of a highly private relationship with God. He calls us to be with him in his tent in order to show us face to face who he is and what he is like. He wants to surprise us with his beauty and overwhelm us with his goodness. That is, I think, what Jesus was looking for at those times when he withdrew to be with his Father. It is what he advises us to do when, in Matthew 6:6, he tells us to go into our room in order to seek and speak with the unseen in secret. He advises us to make an effort to seek that isolation in a room with a closed door. There, alone in his presence, he wants to take us to the depths of our hearts and reveal to us the depths of his heart. Behind closed doors, in the intimacy of a face-to-face and heart-to-heart encounter, we will stand in awe as God the Father reveals himself to us. We may taste of his character and thus come to see who he is.

This gazing upon the beauty of the Lord, which David speaks about in Psalm 27, needs to be learned in private, it is something that nobody else can do for you. You may hear what other people have discovered in their own walk with the Lord and it can and will encourage you. Sharing these things is good but you want to experience them first hand. God doesn't just want you to hear about him from other people, he wants you to meet and hear him personally. Therefore we need to strive towards getting to know him first-hand. David often asks the Lord if he may see his goodness and almost always when he speaks about seeing or tasting God's goodness, it is related to hiding in or finding refuge in God. In Psalm 36:7-8 for instance he says: 'How priceless is your unfailing love! Both high and low among men find refuge in the shadow of your wings. They feast on the abundance of your house; you give them drink from your river of delights.' Knowing God's goodness is reason to seek refuge with him, to draw close and hide under his wings, as Boaz put it in Ruth 2:12. There we are being satisfied by his 'river of delights', there we receive more of what we already knew or experienced, there we go further and deeper. It is deeply private. Again, we may hear others say what God means to them, but hearing of another's experience is always secondary to tasting his goodness or having a drink from the spring of living water yourself.

God wants to reveal things to us about and of himself in the privacy of an inner-room relationship. There we are allowed to see things that aren't normally or naturally visible. We enter, as it were, into another dimension or world, the world of 'unseen things' that are often difficult or impossible to explain. Sometimes David approaches a description of these mysteries when he lyrically writes about what he has been allowed to see and discover of the Lord, but his words are always lacking, for we can never express the magnitude of God.

But we can discover something of it in our hearts! In 'the shelter of the tabernacle' what matters is a revelation of God himself to you or me personally. The things we 'see' there aren't meant for everybody but only for those whose eyes and ears have been touched and opened by the Holy Spirit so that they are tuned in to the Lord. That is precisely what makes hiding in God so precious.

'Gazing upon the beauty of the Lord', as David puts it implies that we need to take time to be with the Lord and to seek his face. Being constantly in a rush and unable to spend time together affects our relationship with the Lord just as it affects our human relationships. The ones who seem to understand this most deeply are people who are madly and deeply in love with each other. Lovers are somehow always able to find lots of time to be together and gaze into each other's eyes! They seek each other's company and long to know and understand each other in depth. Unfortunately this phase often seems to pass rather quickly because we are soon taken up by the hustle, bustle and pressure of life. Many people need to seek counselling later on in their marriage because somehow they have neglected the gazing at and seeking of each other and their relationship has become shallow at its best. They will need to reset priorities and think hard about what they need to do in order to keep their relationship not just going but growing. It is the same in our relationship with God. It is crucial for us not just to know about the inner-room, but to go into it and stay a while. If you want to get to know the Lord deeply it is 'hush' rather than 'rush'!

I think it is important to realise that gazing is an active verb! When a bird-watcher is intent on getting to know a certain bird species, he will spend hours watching his object, attempting to discover each and every detail there is to be known about it. He will do his utmost to catch even just a glimpse of the bird, meticulously registering everything he observes. I personally remember how, when I was working on a TV series on bird life, we had to get up at odd hours to increase our chances of seeing the one bird we were still missing! We made the effort because it was important and we learned to gaze – an interesting and most rewarding exercise.

I have to be about (busy with) my Father's affairs (seeking)

When Jesus' parents found their son sitting in the temple in Jerusalem he was having a discourse with the theologians of his day. He had become so engrossed in this 'Bible study' that all other things had become unimportant, even the departure of his parents who had begun the journey home after the Passover Feast. When they asked him why he was still there in Jerusalem and not with them, he stated his point by saying that he must be about his Father's things. In other words: the things of God were a top priority in his life. And so, in verse 46 of Luke 2 we see Jesus in the temple with the teachers, listening and asking questions. We read that everyone who heard him was amazed at his understanding and his answers, meaning his insight and wisdom. What were they talking about? The Torah, God's Word. They were studying it in depth, discussing what it said and what consequences it had on life.

God's Word was pivotal in Jesus' life. He knew and perceived it, continued to study it and he desired to apply it in his life; his obedience to God's Word was unconditional, time and time again Jesus sought God's will and Word. We see it when Jesus was deeply tempted by Satan at the onset of his public ministry. It was in the desert that he resolutely tested and rejected every one of the three temptations that Satan so defiantly put before him. He appealed to the written Word of God. Three times he answered Satan with the words: 'It is written' (Luke 4:1-12). We see it again in the Garden of Gethsemane, when Jesus was on the threshold of his trial and death. So gruesome was the suffering that was before him that he sweated blood whilst he thought and prayed about it. But even then he chose to obey God and go his way (Luke 22:42b). Obedience to God or 'It is written' was the chorus that echoed throughout Jesus' life on earth. Hiding in God implied also hiding his Word in his heart.

What then, does it mean to be concerned with the things or affairs of the Father? It is a choice to give priority to God's Word and to obedience to it in all possible forms and situations in our lives. Having a relationship with God or seeking refuge in him cannot be separated from the Word. In fact when we love God, we automatically love his Word also. Psalm 119:2 says: 'Blessed are they who keep his statutes and seek him with all their heart' and verse 10 'I seek you with all my heart; do not let me stray from your commands'. Those who belong to God and love him with all their heart cannot do without his Word, they cannot afford to neglect it and in fact they don't want to! God reveals himself through it and means it to be our spiritual food. It needs to find room in us in order for us to grow into fellowship with him as well as for us to grow into the men and women that God intends us to be. The place that God's Word has in our lives says much ,if not all, about our love for him. Let's therefore honestly face the question: Do we love the Word and live with and from it like Jesus did? He says in John 14:21: 'Whoever has my commands and obeys them, he is the one who loves me'.

Bible study too is an inner-room-affair. Of course we profit from what we hear learned and wise Christians say in sermons in our church, at conferences or courses. We also profit from the many Christian books that teach about different aspects of the Christian faith. We need that in order to be sharpened and stimulated in our thinking and study. But we also need to be alone with the Word, studying it prayerfully and meditating on it. We need to read it and be quiet in order to let it sink in and allow the Holy Spirit to help or prompt us as we seek to understand it or apply it to our personal situation. We need to treasure it and carry it with us, maybe in our pocket but always in our hearts.

In 1943 in one of the Japanese internment camps two British women, Margaret Dryburgh and Nora Chambers, made a great impact and in fact changed the morale of most prisoners by bringing music into the camp. Both very musical, they were able to piece together and write down on scraps of paper some of the great compositions of famous composers like Brahms, Mendelssohn, Beethoven and Tchaikovsky. They encouraged the women in the camp to sing the instrumental parts and so organised what became known as a 'voice orchestra'. Voices sang, for instance, the cello solo in Tchaikovsky's string quartet; they sang piano parts or the parts of wind instruments. Mrs. Helen Colijn, one of the Dutch prisoners in that camp, who later wrote a book about those years, says about the voice orchestra: 'This wasn't a women's choir singing songs. It wasn't an orchestra either even though I could hear the violins and an oboe. This was music from heaven, a God-given miracle in a horror-camp.' Ever since I first heard about this voice orchestra (through Mrs. Colijn who was once a guest in my weekly radio programme and later through Dirk Jan Warnaar, who has formed a Dutch voice orchestra modelling that first one in the former Dutch Indies), I have been deeply impressed and intrigued by it. I find it almost impossible to believe that under the given circumstances of deep suffering and starvation in one of the most gruesome Japanese camps, there were people who still had music in their hearts and more than that, who obviously so loved that music that they knew it by heart. They were able to bring to memory the different parts of great orchestral works and write them down painstakingly on whatever pieces of paper they could scrape together. Surely, they must have truly loved music.

Since hearing that story, I have often wondered if we love God's Word so deeply that we would be able to 'piece it together' the way Nora Chambers and Margaret Dryburgh carefully reconstructed the complicated compositions of musical geniuses? Do we know the Bible so well by heart that together we could write down the Gospels, or some of the letters of Paul, or some Old Testament Books? Would we get that far, or would we get no further than some of our favourite Bible verses which we have underlined? Would we seek to remember and write down God's Word because it is like 'music from heaven' to us? As I imagine those starved prisoners, most of them sitting down as they sang because they were too weak to stand, I wonder if God's Word is as dear to us as music was to them?

God's Word is like music from heaven: God reveals himself to us and speaks to us. Whilst we study it, we discover his character through his deeds in history and in personal lives. We discover it in the words he speaks about himself and in Jesus whom we meet in the Gospels as well as through the testimonies and wisdom of those who followed him and became people of God. It is the Holy Spirit who opens our eyes and understanding of it. It is a dynamic and living Word. When we know and obey it, it will move things and us and will become like an overwhelming overture of the great love of our mighty God!

All these things would be impossible without the help of the Holy Spirit whom Jesus calls 'the Spirit of truth' (John 14:17). He is the One who will lead us into the truth and therefore also into understanding God's Word. One may study the Bible for years without ever grasping the truth. As a teenager, I knew a minister who knew the Bible inside out. He was, however, mainly interested in it as a historical document and consequently knew a lot about the background of certain times, about kings and rulers, about wars and social and political affairs. But spiritual things were a mystery to him. When asked about Jesus, he was able to explain to a certain level who he was, but he didn't grasp the deeper truth behind this Person nor could he 'see' the implications or impact of living with him. He 'explained' a lot of things in terms of a good tradition but he couldn't see beyond the historical facts. He isn't the only one. Many people may be highly learned theologians, they study and gain knowledge but whilst doing so they get further and further away from knowing God. Studying the things of God, they overlook God himself who wants to reveal things that exceed human knowledge. Nicodemus was one such theological scholar. A religious leader of his day, he knew a lot but didn't understand much about Jesus, there were things he could not understand or explain. Jesus told him (in John 3:8) that he needed to be 'born of the spirit'. It is fascinating to witness how people who have been born again have their eyes opened to a new understanding of God's Word and therefore of God himself. Once you discover that, you will search for more.

Seeing and seeking then, as David puts it, have to do with being with God. Both words express that it is a dynamic process with the potential of more. We may see God's loveliness but there is a lot more to discover which means that we need to continue seeking.

Come away to be with him

Jesus makes it clear beyond any doubt that walking with God can only become a reality for us through him. I already mentioned what he said to Thomas: 'I am the way and the truth and the life. No-one can come to the Father except through me' (John 14:6). These words are exclusive and radical. Exclusive, however, only in their claim, for the way to and through Jesus is open and accessible, for anyone who chooses to go with him. Jesus also calls himself the door or the gate to God (John 10:7); in other words our relationship with the Father begins with and through the Lord Jesus. This is what he invites us to do when he calls us to follow him in a living relationship with him.

I find it very moving that Mark, when he describes the appointing of the twelve apostles, emphasizes the fact that they were appointed to 'be with him' (Mark 3:14). Of course they were also meant to preach and be useful in other ways whilst proclaiming the Kingdom of God, but their first and foremost calling was to be with Jesus. This fact is echoed by Paul when in 1 Corinthians 1:9 he says that God has called us into fellowship with his Son, Jesus Christ.

It is important that we keep reminding ourselves of our first calling. We usually find it easier to be active and do things. The Dutch are often driven by a Calvinistic trait of wanting to work hard. We know that we are allowed and invited to live by grace, but we often behave as if we still need to earn God's approval and love. Many Christians are over-active in Christian work and church activities and feel that unless they take on even more, they aren't doing enough to be acceptable. Here, however, in Mark 3 we are asked to just 'be'. The Lord is more concerned about our devotion to him than to service. We see this truth illustrated in Luke 10:38-42 where it is said of Mary, who had chosen to sit at Jesus' feet, that she had chosen 'what is better'. Her sister Martha had opted for serving, which in itself was a good thing, but maybe less so at that particular moment. The point made isn't that serving is wrong, but rather that it may never come before or instead of our fellowship with the Lord. He doesn't want a relationship that is based on work, he wants a love relationship where our hearts touch one another. This is what happened when Mary drew near and came and sat at his feet. Friends want to *be* together. Jesus emphasizes that again in John 15:15 when he says: 'I no longer call you servants, because a servant does not know his master's business. Instead, I have called you friends, for everything that I learned from my Father I have made known to you.' His words speak of transparency, of openness without secrets. The friendship Jesus seeks with us leaves no room for hidden agendas and it is built on unconditional love and trust.

We are called to be with Jesus, which brings us back to the concept of the 'inner-room'. Some people translate the call to intimacy with the Lord as 'having a quiet time' and they add certain conditions and rules that need to be strictly obeyed and kept. I remember being told as a fairly new Christian that I had to get up at 6 a.m. at the latest, in order to spend at least half an hour in Bible study and prayer. My prayer had to be divided in neat compartments, it always had to include worship and praise, confession of sins, intercession, etc. Of course these things are good and important and we need to discipline ourselves in Bible study and prayer because if we don't they might just not happen. We don't always long for a personal time with God or we find that our longing or good intentions are easily overruled by other important things. It is amazing what a list of urgent things comes to mind at the very moment when we are about to settle down for some time alone with the Lord. We are thoroughly tempted to go and do them there and then and find that, when we do, we usually don't return to our inner room because other things keep cropping up. If therefore, we don't practise some discipline we may find that our times with God become last in a line of other priorities. Unless we work at creating and setting apart a regular time to be with the Lord, it will never happen. So discipline is necessary. However, more important than golden rules or regulations that are meant to stimulate or guard our regular Bible reading or prayer is, in my opinion, the simple truth that these things should not be a matter of a half hour or hour but rather a life-style. Fellowship with God cannot be translated into a system, it is a life-style of longing for a personal and intimate walk with him. When that becomes a reality and we practise it in our lives, then we will seek times to be alone with him and this longing will grow. For once you have tasted God's goodness you automatically long for more and you will reach the point where you don't only discover that your fellowship with God goes beyond everything else, but also that you can't do without it anymore.

Hiding in Jesus

'How often I have longed to gather your children together, as a hen gathers her chicks under her wings, but you were not willing' (Matt. 23:37). These words, spoken by the Lord Jesus just before the end of his earthly life, express his deep love for a nation that doesn't want him. Jerusalem had killed the prophets and stoned those sent to them by God. Now, finally God's Son himself was standing before them, embodying all the love of the Father and bringing with him the offer of forgiveness, reconciliation and a return to open fellowship with the Father. What he also offered is a hiding place in him, not just to them but also to us. He invites us to come and hide under his wings.

Actually these words of Jesus are quite motherly as he compares himself to a hen who safely gathers her chicks under her wings. Only...the chicks don't want to come, they would rather look after themselves than go to the place of refuge that is offered. John in his Gospel puts it as follows: 'He came to that which was his own, but his own did not receive him' (John 1:11).

Here the Lord God reveals himself in Jesus Christ. Has anybody ever seen God? Of Moses, who was called a friend of God, it is said that he knew the Lord face to face as a friend (Ex.33:11 and Deut. 34:10). Moses, in other words, met the Lord, he knew his close presence, he heard his voice and spoke with him. But did he actually ever *see* him? God's words to Moses in Exodus 33:20 answer that question: 'you cannot see my face, for no-one may see me and live' (see also verses 22-23). Jesus also leaves no doubt when in John 6:46 he says: 'No-one has seen the Father except the one who is from God'. Now, however, things have changed: in his great mercy God comes down to this earth and dwells among people, tangibly and visibly in Jesus Christ. For us, unimaginable yet true, this Man reveals God himself to us. He is, as the Word says, the image of the invisible God (Col. 1:15) of whom John says 'No-one has ever seen God, but God the only Son, who is at the Father's side, has made him known' (John 1:18).

The Lord God has descended to earth in Jesus Christ and he, Jesus, brings with or rather in him into this world all God's characteristics, he is 'full of grace and truth' (John 1:14). When we want to seek refuge in God, we can do so in and through his Son. He suggests that he wants to be that hiding place for us by comparing himself with the mother hen. At the onset of his ministry on earth, he spoke in a synagogue in Nazareth, the place where he was raised. He read from Isaiah and claimed that he was the One whose coming was foretold by the prophet. Indeed

Jesus is the One who came to preach good news to the poor, to bind up the broken-hearted, to proclaim freedom for the captives and release for the prisoners, and he will comfort all who mourn (Isa. 61:1-2). He says in John 10 that he is the Good Shepherd who offers a place of refuge and security to his sheep. He will guide us to green pastures and quiet waters in the midst of a world that is in turmoil.

Jesus is the way and the door to finding refuge with God. Friendship with the Father presupposes faith in the Son, that's where it begins. We have looked at the friendship of David and Jonathan and saw things there that we can now see and experience in perfection in the Lord Jesus. He offers more than just a being with us, he seeks an intimate friendship, something 'confidential' as David points out in Psalm 25:14, and as such he goes much further than any human friendship can ever go. For however deeply friends may be committed to one another, however close they may be, they are never able to go beyond that being near, and very often they will fail even in that, bringing disappointment to one another. Seeking refuge in people will always have limitations, because people are limited and imperfect. Human nearness can be at most a being *with* one another and as such it can never guarantee that ultimate security and wellbeing that we so urgently seek. The Lord Jesus, however, speaks of our being *in* him and of him being *in* us and he reminds us that it is pivotal to keep it that way (John 15:4-5). He in us, we in him. It is fascinating to see in the Psalms that hiding *with* God actually always means hiding *in* God. Not all Bible translations make that clear. When in Psalm 143:9, for instance, we read 'I hide myself in you' (NIV), other translations may read 'To you I run (or flee)'. I think the former translation more accurately describes what happens when we seek refuge with God and surrender to him. I am not hiding behind God, I am hiding in him and this is ultimate security.

12
Hiding Means Trusting

We will only be able to seek refuge with someone we consider reliable and safe. We need to be able to trust that they aren't out to harm us but seek the best for us and, in doing so, we count on their unconditional love and faithfulness. These, however, are the very areas in human relationships where things go wrong and where people deeply disappoint each other. We may have the best intentions, but we do not make the mark in real life. Promises aren't kept, trust is betrayed and people are so hurt and wounded that later on in life they may find themselves incapable of ever trusting again. Sometimes negative experiences on a human level affect our relationship with the Lord. We project our feelings of distrust to him; someone who had a bad father may find it difficult to view God as a loving Father and someone who wasn't loved as a child may struggle deeply later on in life when it comes to believing and trusting in God's love and mercy. A person who was often punished may automatically consider blows or disappointments in life as God's punishment and will fear God rather than trust him. Negative or painful experiences in human relationships can thus work against us when it comes to seeking refuge in the Lord. Our prejudice and fear can affect our walk with God: without actually being aware of it, we may be constantly trying to earn his acceptance and love by our good behaviour and deeds, thus living as fearful servants rather than as beloved children.

In a seminar at a conference for Christian students, I asked people what could withhold them from committing their lives and future to the Lord. I had mentioned several possible hindrances to trusting God and it appeared that one of the main ones was a certain distrust towards God. How do we know that his plans for us are good, and particularly that we are going to like them? 'I like to keep control over my own life,' one of the girls said, 'I prefer to play it safe.' Her words were echoed by others in different ways. 'I'd like to get married,' a student said, 'but maybe God wants me to stay single.' Another said: 'I am afraid that God might want me to give up my studies or even ask me to go to the mission field.' As we talked, we discovered that we are sometimes afraid that God might require things of us that go against our own ideas or wishes. This possibility makes committing our lives to him a rather risky affair. It leads to a certain reserve which conflicts with our calling, for when Jesus asks us to follow him, he requires unconditional trust and commitment.

It is a good thing to consider our view of God and ask ourselves what has shaped our interpretation of who he is. When we realise that our ideas about him are subjective, we are challenged to strive to get to know the God of the Bible rather than the God of our imagination. Two things stand out: God's Fatherhood and his holiness.

The Fatherhood of God

When one of the disciples asked Jesus to teach them to pray, the first thing he told them to do was to say: ' Father' (Luke 11:2). The holy God invites us to call him 'Father' and, as we do so, we affirm not only our sonship or daughtership, but we also appeal to the special and intimate relationship provided in it. The Lord Jesus tells us what that implies when, also in Luke 11, he compares God the Father with a good friend, whom you can always call on. Even in the middle of the night you can knock on his door and be sure that he will be willing and ready to help you and give you what you need. It is quite something to disturb someone at such an unreasonable time. You can't do that with just anybody, it is more likely that there are only one or two people that you would dare to intrude upon so rudely. They are what I call 'back-door-friends': you don't need to formally ring the bell at the main entrance, you can just walk in through the kitchen door. It is like home and according to Jesus, who tells this story, that is how it is with the Lord God. He is Someone near, he is like family, like home. He takes care of us as a father takes care of his children. In Luke 12 we read how people were worried and anxious about small and big things. Christians don't need to be worried or anxious, Jesus says, because 'your Father knows what you need' (Luke 12:30).

In our discussion at the Christian student conference, it was the fact of God's loving fatherhood that brought peace instead of confusion and insecurity. Would he, who calls himself our Father, want to give us negative things? Isn't a father ideally the one on whom you can always count? Doesn't Jesus himself convey that in the 'father example' in the parable of the prodigal son (Luke 15:11-32)?

Our talking and thinking about God's fatherhood was for some people quite emotional. Many people have experienced a very different kind of fatherhood in their own families. I know a young Christian woman who has known and loved God for years, yet she cannot bring herself to call him 'Father', because for her that word is associated with misery and feeling deserted. In our day and age where there is a growing number of one-parent families with absent fathers or mothers, it is increasingly necessary to explain the concept of parenthood and fatherhood more carefully, as is also the case where children have been neglected or abused.

Care and intimacy

What is God's view of fatherhood? In chapter 13 we shall look at
the imagery that he uses to explain it to us. Sometimes God uses
terms that refer to motherhood. They are images of continuous
tender care and cherishing. Paul states in his letter to the Romans
that we are invited to call God 'Abba', which is similar to our
word 'Daddy' (Rom. 8:15). Abba is an Aramaic word that a child,
however little, can easily pronounce. You may be of a different
opinion, but I find that 'Daddy' sounds more intimate than 'Father'.
It is as if God wants to break down any possible distance and
formality by offering us an intimate word like 'Abba'. The holy
God who is to be feared, gives us in his fatherhood the privilege
to come very near. His invitation doesn't imply that we throw our
reverence for him overboard and make him our pal, but we are
invited to draw near in childlike confidence and to trust him
unreservedly. He is the One who says in Jeremiah 29:11 'For I
know the plans I have for you, ...plans to prosper you and not to
harm you, plans to give you hope and a future'. These words,
spoken to exiles in Babylon, testify of God's character and his
love for his children. Once our eyes are opened to these things,
we can leave distrust, doubt and suspicion behind us. 'In repentance
and rest is your salvation, in quietness and trust is your strength' is
what the Sovereign Lord, the Holy One of Israel, says, (Isa.30:15).
God's fatherhood gives us security.

Faithfulness

It is striking that David, who so often met with hardship and
disappointment, repeatedly and emphatically spoke about and held
on to God's faithfulness. In his song of praise in 2 Samuel 22:51
he says the Lord 'shows unfailing kindness to his anointed, to
David and his descendants for ever'. He said this after he had
been delivered from the people who threatened and persecuted
him, in other words after God's faithfulness had been proven.

But he also affirmed God's faithfulness and expressed his faith and trust whilst he was in the midst of great distress. In Psalm 57, a psalm that refers to the moment when David was hiding in a cave in order to escape from Saul, he says 'My heart is steadfast, O God...I will praise you...For great is your love, reaching to the heavens; your faithfulness reaches to the skies' (verses 7, 9-11).

Knowing that the Lord keeps his promises and will fulfil his purposes for us (Psalm 138:8); knowing that he doesn't forsake us or let us plod along on our own or fall prey to circumstances or people; knowing that things are never out of his control, affects us. It gives us the courage to carry on even when our path is puzzling or worse, daunting to us. We can even say that whatever *God* brings about in the lives of his children is always good! In fact throughout our studies we have seen how God is sovereignly orchestrating the events to bring about his purposes and to get us where he wants us to be! David underlines this truth in Psalm 25:10: 'All the ways of the Lord are loving and faithful for those who keep the demands of his covenant'. Knowing that *brings peace* in a restless heart.

Knowing that God is faithful also *stirs us into motion*. When God told Abram to leave his country and people and father's household and 'go to the land I will show you', Abram left 'as the Lord had told him'(Gen.12:1-4). He obeyed and went, certain of the faithfulness of the One who was sending him.

Knowing that God is faithful *makes us persistent*. When God promised that he would make Abram into a great nation (Gen. 12:2), Abram knew and didn't doubt that God could and would be true to his promises. Romans 4:18 recounts how Abraham indeed believed 'against all hope and so became the father of many nations, just as it had been said to him'. Up against all possible human odds of old age and infertility he did not 'weaken in his faith' nor did he 'waver through unbelief regarding the promise of God'(verses 19-20).

Knowing that God is faithful *strengthens our faith*. When Abram had to wait a long time before he saw God's promises to him only partially fulfilled, he grew in faith. We read in Romans 4 that 'he was strengthened in his faith and gave glory to God, being fully persuaded that God had power to do what he had promised' (verses 20-21). When we hold on to God's faithfulness we will sooner persevere than give up.

The holiness of God

Sometimes God's fatherhood is so strongly emphasised that we fail to see his holiness. It isn't, however, a matter of one or the other, they are both characteristics of the same person. Consequently we need to hold on to both: God's fatherhood – where the keyword is love – and his holiness – where the keyword is perfection.

The concept of perfection is sometimes expressed in the four-letter prefix 'omni'. God is omnipotent (almighty), omnipresent (all present),omniscient (all-knowing). These facts make him unique and incomparable to any other living being or greatness, he alone is entitled to be called the Most High (as for instance in Gen. 14:19-20). When the Lord had rescued David from his enemies and from Saul, David said: 'the voice of the Most High resounded' and 'For who is God besides the Lord? And who is the Rock except our God?' (Ps. 18:13,31). The word 'rock' expresses firmness and stability, it is unshakable. The same applies to other terms that David uses to describe his God. He speaks of him as 'the stronghold of my life' (Ps. 27:1), 'a shield around me' (Ps. 3:3) and 'my fortress' (Ps. 59:16). God's holiness is absolute and solid.

The fact of God's holiness and perfection leaves room for no other option than to bow down and stand in deep awe of him. The Bible speaks of the *fear* of the Lord. He isn't someone we can bend to our will, he is the One who takes us by the hand, requiring uncompromising obedience. His law and his ways are perfect, his character unshakable and unchangeable. His promises stand firm. These facts give us *certainty*, that is: we should be free from doubt and reserve and become steadfast and unwavering, even in the face of suffering.

It is true to say that, in the face of suffering, many people start questioning God's holiness. Where some do away with God's justice, others in situations of pain start questioning other aspects of God's character or even his existence. For, if he exists, why then the suffering? What God allows such negative and painful things? What does it reveal about his character or power or reliability? What does his greatness mean in the face of affliction? In our inner struggle we seem to stumble over the same major issues over again. American author Jerry Bridges identifies three main areas of doubt when, in his book *Trusting God*[1], he says that our trust in God is based on God's sovereignty, wisdom and love. All of them aspects of God's holiness, it seems that they are the first ones that we start questioning when we face intense suffering and grief. True, sometimes we feel that what happened to us was a mistake and certainly not God's intention! God must have lost control and let the circumstances run away with him. Here we touch upon questions that refer to *God's sovereignty*. At other times we are unable to reconcile certain events with the goodness of God. We cannot imagine that a loving God would allow a child to be born with a severe handicap or that a marriage end in divorce. This is where the question of *God's love or goodness* is raised. A third possible reaction to the perplexities of life is to start doubting God's wisdom. Does he realise what he is doing to us and what damage he is causing? How do these utterly negative and useless things make any sense? Here we face the issue of *God's wisdom*.

I would like now, to consider the three characteristics mentioned, God's sovereignty, goodness and wisdom, in the light of God's Word. In doing so I acknowledge my indebtedness to

Jerry Bridges for his inspiring thoughts which helped me in my thinking and for his kind consent to make use of some of these.

a) God's sovereignty

When American rabbi Harold Kushner was told that his three-year-old son was suffering from a rare disease which would lead to an early ageing process and death before he would reach the age of fifteen, his world fell apart. The situation he was facing led to an intense struggle about the concept of God's goodness and consequently also that of God's sovereignty. Kushner's book *When Bad Things Happen to Good People*[2], which is a reflection of his thinking, reveals that Kushner finds himself incapable of reconciling God's goodness to the fact that people experience adversity. The only option left to him is to conclude that God loses control at times, resulting in things happening beyond his will. Thus Kushner reaches the point where he is no longer able to believe in God's sovereignty. I quote:

> I believe in God. But I do not believe the same things about him that I did years ago, when I was growing up or when I was a theological student. I recognize his limitations. He is limited in what he can do by laws of nature and by the evolution of human nature and human moral freedom. ... I can worship a God who hates suffering but cannot eliminate it, more easily than I can worship a God who chooses to make children suffer and die, for whatever exalted reason.

At the close of his book he says:

> Are you capable of forgiving and loving God even when you have found out that he is not perfect, even when he has let you down and disappointed you by permitting bad

luck and sickness and cruelty in his world, and permitting some of those things to happen to you? Can you learn to love and forgive him despite his limitations, as Job does, and as you once learned to forgive and love your parents even though they were not as wise, as strong, or as perfect as you needed them to be?

Desiring to hold on to God's goodness but unable to reconcile it with the evil that had befallen him or others, Kushner chose to believe in God's helplessness or powerlessness, thus creating for himself a framework in which he was able to continue to worship God. He made the laws of nature as well as human nature and moral freedom into entities more powerful than God. His conclusion is that God allowed brokenness not only to enter into this world but he himself became subject to it.

Kushner's reaction isn't exceptional. When we experience things that we cannot reconcile with a good God, we tend to say: 'God didn't want this.' These words are true beyond any doubt. From the very beginning God did not want evil to come into our world. The world he created was perfect and what he had in mind for that world and the people living in it was essentially and exclusively good. That 'good' included the freedom that was given to the first people to make choices. Adam and Eve weren't robots or marionettes without a will of their own; they were worthy and responsible people. The very fact that they made a bad choice and that their choice had far-reaching consequences, is an indication of the space that God had allowed them. God showed them what was good. They chose to do what was evil. Of course he could have prevented them from doing so, but he gave these people the freedom to choose, even to choose things that were wrong and against his will. The fruits of that first wrong choice are still present and visible in our world today. But they are not beyond God's control; he has not become incapable of intervening, he is not paralysed by the brokenness of his creation.

So although we are right when we say: 'God didn't want this', our words become untrue when we want to express that certain things that happen are beyond God's control. We then say that things got out of his hand and that he was unable to do anything about them. The implication of this is twofold: not only are we victims or puppets and at the mercy of circumstances or people, but God himself is helpless too. He has become a powerless being who weeps with us in our misery without being able to do anything about it. When this is how we feel, we have, like Kushner, reduced God to human proportions.

Again, it is true to say that God grieves about our distress but his tears are no indication of his powerlessness. When Jesus saw Mary and the Jews with her weep about her brother Lazarus' death, he was as John reports 'deeply moved in spirit and troubled' and 'Jesus wept' (John 11:33,35). Jesus was particularly moved – the Greek speaks of Jesus 'groaning in his spirit' which some scholars connect with being upset or angry – about the fact of death existing on earth. He is the God of the resurrection and the life, the God of eternity who wipes out the temporal. The emotions that Jesus felt when he stood by Lazarus' grave related to the pointlessness and wrongness of death itself as well as to the grief of those present and his own grief over the loss of a very close friend. Jesus' tears, however, weren't tears of powerlessness; a moment later he showed that he is Lord also over death. He is always able to intervene and here in Bethany he did so by raising Lazarus from the dead. In and through that deed he wanted to stir people up to faith in him and his sovereignty. He says in verse 15: 'so that you may believe'. Here is a God who isn't powerless in any sense, he is in no respect limited as Kushner puts it. His sovereignty goes even beyond the grave, our 'last enemy'.

Throughout the Bible we see God's sovereignty. It is as such that he makes himself known. When he appeared before Abram in Genesis 17:1, he said: 'I am God Almighty'. He, who is the creator of heaven and earth, is almighty in *nature*. He is the God of the wind and gales. He is able to still a storm on a lake. He is able to make water come out of a rock and to divide the water of the Red Sea. Countless miracles recorded in God's Word remind us of his great acts in nature. He is also the God of *history*. He proved his sovereignty when he led the people of Israel out of bondage in Egypt and went before them on their journey through the desert and beyond. He is also the God of *individual people*. In our studies we have seen his sovereignty in personal lives. He isn't powerless or thrown when seemingly negative things happen. Even then he follows his own devices. It didn't escape him and it wasn't outside of his will when Naomi, Ruth and Orpah were widowed. Ruth's childlessness wasn't something he couldn't change. He is the One who can close and open a womb. Ruth, who had no children in her marriage of ten years in the land of Moab, would later in Bethlehem have a son from her second husband Boaz. It is said of Rachel, who for many years was unable to conceive, that 'God remembered Rachel ... and opened her womb' (Gen.30:22). When Joseph was sold to a passing caravan by his brothers and ended up in Egypt, his situation and circumstances hadn't gone beyond God's control, Joseph ended up where he was meant to be. God was also present and in control when David was ruthlessly persecuted by Saul. Even when we feel that we are helplessly being dragged along by circumstances or people, he is the Great and Mighty One who reigns. Oswald Chambers in one of his devotional studies rightly says: 'It isn't the world or circumstances that dictate the agenda, it is the great I AM!'

God is almighty and as long as things go well for us and there aren't too many problems, we happily agree with that. But when we are confronted with profound pain and grief, we are tempted to doubt God's sovereignty. It is crucial in those moments, when feelings and emotions overwhelm us, to hold on to God's Word and the testimonies of his sovereignty throughout history. One of the reasons why the Word of God was given to us is to remind us of who God is. It is full of 'memorial stones'. We need to remember them and raise them up in our own lives also: we need to think back to what he did for us and remember how in the past he led and carried us as the sovereign and faithful one. 'Yet this I call to mind and therefore I have hope,' Jeremiah says, 'great is your faithfulness' (Lam.3:21, 23).

b) God's goodness

Where Kushner's personal circumstances led him to believe that God is good but not almighty, Naomi came to the very opposite conclusion. We saw earlier in the Book of Ruth that she kept calling God 'the Almighty', whilst at the same time she described him as the One who had afflicted her and who had brought misfortune upon her – 'The Almighty has made my life very bitter' (Ruth 1:20-21). It seems that Naomi was no longer able to trust in his goodness, a reaction which isn't exceptional and which stems from that age-old question 'Why does God allow suffering?' The Almighty God should be able to do away with pain and if he doesn't, we feel we have good reason to doubt his goodness. Why would a good God allow bad things to happen in our lives? It is inconsistent to his character and therefore not logical and impossible.

When we measure God's goodness to what happens around us and allow events to become a sort of plumbline by which we judge God's character, doubt will soon creep in and it is like a door ajar. God's enemy, the devil, would love to push his way in and open that door wider in order to make room for our doubt to grow into unbelief and subsequently into an aversion towards God. It was his first deed in paradise; there too he sowed the seed of doubt about God's goodness. If God was really good why weren't Adam and Eve allowed to eat from that one particular tree that would make them only wiser? They fell for his preconceived sly plan and the result was that a wedge was driven between themselves and their Creator. Instead of trusting God's goodness and holding on to it they opened themselves to the reasoning of the devil, allowed a trickle of doubt to enter their minds and hearts, and went astray.

When we raise up memorial stones of God's sovereignty and faithfulness, let us also raise up stones of his goodness. We see his love displayed as early as in paradise where God met Adam and Eve after they had disobeyed him. He spoke of a future solution to the human dilemma of separation from God (Gen. 3:9). He spoke of the largest memorial stone of his goodness, the one of the cross. This one deed does away with any doubt regarding his goodness; here we see God's loving response to what happened earlier in paradise, the sacrificing of his only Son in order to save us from our sins. Jesus Christ was willing to go to the extreme of suffering and death and in doing so accomplished the uttermost possible in a perfect deed of unconditional love. Paul talks about this in Romans 5:8 when he says: 'But God demonstrates his own love for us in this: While we were still sinners, Christ died for us.' I cannot possibly measure or understand the depth of Jesus' agony, not a single human experience of pain comes even near what he endured for us. He travelled a deep and lonely road of suffering. On his way to the cross and still even when he hung there, his enemies tested Jesus and challenged his faith in his Father. Surely God would be able to interfere and save him? Surely he would want to do so? Why didn't he, then?

Do you realise that these are questions regarding God's sovereignty and goodness? Do you realise that Jesus also experienced God-forsakenness (Matt. 27:45)? These things did not influence his faith in God nor did they change his decision to drink this bitter cup for our sakes. His life and death speak of unconditional and boundless love; it is the ultimate proof of God's infinite goodness. But there is more: the fact of Jesus' resurrection from the dead effectuates that *I* am not alone and forsaken by God in my suffering the way he was. For even now Jesus, the risen Son who is seated at the right hand of the Father, proves his goodness to me not only by being *with* me in my grief but by also being *in* me with his power. I can, says Paul, know him and the power of his resurrection (Phil. 3:10). He also says:

> But we have this treasure in jars of clay to show that this all surpassing power is from God and not from us. We are hard pressed on every side, but not crushed; perplexed, but not in despair; persecuted, but not abandoned; struck down, but not destroyed. We always carry around in our body the death of Jesus, so that the life of Jesus may also be revealed in our body (2 Cor.4:7-10).

It is Jesus himself who reminds us constantly of God's goodness and love. David too, often emphasised God's goodness as for instance in Psalm 13, which begins with a description of his experience of feeling forsaken by God whilst being persecuted by his enemies. He says in verse 5: *'But I trust in your unfailing love,* my heart rejoices in your salvation.' He says it again in Psalm 52:8 'I trust in God's unfailing love for ever and ever'. His preceding words are very significant: 'I am like an olive tree flourishing in the house of God'. These are the words of a man who could discern God's goodness even in adversity; he acknowledged that it was meant for his growth and never ever for him to pine away. For God's plans for us are good, a 'good' which is not affected by circumstances!

We can't always 'read' God's love or goodness by our circumstances, they often seem to prove the very opposite. Yet David says in Psalm 25:10 'All the ways of the Lord are loving and faithful for those who keep the demands of his covenant'. Sometimes he needed to remind himself of this truth and bring himself to hold on to it. At a moment in his life when his feelings told him that God had forgotten about him and seemed hidden, he stated '... *but* I trust in your unfailing love' (Ps. 13:5). We stand upon the facts rather than our feelings; God is good.

God's goodness comes home to us most deeply when we meet him personally and our hearts are stirred by his love. David talks about that in Psalm 31: 'How great is your goodness, which you have stored up for those who fear you, which you bestow ... on those who take refuge in you. In the shelter of your presence you hide them ... Praise be to the Lord, for he showed his wonderful love to me' (verses 19-21) and in Psalm 63:2 and 3 'I have seen you in the sanctuary and beheld your power and your glory. ...your love is better than life.' In Psalm 90:14 Moses says 'Satisfy us in the morning with your unfailing love.' Words like these – and these are just a handful out of many verses where people of God rejoice about God's goodness – communicate an important truth. God wants us to seek his goodness solely in himself and he wants to be the One who satisfies us. Once we discover this in our hearts, we shall be less vulnerable to the ups and downs of life and less likely to question his goodness when things seem to go wrong. Then we shall be able to say with the author of Psalm 94: 'When I said, "My foot is slipping", your love, O Lord, supported me' (verse 18).

c)God's wisdom
Our doubting God is often brought about by our inability to explain our pain. We need to be able to fit it in somewhere in order to be able to accept it. What we are actually looking for is the reason or wisdom behind events, and that is exactly where our problem lies: being as limited as we are we shall never be able to fathom all events; one needs the perspective of eternity for

that! Yet when we reach our limits, it sometimes is the Eternal One we blame and his wisdom we question!

God's Word leaves no doubt about the fact that people have no idea about God's nature and thinking. The Lord himself says by the mouth of his prophet Isaiah 'For my thoughts are not your thoughts, neither are your ways my ways... As the heavens are higher than the earth, so are my ways higher than your ways, and my thoughts than your thoughts' (Isa.55:8,9). The same thought recurs in Paul's letter to the Romans where he says: 'Oh, the depth of the riches and the wisdom and knowledge of God! How unsearchable his judgements, and his paths beyond tracing out! Who has known the mind of the Lord? Or who has been his counsellor?' (Rom. 11:33-34). When David in Psalm 139 recounts how God knows him through and through, he cannot but say: 'Such knowledge is too wonderful for me, too lofty for me to attain' (verse 6).

All of these and many more texts leave no doubt as to God's infinite wisdom. It is impossible and will therefore never happen that God will be at his wits' end not knowing where to go or how to handle things. People can get themselves in a fix, but God is never perplexed. There are many things we can't understand, but that doesn't mean that they are beyond God.

The prime example of our foolishness and lack of understanding is our reaction to the incarnation of Jesus Christ, God's Son. One of the human errors of his day was that people wanted to ascribe to him a political role as the liberator of the Jewish people who were suffering under the yoke of Rome. At one point they wanted to make him their king, after all he himself often spoke about 'his Kingdom'! He did indeed but they misunderstood his intentions. When finally Jesus was sentenced to death on a cross, many people saw therein a proof of his failure to fulfil his mission. Not only his enemies came to that conclusion but also a number of his followers, who were unable to understand what was happening, did so. They had to face their own disillusionment. It was only later, after the resurrection, that they discovered that what had actually happened was 'what your will and power had decided beforehand should happen' (Acts 4:28). Paul says that the crucifixion of Jesus is 'God's secret wisdom, a wisdom that has been hidden'. It is 'not the wisdom of this age or of the rulers of this age'. He says: 'None of the rulers of this age understood it, for if they had, they would not have crucified the Lord of glory' (1 Cor. 2:6-8). Finite man can never understand the infinite God! But with the help of his Spirit they can develop spiritual eyes and gain heavenly wisdom.

Simon and Helen's marriage has remained childless. They love children and are involved in a children's ministry. Why weren't they able to have children themselves? I don't know. Nor do I know why Helen got multiple sclerosis when she was about forty years old. Even though it isn't possible to foretell how things will develop, MS is a progressive illness and those suffering from it will face increasing disability. It is likely that Helen will become more limited in what she can do, her own life as well as Simon's and their joint ministry will be affected by her condition. I am unable to discover God's wisdom in this situation. In my opinion this couple would have been super parents. I also think they are both needed in what I consider a crucial ministry; children need to hear the message of the gospel in today's secular society. In my thinking about and expressing these things I am actually saying that I doubt God's wisdom in this particular situation.

What do Simon and Helen think? They have gone through a difficult and discouraging period when their wish to become parents wasn't fulfilled. It takes time and effort to come to the point where one accepts that. It is difficult to see other people having children, to rejoice with them and to enjoy their children without feeling hurt or jealous. Simon and Helen reached that point. They grew into their shared ministry and thoroughly enjoy it. Then came multiple sclerosis. I met them a couple of years after the illness had been diagnosed and almost twenty-five years after we first met at a British Bible College where we spent one year together. I met two people who are very different from the ones I knew twenty-five years ago. The change in them is more than the usual. Yes, they have become a little older, a little wiser and a few grey hairs have appeared. Much more important than that, however, is their personality that radiates more of God, a marriage that has become stronger, a deep spiritual unity, a deep love for Jesus and peace that passes understanding. These two people testify of God's intervention in their lives and actually say that they wouldn't have wanted to miss it at any price. Humanly speaking things might have been better; we consider childlessness and illness negative things. But when I look at them from the perspective of eternity I realise they have been blessed. The wonderful thing is that this is how Simon and Helen themselves feel about it. If twenty-five years ago they had been allowed to map out their own route in life, it would have probably been quite different from what it turned out to be. However, God in his endless wisdom thought it good to do what is ultimately wise and good. I wouldn't dare to say these words, let alone write them down, if Simon and Helen aren't saying the very same thing themselves.

When confronted with the perplexities of life, we must not and should not draw conclusions from them regarding God's wisdom. We need to realise that as long as we live on this earth we shall never be able to get a clear view of the Great Plan and understand God's wisdom. The only thing we can do is to learn to trust and to surrender to the One who does know all things! Jeremiah says: 'This is what the Lord says: "Let not the wise man boast of his wisdom or the strong man boast of his strength or the rich man boast of his riches, but let him who boasts boast about this: that he understands and knows me, that I am the Lord, who exercises kindness, justice and righteousness on earth."' (Jer. 9:23,24). In other words: human wisdom, strength or richness are relative, what really matters is understanding and knowing God. Again it is David who shows us the way to a childlike trust as we hide in God: 'Lord,...I do not concern myself with great matters or things too wonderful for me. But I have stilled and quieted my soul; like a weaned child with its mother, like a weaned child is my soul within me' (Ps.131:1-2).

Believing in God's justice, sovereignty, goodness and wisdom imply a surrender of my will and mind. We can try and may in fact understand things up to a certain level but then we reach our limit. We may try to explain suffering in terms of 'good' that comes out of it and sometimes in doing so, in our helplessness, we give answers or solutions that are glib. The fact is, suffering will always be a tragic thing even though it can bear good fruit and teach us valuable lessons. Sometimes, it doesn't, at least not that we know of or are able to see. And yet God is God.

Seeking refuge with our questions

Seeking refuge with God implies admitting our own helplessness and short-sightedness and trusting his character. I find Job's words, spoken after years of misery and not understanding, incredibly moving and true:

> I know that you can do all things; no plan of yours can be thwarted. You asked, 'Who is this that obscures my counsel without knowledge?' Surely I spoke of things I did not understand, things too wonderful for me to know....My ears had heard of you but now my eyes have seen you. Therefore I despise myself and repent in dust and ashes. (Job 42:2-6).

Where some people, perplexed by negative or cruel circumstances, question God's justice, others, like Kushner, do away with their faith in God's sovereignty. Likewise, Naomi's doubt about God's goodness has been felt by many who, like her, faced personal tragedies larger than life. And who of us never ever questioned God's wisdom in the face of circumstances too painful to be true? Questions will never end, they go with life. In fact it seems that as I get older the number of questions I face increases rather than decreases. Yet, strangely enough, the need to find fitting answers at any price becomes less urgent, not because it isn't important to find them, but rather because I am beginning to understand that as long as I live on this earth I shall never be able to reach the point where everything is clear and solved!

The fact that I admit my perplexity doesn't mean that, like an ostrich, I stick my head in the sand and avoid questions. Sometimes I do question but find that my own ignorance and respect for God's holiness silence me. Who am I to keep asking? We are never in a position to call God to account for things we cannot understand. We simply don't have the right to ever reproach him or ask him to justify his deeds. Such questions are based on a serious misconception: we feel God owes us something and therefore we can make him accountable for his actions. When we think about God that way, we reduce him to our human level, making him into someone equal to us. But God isn't a human being, he is the Holy One. We have no right to questions, yet we are invited to come to him and pour out our hearts before him. When I do that I sometimes find my questions being drowned in God's love. In my hiding in him I find rest and can only 'let go and let God'. The great bonus is that as I do that, he shows me more of himself.

In Psalm 73 (which I already mentioned in chapter 2) we see the same thing happening. Asaph, after summing up his list of complaints about God's injustice, goes into God's sanctuary and there, he says, 'I understood' (verse 17). His eyes were opened and he saw the things he was so upset about in their right perspective, he came to see that the apparent wealth and happiness of the wicked that he thought unfair wouldn't lead to anything ,and so he became aware of the relative worthlessness of the very things he envied. But much more important than that is that he discovered the most precious thing of all, namely that of the privilege of knowing God. He says in verse 23 'Yet I am always with you, you hold me by my right hand. You guide me with your counsel, and afterwards you will take me into glory'. This may sound glib, but is nevertheless true: knowing God and belonging to him with all that it implies now and forever, surpass all things, however painful and perplexing, that we encounter here on earth. It is a truth we discover when we enter the sanctuary of God, at that very moment and time when we take off our shoes of questions and pride and enter into his presence to seek him for himself and not merely to find answers or solutions to life's questions. The latter is never guaranteed; in fact, even in the light of Christ, perpetual mystery remains.

What both Job and Asaph discovered and expressed is God's purpose with us. He wants us to see him rather than just to know about him from hearsay. He wants us to know him as the all-just, the Almighty, the all-good, and all-wise; as Father and as one who is totally and perfectly reliable and trustworthy. Translated into New Testament language, he wants us to have fellowship with his Son Jesus Christ. Being with the Lord is both our destiny on earth and our eternal future. All the things we experience or face during our earthly lives can serve to our getting to know him more deeply and love him more dearly. At first that may sound contradictory. Problems tend to alienate rather than bind together. With God, however, it doesn't work that way. *Often it is when we have come to the end of ourselves and have hit rock bottom that we seek God's presence most urgently and meet him in depth.*

René

At the end of this chapter I want to share the experience of an American couple whose daughter aged thirty-four died in an accident in 1991. René was a vivacious young woman, very talented and enthusiastic in her faith. After graduation from university and studies at a European Bible School, she began working with young people. It was at a Young Life summer camp in the US that she had a fatal accident.

When I met René's parents and they told me about their daughter's accident and death four years earlier, I was particularly intrigued by a remark of her father, Charles Piersee. He said: 'If we hadn't firmly believed in and held on to God's sovereignty, we wouldn't have survived René's death.' When I asked him what he meant, he told me their experience. René fell from a great height during an activity with a so-called zip line. This is a high structure from which a cable is attached that is anchored in water below. A person wears a harness that hooks onto the cable, whereupon he or she slides down into the water. In René's case, the cable she was attached to didn't hold her because it wasn't fastened properly. When her parents were informed about her accident, René was being moved to the nearest large hospital. There tests confirmed her cerebral death. At that first moment of deep shock one question stood out: Why? But there were many more questions to be faced.

Upon their arrival in hospital René's parents were almost immediately confronted with the request to give permission for René's organs to be used as donor organs. While awaiting their decision, doctors had kept their daughter attached to all kinds of tubes and machinery in order to keep her organs alive. Seeing her in that situation led to an intense struggle about the correctness of the doctor's diagnosis (had she really died?) and about the possibility of a miracle of healing (would that be beyond God's ability?).

'We had to make a choice there and then to trust,' said René's mother 'and that is what we kept concentrating on and what kept us going. So overwhelming was the situation that our mind seemed to go numb. It wasn't until later that we had "room" to think about the many questions that we were then swamped with. Questions about the meaninglessness of this accident. Questions about the point of such a cruel and abrupt end of a valuable life. We had to consciously accept in faith that God was in control of this situation. Somehow we were kept from going under in despair. Friends spontaneously started a prayer chain and we felt that we were being held and carried in our grief. Later on God even made us meet a mother who had also lost a daughter in a sky diving action. We had many similarities and were able to share our pain and questions with her. It is extremely helpful to have someone truly understand.'

René's father said that five things stood out for them:

We decided that we didn't have the right to doubt God's ways and to call him to account for our daughter's death. In my prayers I expressed that as a servant of the Lord I have no say in the matter. I needed to say it out loud because I realised that Satan was trying to use our whys to somehow get into this situation and undermine our faith. There were so many whys. Our daughter was so promising, so talented. She got the most out of life. And she served God.

The closer we are to God, the fewer questions we have. In our lives and walk with him we learn to accept whatever he brings on our path, because what we encounter can be an instrument in his hand to mould us and shape us into the person he means us to be. We were both sixty years old. We had quite some life experience. We also knew that we weren't the first parents to lose a child.

Satan is God's opponent who wants to disrupt and hinder the plans God has for his Kingdom. It wasn't only René who was involved in Christian ministry, we too were involved in work for God's Kingdom. In our own ministry amongst military people we stood on the threshold of a very important and strategic conference. I was to be one of the speakers at that conference. Would I have anything left to say?

We consider our life a pilgrimage where it is of the utmost importance that we keep our eyes focused on God's final plan, independent from things that happen en route. In our deep grief we kept praying for something good to come out of the death of our daughter. We also prayed continually for compassion as spoken of in Lamentations 3:32 'though he cause grief, he will have compassion according to the abundance of his steadfast love' (RSV).

For our daughter's funeral we chose the words from Psalm 84:5-7 'Blessed are the men whose strength is in thee, in whose heart are the highways to Zion. As they go through the valley of Baca they make it a place of springs; the early rain also covers it with pools. They go from strength to strength...' (RSV). We founded a memorial fund and asked people to donate money rather than give flowers at the funeral so that we would be able to continue René's dream to share the Gospel with young people.

What a privilege to meet this godly couple and to hear René's mother say: 'The Bible calls us to trust God's sovereignty, love and wisdom. I needed to accept his way with my daughter even though it goes totally against my feelings and my will. I loved René so much.'

Since René died, her parents received about one hundred letters from young people from all parts of the world who had in one way or another been touched by their daughter. For some of them René's death was a turning point, it led to a decision to follow Christ. They said things like: 'I want René's dedication in following the Lord in my own life' and 'I became whole because René gave so much of her time to me'. One person said, 'René believed in me when no one else did'.

A few years have passed. It still hurts and the feeling of loss will last a lifetime. Charles and Carol will forever miss their daughter. But the sting has been taken out of their grief. They now say: 'It is as if things were guided. René had completed a couple of things in her life. She stood before a great change in her career. She had wound up certain matters, she had been reconciled with people, things had been spoken about openly. It is as if certain preparations had been made and she was ready to go'.

René's parents have kept going. God blessed their decision to keep trusting him. They have found rest in their hiding with him. They have come to see beyond the here and now and have discovered the fruit of what seemed senseless: a harvest of young people who chose to follow God and make spiritual growth their aim.

Notes

1. Jerry Bridges, *Trusting God*, NAVPRESS, Colorado Springs, USA, 1988.
2. Harold Kushner, *When Bad Things Happen to Good People*, Pan Books, 1982.

13

What Happens When We Hide in God?

We have seen how Ruth came to hide under the wings of the Almighty (Ruth 2:12) and how hiding in God implies trusting him. Once we realise the magnitude of the fact that God is both the Holy One and our Father-Friend, we know beyond any doubt that there is no better foundation upon which to build our life, nor a better hiding place. In this chapter I want to consider what we encounter when we draw close to the Lord and hide in him. We shall look at three main concepts: care and protection; unconditional acceptance; and rest and refreshment. We shall also consider words which in the Bible are used in connection with hiding in God as well as which underline the three ideas just mentioned. 'Hiding' and 'wings' are the two main concepts that I use as a starting point.

The Hebrew word *hasah* that is translated as 'take refuge' in Ruth 2:12, occurs thirty-seven times in the Old Testament, mostly in the psalms. Usually the word is conjoined with another word that reveals something about the type of refuge or about the character of the One in whom we hide. These are words like tent (movable, not bound to one place), dwelling (a temporary place of refuge), fortress (massive, defensive), shield (personal) and refuge (protection and safety).

In Ruth 2:12 hiding is connected to 'the wings of the Lord' (the Almighty). The Hebrew word *kanap* used here for wings, occurs 111 times in the Old Testament, where quite often it is used in connection with 'shadow' or 'shade'. Let us first consider the word wings and attempt to discover what the Lord wants to convey through this concept. What do I find when I hide under the wings of God?

Care and Protection

The first occurrence of the Hebrew word *kanap* (wings) is in Exodus 19:4 where God speaks to Moses on Mount Sinai: 'You yourselves have seen what I did to Egypt, and how I carried you on eagles' wings and brought you to myself.' The metaphor of the eagle recurs in the Song of Moses in Deuteronomy 32:10-12: 'he found him... he shielded him and cared for him; he guarded him as the apple of his eye, like an eagle that stirs up its nest and hovers over its young, that spreads its wings to catch them and carries them on its pinions. The Lord alone led him'.

Watching an eagle soaring high in the sky is an awesome display of strength and 'presence'. We find this bird mainly in rocky areas; his wings have a wide span and he has a prominent head with a conspicuous beak and very sharp eyes. Quite capable of carrying a large and heavy prey to great heights, the eagle is a so-called 'top-predator' implying that he is at the top of the food chain and doesn't have natural enemies. No one in his territory is a match for him, he is unbeatable. But there is another side to him as well! When we read Exodus 19:4 and Deuteronomy 32:10-13 and see the tremendous *power* of this terrifying bird of prey, it is quite a surprise to find that he is also a *tender* and protective parent.

The text in Deuteronomy 32:11 seems to suggest that the parent eagle catches its young whilst in flight, carrying it on its pinions. Although this behaviour has never actually been observed (or so I was told by an ornithologist!), it is generally agreed that it could well be true. The eagle certainly has the strength, pliancy and swiftness to be able to do so, and carrying young is an act not unusual in nature. The carrying has a different meaning too, though. When the parent eagle flies underneath the young, the movements of their wings produce an updraught or air current which lifts the young one. The eaglet is, as it were, being carried while flying himself, thus making it into a beautiful joint effort.

The eagle is known to go to great lengths to care for his young. During a powerful gale, he will stand erect on the nest, wings spread out, in order to protect his brood from being blown away. He is also known to feed his young whilst in flight. But he isn't overprotective! When the young start to grow feathers and the wing exercises begin, some discipline is carried out; sometimes the parents starve their young for several days until sheer hunger drives them to risk their maiden flight and learn new things. In their providing protection as well as a stimulus to venture out, the parents create a healthy environment for growth towards maturity.

In the above mentioned verses in Deuteronomy 32, the Lord God compares himself to the eagle. He too is to be greatly feared by his enemies (Egypt), but he also tenderly protects, carries and guides his young (children). Note the words: he *found* him, he *shielded* him, he *cared for* him, he *guarded* him, he *led* him…, all of them active verbs which convey a deep love, compassion and care. They also speak of God's omniscience; there is no place where he is unable to spot or touch us, we are never out of his sight or reach. David underlines this colossal truth in Psalm 139:7-10 when he says: 'Where can I go from your Spirit? Where can I flee from your presence? If I go up to the heavens, you are there; if I make my bed in the depths, you are there. If I rise on the wings of the dawn, if I settle on the far side of the sea, even there your hand will guide me, your right hand will hold me fast' and in verse 5 he says: 'You hem me in, behind and before; you have laid your hand upon me.' In Deuteronomy 33:26 and 27 the same truth is communicated: 'God ...rides on the heavens to help you and on the clouds in his majesty. The eternal God is your refuge, and underneath are the everlasting arms'.

Care and protection: A fertile soil for growth

How does God's promise of his everlasting arms being permanently underneath us affect our daily life? As is the case with the eagles' young, God's children are provided with constant and deep parental care and protection. The certainty of God's continuing presence creates a safe base from where we can venture out doing whatever God asks of us or brings about in our lives. We can do this *in confidence*, knowing that our heavenly Father hovers over, around and underneath us ready to catch and carry us. Sometimes the Lord asks us to do things and to take steps of faith that involve jumping into the unknown. We do so trusting that he is there to help us. Just as the eagle hovers in the air, keeping his eyes fixed on his not yet adult or mature young, so the Lord is present 'in the heavens and on the clouds', watching over his children. What a magnificent imagery! Thus secure and protected, we are given all ingredients necessary to grow from childhood into maturity, becoming men and women of God. Our training school may last a lifetime and some jumps are terrifying, but they are necessary for our spiritual growth.

Knowing all this, there are still situations in life that we would rather avoid or at least postpone instead of venturing into them. It can be an operation or a sickbed, a difficult confrontation in a conflict situation or a weighty decision that needs to be made. It can be circumstances in which we feel lonely and deserted. Our desire to flee from problems, difficulties or things we dread is a natural human reaction. When in distress, we can long for the security and carefree existence that we knew as children, we would much rather stay in the nest, safe and secure in the shelter and protection of our parents, than be confronted with the pain of life. Sometimes this desire can be so strong that, even as adults we can relapse into dependent or escapist behaviour in order to get away from reality. Sometimes we seek security with others, hoping that they will carry or protect us.

When we are tempted to lapse into such dependent behaviour, we need to remind ourselves of the promise of God's everlasting arms underneath us. But what does that mean to me? How real is it, how 'familiar' is the Lord to me? Is he my 'home', my security? If indeed my safety is rooted in God and not in a person or place (or even myself), then my whereabouts or circumstances don't matter. The Lord who is 'riding on the heavens as my helper and on the clouds in his majesty' isn't restrained to one particular place or situation, the promise of his everlasting arms carrying me is always valid. Actually, God's presence in my life guarantees that his secure refuge is always with me. I can at all times call on it; the door to God's hiding place is always open.

Sometimes the reality of what is physically and visibly present is so strong that it can overshadow God's truths. At such times we need other people to remind us of the divine reality. Once whilst abroad I was confronted with a series of unexpected calamities. I reached the point where I was tempted to just pack my cases and return home. It was an immature attitude, a wish to escape from problems. Fortunately there was someone who both comforted and encouraged me to stay and face the situation. Whilst doing so she reminded me of God's everlasting arms and assured me of her prayers. Rather than stimulating me to seek my security in circumstances or people, she challenged me to get on with it and to trust that God was with me. And so, 'starved' of people to hold my hand, I was forced to jump and – to land into God's arms!

Sometimes we need to reach rock bottom, or allow ourselves to fall very deeply in order to become aware of the reality of

God's arms underneath us. We need to jump off the mountain of human certainties and let go of them in order to discover God's presence and protection. Sometimes God himself takes away the securities we hold on to in order to bring us to himself and teach us about ultimate security. We need empty hands to reach that point where there isn't any other option except to fall into God's arms. We fall, as it were, through the storm down to the bottom of life's raging sea. Having been thrown about by the waves, exhausted and fearful of perishing, we suddenly find ourselves enveloped by unperturbed stillness. Similarly, if we allow ourselves to fall so deeply that we land in the arms of the everlasting Father, we shall find ineffable peace and rest in the midst of turbulence. God provides calm *in* the storm, not *after* the storm!

Safe places

When we consider God's care and protection, we look at that stable basic security which is provided for in our relationship with the Lord. It is conveyed by solid words like stronghold, fortress, rock and refuge, all of them metaphors used in the Bible to portray God. Interestingly, these words are often mentioned in the context of hiding in him.

When in danger or distress, we indeed seek 'strongholds', safe places or people to protect us. In the old days fortresses or castles were considered generally as places where people could run to when they were in danger. Once inside, the gateway was locked and fortified and strong men took their positions to defend the fortress and all who had come to find refuge there. They didn't always succeed – human protection, however well-prepared or organised, is always limited. Throughout time there have been many people who did all they could to protect others, going even as far as risking their own lives; yet they were nevertheless unable to give a hundred percent guarantee that no one would perish.

During the Second World War, many who offered people a hiding place in their homes lost their own lives. Some of them were Christians who had put their hope in God, expecting his help and protection; yet they themselves were taken prisoner and killed. What does that say about safety under the wings of the Almighty?

Dutch evangelist Corrie ten Boom was sent to a German concentration camp, because she, with her father and sister, had hidden people in her home in Haarlem. Her father died in prison in Scheveningen, her sister later died in the concentration camp where Corrie also stayed. The experiences of the ten Boom family were published in a book of which a film version was made later: *The Hiding Place.* This family, who themselves were hiding in God, offered others a place of refuge in their home, which resulted in intense suffering and the death of several of them. Corrie ten Boom, who did survive, was over fifty when she was released from the prison camp. Amazingly, she dedicated her remaining years to evangelism, speaking of God's goodness. How could she ever keep calling God her hiding place after having gone through such great affliction and after seeing her sister, father and many others perish in extremely cruel circumstances?

Corrie ten Boom was able to do so because she had tasted God's goodness in good times as well as in the darkest circumstances. She was able to witness about his presence and love even in a concentration camp, because God was tangibly present, even when he did not rescue people from their wretched circumstances, even when Corrie and her sister stood before their tormentors, emaciated and in agony of death. God's deliverance or rescue wasn't so much physical, it was of a totally different order; he blessed Corrie, as well as her sister and father and many others with and through his presence. She knew of 'hiding in God' and thus he became her safe place of refuge in the midst of pain and misery.

When American author Gordon MacDonald, in his book

Restoring Your Spiritual Passion [1] writes about so-called 'safe places', he is actually speaking of hiding in God. Sometimes we seek God's presence in a particular place, we retreat to a convent or to some other quiet and secluded spot. Our fellowship with the Lord, however, isn't restrained or bound to a certain place. The best and safest place, says MacDonald, is a heavenly one which, in fact, we carry in and with us and which we can call upon by seeking God's presence. This can happen anywhere, in a prison camp, in our car, at a sick bed, when at home, whilst on the phone or out walking the dog. Talking with our heavenly Father is natural and can therefore happen anywhere. We can at all times and in all places call upon God and the place where we are at that moment becomes a 'safe place', because it is covered with God's presence.

Does being in a 'safe place' as it is described here, automatically remove us from any possible danger zone? No. The safety we are talking about is linked with God's presence rather than with the absence of danger; it is a safety that transcends the immediate. The very fact that God is an eternal God adds an extra dimension to my life and makes me see the events that I encounter – even life threatening events – in a different light because I know that what happens here isn't final. I know that death is not the end for a Christian and I know that nothing can separate me from the Eternal. In fact the Eternal can step right into the immediate circumstances, giving me strength and hope that go beyond what I face and presently go through. However painful my circumstances, they are never greater than the One in whose hands I have placed my life. He holds the past, present and future, and therefore in hiding with him – and only there – I find absolute and ultimate safety.

We need to develop spiritual eyes in order to understand this glorious truth of being in a safe place. It is movingly illustrated by Stephen, the first Christian martyr in history. We read about him in Acts 6 and 7 where he is described as someone 'full of the Spirit and wisdom' and 'full of God's grace and power' (Acts 6:3,8).

Stephen was appointed by the disciples to look after the widows who were being neglected. We read that he did 'great wonders and miraculous signs among the people' (Acts 6:8), but then opposition arose and Stephen was brought before the Sanhedrin, accused of speaking against the law. He faced an unfair trial with false witnesses, but nevertheless gave a brilliant speech. What he said so infuriated his opponents, that he was dragged out of the city to be stoned. We read that just prior to being carried out, Stephen looked up to heaven and saw 'the glory of God, and Jesus standing at the right hand of God' (Acts 7:55). What happened here is that Stephen was given a 'safe place'. Not only did he experience God's presence and nearness, but God gave him an extra blessing of a view into heaven where Jesus was *standing* at the right hand of the Father. We read mostly – if not always – that Jesus is *seated* at the right hand of God. This makes his standing up here both fascinating and moving. It proves his intense love for and involvement with his disciple Stephen, who was going to be killed in a very gruesome way within a matter of minutes. It is as if Jesus here was underlining his commitment to Stephen: 'I am with you and I am praying for you.' The security this gave him enabled him, whilst he was being stoned, to say something which paralleled the words of his Saviour when he was dying on the cross. He said: 'Lord Jesus, receive my spirit' and then 'Lord, do not hold this sin against them'. In this moment of utter terror, whilst dying, Stephen completely surrendered himself to the Lord, on whom he had fixed his hope, and in this moment of total and ultimate safety with the Lord, he found room to intercede and ask forgiveness for his torturers and murderers (Acts 7:59, 60).

Safe places are like a cocoon that the Lord spins around us[2]. It is nothing magical, our feet are still on the ground, but we are as it were, enwrapped in the heavenly reality. We are not taken out of the world but we are protected in it (John 17:4). When alone in a hospital bed or facing great stress at home, when unloved in marriage or distressed for whatever reason, we can, spun in the invisible cocoon of God's arms around us, know peace in the midst of turmoil. We can call these safe places upon us as we call upon the Lord. We can also do this for other people in our intercessory prayers for them. As we practise this, we will increasingly discover that the safe places of God's presence give us space in the midst of distress.

Unconditional acceptance

When Boaz said that Ruth came to 'hide under the wings of the Almighty' (Ruth 2:12), I envisage in the context of her particular circumstances of uncertainty and confusion, an experience of being held and comforted. The idea of hiding under God's wings conveys security and warmth, maybe what one finds there is what Americans call 'TLC' (Tender Loving Care). We can come to him as we are, without fear, without pretence, knowing that we'll be lovingly accepted. David speaks about it in Psalm 61:4 where he says: 'I long to...take refuge in the shelter of your wings' and in Psalm 91:4: 'He will cover you with his feathers, and under his wings you will find refuge'.

In Luke 15 Jesus tells the parable of the prodigal son, who left his home to spend an outrageous time in a far-away country. When things turned against him there and he was confronted with cruel people and circumstances, he came to his senses and decided to return home. The discipline of pain and hardship made him seek his father! He did so feeling guilty and unworthy and he prepared a repentant speech; on his arrival he intended to ask his father for a humble job as one of his servants. But it didn't go quite the way he had anticipated: the father saw his son coming from afar, ran to meet him and then gathered him in his arms, smothering his words as he pressed him against his heart. There is overwhelming power released by unconditional and loving acceptance! The prodigal found in his father's embrace security, forgiveness and comfort. It is quite awesome to realise that in this parable, Jesus was actually drawing a picture of our heavenly Father.

The prodigal son came home of his own accord and was received with open arms. Zacchaeus, a chief tax-collector at Jericho, was prompted by Jesus himself to do the same. Having climbed into a sycamore-fig tree in order to have a good view of the Lord – and stay out of view himself? – he was spotted by Jesus, who then invited himself to his house. What a gentle way to meet a sinner! Rather than confronting him publicly with his lifestyle– Zacchaeus undoubtedly had abused his position on occasions to enrich himself – Jesus gave him the honour of a personal request to stay at his house (see Luke 19:1-10). The woman who was caught in adultery was treated likewise. As she stood, surrounded, by eager accusers, Jesus told her that he did not condemn her. Instead he offered her a new start when he told her to go home and sin no more (see John 8:1-11). I am sure that is exactly what she did! Meeting the Lord and experiencing his total and unconditional love and acceptance is so overwhelming that it disarms us. Hiding in God's arms isn't only an experience of being pampered, it is also an experience of being sorted out! Deeply convicted about our own unworthiness, we drop our masks and long to change. Zacchaeus didn't only feel the urge to repay people for what he had unlawfully taken from them, but he wanted to do much more than that, he wanted to repay them four times over!

Do we know what it means to be held by our heavenly Father, to come running home and be met by his loving embrace? Do we dare to be a *child* of God and come as we are, masks off? Have we ever met his love in such a way that burdens have literally been lifted, that pain has ebbed away and guilt been dealt with? Do we know what it means to stay in his presence and feel his love and forgiveness become true to us, can we honestly say we know it rather than just know about it?

When the father of the prodigal embraced his son, I imagine he was initially holding someone apprehensive and tense. But then as he held him, the young man realised there was no need to be afraid and he relaxed. He hadn't expected a welcome like that, he had assumed he would have to earn his way into his father's house again, having made such a mess of his life and having wasted all he had been given. Guilty like Adam, he was ashamed of his nakedness and wanted to cover it up by an offer of good works. But his father took him in his arms and ordered a set of festive clothes to be fetched for him and a feast to be organised. And meanwhile he held him. Here is an image of our heavenly Father who lovingly picks up his child, holding him and offering the wordless comfort of his nearness. Every one of us knows that inner longing to nestle against someone and to let go, and here is an invitation to do that with our heavenly Father. We rob ourselves of something very precious if we don't learn to pour out our hearts before the Lord without holding back in any way. As we come to him with our sins, however ugly and shameful, we will find a spacious place where we are allowed to call things by name without being rejected for it. He responds with wide-open arms and loving forgiveness, thus offering us optimum conditions for change.

We are also offered healing and can go to Jesus with the wounds which were caused by our sins, by others or by 'life'. It doesn't make any difference whether we go to him with wounds big and stinking, with a complicated injury or just a superficial scratch. Maybe we have always heard or felt that we need to pull ourselves together and not whine, we were taught to hide our pain and be casual about it, but we can also choose to bring it to the Lord and learn to receive his comfort. Hiding in God means resting with him, letting go and letting God! He offers us his quiet presence and loving arms around us, but we need to sit down and stay with him in order to learn and discover what this means. Malachi tells us that there is healing under the *wings* of the 'sun of righteousness' (Mal. 4:2). When we go to the Lord with our ailments, we will be held and cared for, our wounds will be cleansed and dressed. 'The Lord is close to the brokenhearted and saves those who are crushed in spirit', says David in Psalm 34:18 and Psalm 147:3 says: 'He heals the brokenhearted and binds up their wounds.' The Lord himself wants to '...bind up the injured and strengthen the weak...' (Ezek. 34:16). These are the words of the Good Shepherd and he speaks like a mother. Of Jesus, our Shepherd, it is said that he shall come 'to bind up the brokenhearted...to comfort all who mourn...' (Isa. 61:1,2). Isaiah 40:11 tells us that 'He gathers the lambs in his arms and carries them close to his heart (or: in his bosom)'.

In Mark 10:16 we see Jesus embracing children: 'He took them in his arms, put his hands on them and blessed them.' The grown-ups wanted to prevent the children from coming near. They felt other things should have priority. Jesus, however, clearly stated that he had room for little ones even if they only came for no other reason than to be with him and to feel his touch. He gave them more than what they asked for: they went away blessed. When we are encouraged to be like children in our relationship with the Lord, here is one example of what that could mean. Children can be quite unpretentious in the way they climb on to their mother or father's lap. They reach out for a cuddle, they want to be held. They come with confidence, not expecting to be turned away. The prostitute, who made a fool of herself by throwing herself onto Jesus at a dinner party, was welcomed with open arms. Ignoring the snickering and whispering of the Pharisees, Jesus allowed her to draw near and touch him. Rather than rejecting her and disapproving of her behaviour, he stood up for her in the face of the harsh criticism of those present. She, who was used to being rejected publicly, was affirmed, forgiven and restored (see Luke 7:36-50). She went with confidence and was not put to shame (see also Ps. 34:5). Do we, as children of God, have the kind of relationship with our Abba where we feel safe and free to go to him and snuggle up to him for no other reason than simply to be near him? If we learn to do this we shall be deeply blessed!

'My soul longs for you' are words which are often spoken by David in his psalms. They express who he was: a man of God, who could be as a child with his heavenly Father. He longed for contact and knew that there was unconditional love and acceptance even when he had done wrong. 'I am,' he said, '...like a weaned child with its mother, like a weaned child is my soul within me' (Ps. 131:2). David felt totally relaxed in God's love. Do we feel the same way? Do we seek him for who he is, simply because we long to be with him and not because we need something of him? Once we have tasted God's goodness, we will long for more. Once we have learnt to trust and hide in God, we will long for these precious intimate moments alone with him. There we will meet the countless blessings that flow from his presence and, safe in his unconditional love and acceptance, we will find that we are forgiven and healed, restored and straightened up so that we can go forward.

Held and loved by God: A fertile soil for change

In the first part of this chapter I spoke about wings as the imagery of care and protection and as good soil for growth. When we talk of wings as a picture of being held in loving acceptance, we have come to the environment or soil which can produce change. Change is sometimes more difficult and painful than growth, because it involves the necessity to turn around and do things differently. This can leave us quite vulnerable as well as defensive. It requires courage to admit failures or shortcomings. We all know that pressure can be counterproductive in that it makes us withdraw rather than open up, and that we sooner defend ourselves and deny the wrong rather than admit the truth. It is biblical and necessary that we are confronted with our sins, but nowhere is it more freeing then when this is done by the Lord himself, in a personal encounter with him. I dare say too, that never is it more loving than when it is done by him, for his rebuke always comes within the framework of his standing offer of forgiveness, cleansing and a new start. He rebukes us within the context of unconditional acceptance, never to destroy us but rather to heal and restore us. It is good to hide under the wings of the Almighty and there to become aware of things that must and can change, and to find the power to do so.

Rest and refreshment

While studying the word 'wings' in the Bible, I found it often linked with the word 'shadow'. This word occurs for the first time in Genesis 19, where we read how two angels arrived at Sodom and were invited by Lot to spend the night in his house. When they were threatened by men from the city, Lot protected his angel-guests, saying 'they have come under the protection of my roof' (verse 8). The Hebrew word used here for protection is *sel* which is also translated as shadow, shade, protection or shelter! We see it used again in Psalm 17 where David, who was pursued, asked of God: 'Keep me as the apple of your eye; hide me in the *shadow* of your wings from the wicked who assail me, from my mortal enemies who surround me' (verses 8 and 9) and also in Psalm 57, which refers to the period when David fled from Saul into a cave (described in 1 Sam. 22:1): 'I will take refuge in the *shadow* of your wings until the disaster has passed.'

Shade in the Middle East means something quite different from what it does in most of Western Europe. We don't very often experience that singeing heat that makes people retire into their homes at midday in order to find some cool and rest behind closed shutters. When looking at the sun-worshippers on foreign beaches, it seems that many people prefer the sun and sunburn above the coolness of a shady spot. However, in countries where temperatures usually soar around noon, people are wise enough to adjust their lifestyle and make refreshing shade and coolness and their siesta a higher priority than surrendering to an exhausting heat. When the sun is high, a shepherd will lead his herd to shady spots in order to protect his sheep or goats from the sun and provide rest and refreshment for them. Shade is an absolute necessity.

When I consider the benefit of shade in hot countries and compare them to what is provided in the shadow of God's wings, I find a remarkable parallel. God's wings protect us against evil (the burning sun), underneath them we find rest and are refreshed (shade). As earlier in the chapter we have already considered what protection involves, we will now concentrate on the aspects of rest and refreshment.

In Matthew 11:28 Jesus calls us to 'Come to me, all you who are weary and burdened, and I will give you rest'. In other words, 'Come from the stifling heat of life under the shadow of my wings. Come near, lay down your worries and let go of everything that is going on "outside". I don't only want you to rest, but I want to give you a rest so deep that it touches your soul.' What Jesus is speaking about here isn't physical rest (important though that may be), but inner rest. When we sleep or keep our siesta, we do rest physically, but the restlessness deep down in us remains untouched; it is possible to be rested without being at rest. The latter is what God wants to deal with. Therefore, when we wish to find peace for our souls, we need to seek *God's* shade. It is a principle that David repeatedly underlines in his psalms; in resting or hiding in God he finds all that he needs, his whole being is being satisfied by God. Psalm 23 sums these things up in its first three verses (and here we have the imagery of the shepherd, leading his sheep to shady places): 'The Lord is my shepherd, I shall lack nothing. He makes me *lie down* in green pastures, he leads me beside quiet waters, he *restores* my soul'. Jesus says: 'I want to give you rest for your soul', David says: 'He restores my soul.' These two things go together: in God's presence I find rest and restoration, which strengthens me to go forward.

There is more that happens under the shadow of God's wings: we find rest, we are refreshed, but we are also fed. David says in Psalm 36:7-9a: 'How priceless is your unfailing love! Both high and low among men find refuge in the shadow of your wings. They feast on the abundance of your house; you give them drink from the river of your delights. For with you is the fountain of life...'

The 'abundance of your house' refers to the quality of food that God gives us. True, the abundance of fats and rich food is being avoided in our day and age, but here in God's Word it expresses that what God gives to us is the very best that man can get. It reminds me of God's promise (in Isa. 25:6) to prepare a feast of rich food for all peoples, 'a banquet of aged wine - the best of meats and the finest of wines'. It is a picture of feasting and abundance, of enjoyment and being satisfied. How many of us know such pleasure, such refreshment and satisfaction from the Lord? Sometimes we just visit God briefly, we only allow the shortest time possible to present him with our desires, to pray for family and friends and maybe even for the mission field. But who of us stays long enough to taste of God's goodness and to enjoy his presence; who allows time to just be near and be refreshed in the coolness of the shadow of his wings, to eat and drink of what God provides for us? 'Open wide your mouth and I will fill it', says the Lord God (Ps. 81:10) and David says, 'For with you is the fountain of life', in other words 'I need to seek your presence in order to be refreshed'. It is the same message that Jesus conveyed in John 4 when he met that thirsty woman at the well at Sychar: 'You draw water here but that water only quenches your thirst temporarily and you will have to return time and time again and draw new water. I, however, want to give you water that satisfies; once you drink it you will never be thirsty again. Indeed, the water I give will become in you a spring of water welling up to eternal life.' Later on, in John 7, he said the same thing over again: 'If a man is thirsty, let him come to me and drink. Whoever believes in me as the Scripture has said, streams of living water will flow from within him.' John then added: 'By this he meant the Spirit, whom those who believed in him were later to receive'(verses 38 and 39).

To us, who live in the days after Jesus' life on earth and his resurrection, the fountain of life that David describes is given in and through Jesus. He is the fulfilment of God's promises that will become a reality in our lives through the Holy Spirit, who will be with us forever. In Jesus we meet God's goodness: when we walk with him we'll know that he is the fountain that satisfies. But Jesus also refers time and time again to that other important source of food which is God's Word. We need to feed ourselves from it in order to grow in our walk with God. One could say that the Bible is filled with rich food, the best of meats and the finest of wines. It has so much good for us in store that we need to allow ample time to discover it all! Therefore we need to make sure we 'eat' regularly and deeply from God's Word in order to grow spiritually.

Elijah and Jonah

When considering the shadow that God provides as protection against the heat and as a means of refreshment and satisfaction, I am reminded of two people who were given this unexpectedly when they weren't seeking it. The first person is the prophet Elijah, whom we meet in 1 Kings 19, a depressed man. He had done his utmost for God, but had reached the point where he felt he was quite alone and deserted. In verse 10 he sums up what had happened, he speaks of his own zeal and complains about Israel's unfaithfulness and, after listing a few more details, he finishes by saying that he is the only one left and people are trying to kill him. Like David, Elijah was fleeing and fearing for his life, he too was pursued by enemies (verses 1-3). But whereas David was often the one who sought God in oppressing circumstances, desiring to hide in him, Elijah withdrew in his distress. He had found a broom tree in the desert to sit under (he was looking for shade!). There, filled with fear and self-pity and desiring to die, he fell asleep (verses 4-5). Subsequently two things happened: first, the Lord sent an angel who touched him and encouraged him to get up and then gave him food and drink. That actually happened twice. We then read that Elijah got up, ate and drank and following that, 'strengthened by that food, he travelled for forty days and forty nights until he reached Horeb, the mountain of God' (verses 5-8). Here we have a practical example of an encounter with God in the *shade* of a broom tree, where Elijah was provided with coolness – rest and refreshment – and food that enabled him to persevere and go on.

The second thing that happened is that the word of the Lord came directly to Elijah when he spent the night in a cave – a place of refuge. The Lord asked Elijah: 'What are you doing here?' (verse 9), thus offering him the opportunity to pour out his heart and express what he felt. Elijah's response was one of despair; he complained about his circumstances and maybe also about God: his statement that he had been very zealous for him but seemed to have only been left with loneliness and a fear of death, has the hint of an accusation. Then the Lord came to Elijah in person, not in a dramatic way of overwhelming signs of nature as sometimes is the case, but in a 'gentle whisper' (verse 12). The Hebrew expression used here is of an unspeakable tenderness, the AV translation speaks of a 'still small voice'. The Lord met with Elijah, he himself came to him. Recognising God's whisper, Elijah covered his face and again he heard the words: 'What are you doing here, Elijah?' (verse 13). Again Elijah opened his heart before God and then he was commissioned to return the way he came and go to the Desert of Damascus (the Syrian desert). His arrival there marked the beginning of some great events (verses 14-18).

Now let us consider another prophet, Jonah, whose colourful story most people are familiar with. It starts off with God commissioning him to go out and preach to the city of Nineveh and Jonah's unwillingness to do so. Rather than obeying, he chose to flee not only from God's calling but also from God himself (Jonah 1:3). This led to a hair-raising adventure in a raging storm at sea, which Jonah survived only because God intervened; when Jonah was thrown overboard by the sailors, he provided a great fish to swallow him and save him from drowning. Then, from 'inside the fish' (Jonah 2:1) Jonah thanked God for coming to his rescue, he praised him and promised to fulfil his task. Do note: praise and thanksgiving in what must have been a most unpleasant place to be, the insides of the fish! God can obviously turn even the most dreadful habitat into a safe place of refuge and there surprise us with a precious encounter with him. He isn't confined to a certain spot or time, he meets us where we are.

In Jonah 3, after Jonah had been 'vomited on to dry land' by the fish, he was again commissioned to go to Nineveh to preach against that town and inform the people of God's wrath. When Jonah obeyed and all of Nineveh was converted, God had compassion and reversed his plans; he did not bring upon this town the destruction that he had threatened (verse 10). This very act of grace upset Jonah, he was 'greatly displeased'. In his reaction to God, he angrily expressed that what happened did not surprise him because it was in line with God's character: 'I knew that you are a gracious and compassionate God, slow to anger and abounding in love, a God who relents from sending calamity' (Jonah 4:2). In other words, 'I could have known that this would happen and that is why I wasn't too keen to obey you in the first place. I don't know why I took the trouble to spend my time and energy preaching to Nineveh, this really upsets me and all I want now is to die' (Jonah 4:1-3). Following his lament, Jonah went to a place east of the city and made himself a shelter to provide shade (verse 5). In his situation of empty-handedness caused by his own disobedience, he went his own way and sought *his own shade* –solution to his problem. It was then and there that God met him, firstly with the question: 'Have you any right to be angry?' (verse 4). It is the question of a God whose love for someone isn't in any way limited, not even by that person's stubbornness (or childishness!). What happened next was in no way related to or dependent upon Jonah's response or repentance, it was based solely on God's unconditional grace. We read in verse 6: 'Then the Lord God provided a vine and made it grow up over Jonah to give shade for his head to ease his discomfort...' Here God gave Jonah the wonder of *his shade* to refresh him and to show him his goodness in order to make him realise his short-sightedness. Jonah, however, didn't comprehend God's message of grace and therefore God removed the shade in order to make him see what was happening. It resulted in a burning headache which made Jonah feel so faint that he again longed to die in order to be released of all his trouble (verse 8). It was then, in the blazing and stinging sun, that God communicated a lesson that he had initially wanted to share in the refreshing coolness of his shade.

Rest and refreshment: A fertile soil for perseverance
Sometimes we are hampered by our own negative attitude to grasp God's message or to see his love. Sometimes, in our anger or bitterness, we create our own place of refuge, away from

God. Sometimes, when we run away from hiding in him, he needs to teach us a hard lesson and confront us through painful circumstances with his mercy and grace. In doing so he gently beckons us to return to him, our true source of 'shade'.

We will know times of barrenness, times of empty hands, but even then the Lord, in his great mercy, will satisfy us. We read in Isaiah 58:11 'The Lord will guide you always; he will satisfy your needs *in* a sun-scorched land and will strengthen your frame. You will be like a well-watered garden, like a spring whose waters never fail'. Even at times when, for whatever reason one does not seek God but maybe withdraws instead, he himself comes out to meet us, offering us a hiding place in him with all that it entails. In Elijah's case there was refreshment (sleep and food), room to unburden his heart and a new perspective, things that made him get back on his feet and enabled him to persevere. On top of that he had gained the precious experience of a deep personal encounter with the Lord.

Going on with a difference

We have looked at three things we meet when we hide in God: care and protection; unconditional acceptance; and rest and refreshment. They are the soil that brings forth the fruits of growth, change and perseverance. But there is more, hiding in God leaves a visible mark on people, both outwardly and inwardly.

After Moses (who knew what friendship and hiding in God meant) had spent forty days and nights with the Lord, in a personal encounter in a place of refuge on Mount Sinai, he returned to the Israelites, his face 'radiant because he had spoken with the Lord' (Ex. 34:29). Moses shows how those who know the Lord change into people who radiate the wonder and happiness of a personal knowing of God. What happens in the secrecy of hiding in him, cannot remain hidden, it leaves an ineradicable impression upon lives!

We do not only become radiant people, when hiding in God, we also become stronger people. At the onset of this chapter we considered the metaphor of the eagle that God used to describe himself. This imagery recurs in Isaiah 40 with one difference: the eagle here is a picture of the *people* who hope in the Lord. Isaiah states that God 'gives strength to the weary and increases the power of the weak. ...those who hope in the Lord will renew their strength. They will soar on wings like eagles; they will run and not grow weary, they will walk and not be faint' (verses 29-31). David says in Psalm 103:3-5 that God's forgiveness and healing, his love and compassion and the fact that he satisfies David's desires with good things meant 'that my youth is renewed like the eagle's'. He comments in Psalm 138:3 'You made me bold and stout-hearted', which in the RSV translation reads 'My strength of soul thou didst increase'.

How do we get this strength? It is not a matter of the Lord simply handing it over to us; there is more to it. When looking at Isaiah 40 again, we read in verse 31 that it is 'those who hope in the Lord' who will receive this strength. This hoping in (also translated as 'waiting upon' or 'eagerly awaiting') is derived from a Hebrew word which speaks of being intertwined. We need, in other words, to become more intertwined with the Lord. We need to hide more and more deeply in him and this is how we receive this strength.

This picture of strength is also found in Hebrews 12, the chapter that follows a list of people who portrayed great faith, the so-called 'cloud of witnesses'. In Hebrews 12 we are summoned to be faithful as well as to persevere. The life of a believer is described as a race that we must run with a minimum of luggage ('everything that hinders and the sin that so easily entangles', v 1). Our only chance of persevering to reach and cross the finishing line is that we run with our eyes solely fixed on Jesus, the author and perfecter of our faith, who has conquered death and is seated at the right hand of God. 'Consider him', we read, 'so that you will not grow weary and lose heart' (verse 3). In verses 12 to 13 we are summoned to strengthen our feeble arms and weak knees and to make level paths for our feet, 'so that the lame may not be disabled, but rather healed'. As we are given strength by the Lord, we need to take the weaker ones amongst us along, in order to keep them from dropping out en route ('so that what is lamed may not be put out of joint' is how the RSV puts it). Again I envisage Ruth travelling with her mother-in-law Naomi. In her own hiding under the wings of God Ruth had found ample strength, not just for herself, but also to help her mother-in-law along and support her where she, in bitterness, had become weak and was in danger of lagging behind.

And so, as we learn increasingly to hide in God, to seek and stay in his presence, we grow into people fit for service, people who radiate and communicate that which they themselves have been given by the Lord. We, who have come to know God as our place of refuge, are commissioned to function as such in a world where people are drifting and seeking security. We can reach out to them in his name and act as road signs to the one who offers ultimate security. We grow into people who reflect God's character in the way we welcome, love and forgive others. Having ourselves found rest and strength with him, we can in turn offer those very things to those straying, young or weak as we invite them to come to his pastures and rivers of delight. Born-again Christians are to be an attractive mystery to others because of the quality and energy of their lives which reflect the glory of their Lord. Jesus asks us to be visible lights in a world and age of darkness. Our light becomes stronger when we become increasingly and inseparably attached to the main Source and when we keep having our batteries checked, fixed and recharged under the wings of the Almighty.

Notes

1. Gordon MacDonald , *Restoring your Spiritual Passion* , Highland Books.

2. The idea of a cocoon spun around us is in no way related to today's trend of 'cocooning' where people withdraw in their own private world, comfortably hemmed in by the walls of their homes. Christians are sheltered by God's love, but they are commissioned to go out into the world rather than to withdraw from it. When Jesus prays for his disciples in John 17:15, he says: 'My prayer is not that you take them out of the world, but that you protect them from the evil one. They are not of the world, even as I am not of it. ...As you sent me into the world, I have sent them into the world.'

14
Lord, Teach Us to Hide in You

There is a childhood into which we have to grow, just as there is a childhood we must leave behind. One is a childishness from which but a few of those who are counted wisest among men have freed themselves. The other is a childlikeness which is the highest gain of humanity.

During the Dutch famine-winter of 1944, author Else Vlug was one of many children who were sent to the country to find shelter and food with a farming family. Although the children badly needed this time of recuperation and benefited from it, many of them were plagued by feelings of homesickness. Else was one of them; somehow she felt desolate and lacked the emotional warmth and security she needed during this time away from home. Her distress and loneliness made her put into practice what she had been taught for as long as she could remember: she went to find refuge in the Lord. Far away from home and everything that was familiar to her, there was just that one option left, that of seeking her heavenly Father. She came to him open-minded and trusting; there was no reason to have any reservations for she had only heard good things about God. Indeed, Else wasn't disappointed, what she believed became a reality: God became her shelter and home.

In our relationship with God we need to have the attitude of child-wonder. A child doesn't have major questions about how to approach God or how meeting with God 'works' in practice, neither does it speculate about whether it is really means for her or him. A child comes with confidence and expectancy. They just walk in without even knocking on the door. This childlikeness in attitude, this natural and pure way of coming to God, is what Jesus talks about in Mark 10:13-16, where he says: 'Anyone who will not receive the kingdom of God like a little child, will never enter it.' He said that whilst people were bringing little children to him. In a way they disturbed his programme, but rather than sending them away, he took them in his arms and blessed them.

When, during that oppressive winter of 1944, Else Vlug came empty-handed to hide with the Lord, she experienced the same thing and learned a lesson that has never left her since. God proved his faithfulness to that little girl and met her on her level of understanding. He comforted her and filled her hands with small things that made her happy. He showed her his greatness and goodness in the miracles of nature, through things she discovered in and around the farm. Now, fifty years later, Else has grown in faith and trust, despite the pain and problems that are part and parcel of life. She knows from experience what hiding in God means and she has come to know the Lord as one who is totally trustworthy. David says in Psalm 25:3 (words that will later be cited by Paul in his letter to the Romans): 'No-one whose hope is in you will ever be put to shame'. Once we learn to hide in the Lord, we will not only find that we are never put to shame, but we will be surprised and overwhelmed by his goodness.

Sadly many of us have lost that childlike trust. We have learned by bitter experience that it is wisest to enter into relationships with some reserve. Our trust is conditional and cautious, we feel uneasy about being dependent and feel extremely hesitant and vulnerable when it comes to surrendering ourselves to another person. This attitude can affect our thinking about God. We saw earlier how we sometimes struggle with a certain distrust and doubt whether God really wants the best for us. Deep down we may feel that it is safer to keep control over our own lives and future. But it isn't! In our limitedness we don't realise that people are incapable of functioning as independent beings. We were simply not created to live that way; we are destined to walk with God. Therefore, in our supposed independence, we are bound to make mistakes that are destructive. We choose that which is wrong and become enslaved to it. Dependence as God has meant it, however, frees us instead. The Bible is quite emphatic about the fact that it is our nature to crave for and go after things that are wrong and worthless. They are not neutral or innocent, they bind us and lead to destruction. When we follow the Lord, however, we travel a road that brings us to our destination; it sets us free and leads to eternal life in fellowship with him.

Life is meant to make us know God and to be formed by him into the people that he means us to be. In order for that to happen I must put off things that hinder that process. I need to unlearn my automatic desire to trust myself and to live life and make decisions on my own. I need to lose myself in order to gain him. I must reach the point where I know that my own strength is not sufficient, in order to discover how great his strength is in me. I must, in other words, learn to be dependent. Sometimes suffering is used as a means by which we learn this. Joseph experienced time and time again that what he had succeeded in building up, was broken down again. When he thought he had found security with people or in a certain position, he found those very things slipping through his fingers. The combination of those incidents made him into a man of God, whose happiness didn't depend upon relative things but upon his relationship and walk with the Lord. He became a man full of the Spirit. Many people will join him in witnessing that through, their suffering they learned to be dependent upon God, which resulted in their finding precious treasures and riches that they hadn't thought possible! Dependence upon God doesn't rob us of good things, it enriches us.

In Mark 1:14-20 we read that the first disciples left everything in order to follow Jesus. Indeed, following Jesus requires self-denial, which means that I release any claim to my own rights. My desires will not automatically be fulfilled, nor will my plans automatically come to fruition. I surrender myself, my desires and wishes to Christ. That doesn't imply that I become a helpless slave without a will of my own. I follow a Master who says: 'I no longer call you servants, because a servant does not know his master's business. Instead, I have called you friends' (John 15:15). But it goes even further than that! Paul says in Romans 8:15 'For you did not receive a spirit that makes you a slave again to fear, but you received the Spirit of sonship'. Seen in the cultural context of those days, we are slaves who have been first ransomed and then adopted by their master. We are dearly loved children of our heavenly Lord (Eph. 5:1) – an overwhelming truth! It is within this framework of a love relationship with God that we learn to be more and more dependent upon him. We learn this as we walk through life with him, which is a journey into a 'life to the full' (John 10:10). This life starts here on earth but its climax will take place when we join our Lord in heaven. If we want to reach our destination, uncompromising obedience and dependence are required of us, no arguments against that! 'Follow Me' implies absolute and total surrender and commitment. These things become less difficult when we know who calls us.

When the first disciples – Peter and Andrew, James and John – left their nets and fishing business in order to follow Jesus, they left their human securities behind. They made a choice for a greater security, one that Peter describes in John 6:68. It was a decisive moment; people realised the price of following Jesus and deserted him. When Jesus asked his twelve disciples where they stood ('You do not want to leave too, do you?'), it was Peter who replied: 'Lord, to whom shall we go? You have the words of eternal life. We believe and know that you are the Holy One of God.' Similar words of his are recorded in Matthew 16:16, where Jesus asked Peter who he thought he was? Peter replied: 'You are the Christ, the Son of the living God.'

Getting to know God

It is possible to know a great deal about the Lord and to have gained an impressive amount of knowledge about matters of faith, without knowing personally the very One whom it is all about! One can, so to speak, know God's Word from cover to cover, lead Bible studies or preach, one can publicly defend biblical values, but these activities, however good in themselves, are no guarantee for knowing God personally. We can do a lot of Christian things with great integrity and sincerity without ever knowing in our hearts who God is and what he is really like.

Jim Packer in his book *Knowing God* [1], comments: 'A little knowledge of God is worth more than a great deal of knowledge about him.' This is a formidable truth. Some people may be highly knowledgeable about God's Word, they may be capable of deep theological dispute without, however, knowing God. Their level of reasoning and thinking is quite impressive, but somehow God himself isn't heard even though he is the subject matter. There are also those, who aren't scholars, nor have they studied theology, yet their words contain a wisdom so profound that it can only be inspired and given by the Lord himself. They are deeply spiritual people who know what it means to sit at the feet of the Lord and to hear his voice in their hearts. In their personal walk with God they have been shaped and taught by his Spirit.

Packer adds something which is very relevant and challenging, particularly in the context of this book, where we look at suffering and at learning to trust and hide in God. He says:

> The question is not whether we are good at theology, or 'balanced' (horrible, self-conscious word!) in our approach to problems of Christian living; the question is, can we say, simply, honestly, not because we feel that as evangelicals we ought to, but because it is plain matter of fact, that we have known God, and that because we have known God the unpleasantness we have had, or the pleasantness we have not had, through being Christians does not matter to us? If we really knew God, this is what we would be saying, and if we are not saying it, that is a sign that we need to face ourselves more sharply with the difference between knowing God and merely knowing about him.

How and where does getting to know God start? It begins with making room for him and listening. It means that I open my heart, eyes and ears to him and set all that I have on discovering him. It means that priorities will change and that some activities will be shelved or postponed, in order to read God's Word, not as an academic Bible study in the sense that I gather information and knowledge about God, but as a spiritual search aimed at discovering all I can about God's being and character. I want to find out who he is and what he is like, I want to listen and search God's heart. I want to find out more about his purposes both generally and personally and learn to apply his Word to my life, in obedience. I also want to learn to have fellowship with him, to sit at his feet and drink in his presence, I desire to learn to communicate with him, to pray, with and without words, speaking as well as listening. All these things imply that my being a Christian grows into more than Sunday worship at church and takes a different direction from gaining information about him; I want to know God personally and want to take the responsibility to seek him myself and to press forward in order to grow in my friendship and walk with him. I long to be able to say that I don't know God just from what I have heard others say about him or from what I have read, but that my own eyes have seen him. In other words I want to know him first-hand! I desire to stop being religious and become spiritually real.

When we earnestly seek God we will find that he rewards us (Heb.11:6). James 4:8 says: 'Come near to God and he will come near to you.' God will answer us by coming to us, revealing himself to us and thus enabling us get to know him better. It is then that a wondrous reciprocity takes effect: as we meet the Lord we will long for more and as we long for more, we will seek and meet the Lord again.

Maybe it all began with a decision of our will, but then it becomes our heart's desire; we long to get to know the Lord better. In Psalm 27:4, which I mentioned earlier, David expresses how crucial and precious his encounters with the Lord have become. He says: 'One thing I ask of the Lord, this is what I seek: that I may dwell in the house of the Lord all the days of my life, to gaze upon the beauty of the Lord and to seek him in his temple'. The RSV puts it like this: 'to behold the beauty of the Lord and to inquire in his temple.'

Here again are the two major activities that play a role in getting to know the Lord: being with him and gazing upon his beauty, and inquiring in the temple. The two sides of the coin, knowing of and knowing about God, should be interactive, but the main aim is always knowing God. David, in Psalm 27 shows that, once we have come to know him, we shall find that our priorities shift. All other things become of lesser importance – which is not the same as unimportant – there is an urgency of wanting to be with the Lord. We are pressing on towards that goal. We shall reach that point where life without him is unimaginable. While once we knew in our minds that man cannot live without God, this now becomes a truth that is rooted in our hearts. David says in Psalm 16:2 – 'I said to the Lord, " You are my Lord; apart from you I have no good thing"'. When we confess that we cannot live and cope without the Lord, we actually state our complete helplessness and our total dependence upon him.

Years ago I bought a small book that contains letters, thoughts and spiritual principles of Brother Lawrence, a French monk who lived in the seventeenth century, and who in his monastery kitchen discovered an overwhelming delight in God's presence [2]. His life was dominated by one main ideal, namely that of always living in God's presence. In striving after this he appealed to the fact that God is in a believer and that he commissions the believer to remain in him (John 15:4). The former we have to constantly keep in mind and before our eyes, whereas the latter requires learning. It is for that reason that Brother Lawrence speaks about '*Practising* the presence of God', thereby indicating that a walk or fellowship with the Lord never happens automatically. Concerning ourselves with spiritual matters goes so drastically against our very nature that we need schooling and discipline in order to learn it. One of the first things we need to learn is that we thoroughly anchor ourselves in God's presence by pursuing continual contact in an ongoing and open conversation with the Lord. In speaking of these things Brother Lawrence is pointing at the importance of prayer and it is indeed our prayer life – our communication with the Lord – that is very telling regarding our walk with and our knowing God. Look at what he says, in a section entitled 'Practices Essential to Acquire the Spiritual Life':

> The most holy practice, the nearest to daily life, is the practice of the presence of God, that is to find joy in his divine company and to make it a habit of life, speaking humbly

and conversing lovingly with him at all times, every moment, without rule or restriction, above all at times of temptation, distress, dryness, and revulsion, and even of faithlessness and sin. We should apply ourselves continually, so that, without exception, all our actions become small occasions of fellowship with God. What can God have that gives him greater satisfaction than that a thousand thousand times a day all his creatures should thus pause and worship him in the heart.

We need perseverance in order to make these things our habit and we will soon discover as we enrol at God's Discipleship Training School that perseverance is indeed emphasized as a characteristic that needs to be developed. It affects other major subjects in the curriculum like Bible study, prayer and obedience. Perseverance isn't something that is easy to grasp, it is gained mainly by exposure to hardship. The Lord at times gives us apprenticeships or other special periods which we will find far from easy or even painful, yet they bear good fruit in our lives. Again and again the Lord surprises us with his presence, goodness and blessing – things that become so precious to us that we will press on and seek moments of a personal encounter with God, not because this is what he expects of us, but because we ourselves long to meet him.

As we get to know the Lord more deeply, we will find a precious friendship developing. This may firstly have been just theory or hearsay, but now it becomes our personal experience and is tangible, not just for us but also for others as our fellowship with God becomes visible in and through our lives. It is then that we come to know that deep joy and peace that are fruits of a walk with God and of knowing him. Sometimes, out of sheer joy and overwhelming gratefulness, we may, in our praise and adoration, forget all and everything around us. 'David...danced before the Lord with all his might', according to 2 Samuel 6:14.

His wife thought his behaviour abominable, she despised him for it.

Something similar happened in Luke 7:36-50, where a prostitute violated all the laws of etiquette and decency by gatecrashing at a dinner where Jesus was the guest of honour. She disrupted the dinner and all that was going on by bursting in and then anointing him with perfume and she did so with a lot of hullabaloo for she cried her heart out and washed Jesus' feet with her tears, wiping them with her hair and then kissing them. Again: what a terrible show, highly embarrassing! But Jesus, facing the harsh criticism of those present, simply said: 'She loved much.' We are quick to criticise ruthlessly what we consider extreme or inordinate behaviour, but God sees the heart which may be so full of him that it flows over in unexpected ways!

God delights in the adoration and praise of his creation. Even nature is called to rejoice: 'Let the heavens rejoice, let the earth be glad; let the sea resound, and all that is in it; let the fields be jubilant, and everything in them. Then all the trees of the forest will sing for joy' (Ps.96:11-12) and 'Let the rivers clap their hands, let the mountains sing together for joy' (Ps. 98:8). I call that exuberant! It reminds me of a conference where joy was one of the major topics. In the closing meeting a hymn was chosen that fitted this theme and whilst people were singing it rather solemnly, suddenly the door burst open and a train of young enthusiastic people came in, clapping their hands and carrying musical instruments and colourful balloons. The singing changed into jubilant and joyful praise. Some people considered this abundant behaviour rather irreverent, others felt that these young people had understood the message.

When in Matthew 11 the Lord Jesus says: 'Come to me... Take my yoke upon you and learn from me' (verses 28-29), his words are those of a teacher summoning his students to be apprenticed by him. We saw earlier that following Jesus requires a training school and a learning process. We don't go through it alone, we join ranks with others as we study and learn within the context of a fellowship of believers. Regular contact with fellow-believers is something we must never neglect. We cannot function without one another and, where possible, we need to keep in touch and seek each other. The first Christians exemplify this and their history, recorded in Acts, is an ode to the 'fellowship of the saints'. Acts 2:42 says: 'They devoted themselves to the apostles' teaching and to the fellowship'. Where solitude is both necessary and of great value in our personal walk with God, isolation is dangerous. It is possible beyond any doubt to 'survive' when one is alone as a Christian; those who have been imprisoned in solitary confinement witness to this fact, their barren circumstances did not automatically undermine their faith, in fact these people often came out of prison as stronger Christians than they were before. The same applies to people who, for any other reason, may be isolated from fellow-Christians; they don't necessarily lose their faith! However, set apart from others we are more vulnerable to become weak, we are like coals that are taken out of the burning fire; as long as they are in contact with other coals they keep glowing, but once they are set apart, they are no longer warmed by the glow and heat of the other coals and they go out. As long as we kindle and keep up our fellowship, we shall be warmed and enriched.

Hiding in God

Is knowing God similar to hiding in God? It may be the starting point or the fruit of it, but mostly it will be a case of reciprocity. We have seen that certain circumstances may drive us to God; our helplessness and grief make us seek refuge in him. Subsequently, we discover how good it is to hide in the Lord, because in the sanctuary of a personal encounter we see him with our own eyes. It can, however, also be a matter of a growing process of faith and trust, which make us hide more and more deeply in him. Hiding is the practice of drawing and being close to the Lord, expecting everything from him because we have discovered that he is the only one who can satisfy us. Some learn this the hard way through suffering, whereas others seem to learn it more easily.

Does hiding in God ever end? Is it ever completed? When we translate it as hiding from danger and consider the hiding-place as a temporary shelter, then we lower hiding in God to a series of limited moments or 'snapshots'. It is the same as limiting our prayer life to moments of crying out for help. Such prayers in need are not wrong in themselves, but they should never make up our total prayer life. Rather they should be part of a lifestyle of prayer, just as our seeking refuge in God should grow into a constant attitude, rather than be a matter of isolated moments, few and far between. The wonder and delight of real friendship with God cannot be compared to occasional feelings of his presence in prayer. If we seek God only at times of need, we miss out a lot and don't honour God who desires us to walk with him rather than have us visit him incidentally. In a love relationship it won't do to just meet and talk now and then in a haphazard manner. We need to keep in touch, and talking and our communication must grow in frequency as well as in depth. It must become our heart's desire to maintain a vital connection with Christ and to see to it that nothing interferes with that. This will bear the fruit of a deepening love. Friendship with God is a dynamic process. In practical everyday living it means that in all things I become increasingly dependent upon the Lord and that in all things I seek him increasingly, because I love him increasingly and am unable as well as unwilling to live without him.

'Whom have I in heaven but you? And there is nothing on earth that I desire other than you. My flesh and my heart may fail, but God is the strength of my heart and my portion forever,' are Asaph's words in Psalm 73:25,26. He adds (in verse 28): 'But as for me, it is good to be near God. I have made the Sovereign Lord my refuge; I will tell of all your deeds.'

It is my desire that these words of Asaph will echo more and more strongly in our hearts. If this book may in some way contribute to that process and stimulate us in our seeking to learn to hide in God, it has served its aim.

Notes

1. Jim Packer, *Knowing God*, Hodder and Stoughton, 1973.
2. Brother Lawrence, *The Practice of the Presence of God*, tr. E.M. Blaiklock, Hodder and Stoughton, 1981.